Meetings with
Remarkable Muslims

Meetings with Remarkable Muslims

A COLLECTION

Edited by BARNABY ROGERSON
and ROSE BARING

London

Eland Publishing Ltd, 61 Exmouth Market, London ECIR 4QL

First published by Eland Publishing Limited in 2005

Copyright © Contributors, as acknowledged

ISBN 13: 978 0 907871 64 4
ISBN 10: 0 907871 64 X

All rights reserved. This publication may not be
reproduced, stored in a retrieval system or
transmitted in any form or by any means, electronic,
mechanical, photocopying, recording or otherwise,
without permission in writing from the publishers.

Dust jacket designed by Robert Dalrymple
IMAGES Front Cover: Mosque Keeper, Gao, Mali © Barnaby Rogerson
Commandant Ahmed Shah Massoud © Webistan/CORBIS
Woman smokes at Cannabis Harvest © Françoise de Mulder/CORBIS
Back Cover: Ghanzi, Afghanistan, 1991 © Steve McCurry
Inside flap: Youssou N'Dour Singing in Concert © David Katzenstein/CORBIS

Text set in Great Britain by Antony Gray
Printed and bound in England by Antony Rowe Ltd, Chippenham, Wiltshire

Contents

Part III: Ghosts

About the Contributors

Introduction

Meetings with Remarkable Muslims is a collection of travel writing which delights in cultural difference yet celebrates our common humanity. It arose out of the marches in London against the invasion of Iraq. Realising that the lies, half-truths and manufactured fears by which this war had been sold to the public were backed by the images of the Islamic world latched onto by our media – of bearded fanatics, suicide bombers and veiled gunmen – it seemed important to offer a broader, truer picture. As anyone who has travelled regularly within the Muslim world will know, this perception is wilfully – even perhaps maliciously – false.

In the search for contributors, one decried the project as absurdly patronising, others were unable to choose between the many remarkable Muslims in their lives. But the vast majority agreed at once, and became so fired up by the project that they began to suggest and encourage others. As a result, *Meetings with Remarkable Muslims* became a much richer, more enchanting, more uplifting and disparate collection than was originally envisaged. It has become a testament to friendships and to the chance encounters that unexpectedly enhance our lives. It is also about how the Islamic world continues to enchant, delight and bemuse the West. It has no political subtext, follows no academic discipline and sharpens no doctrinal axe.

The collection is about Muslims who are remarkable to the extent that they are remembered and continue to inspire the lives of those who met them. There are no world-famous presidents, revolutionary colonels or publicity-hungry preachers in this world-view. Instead it is the porters, drivers, smugglers, musicians, teachers, mothers, neighbours and restauranteurs who are cherished for the example of their ordinary lives. A few are empowered and transfigured by a religion that motivates every action of their lives, but most are like the rest of us, trying to love, survive, take some pleasures and make some sense of it all. There are also a few genuine heroes – commanders of the Afghan resistance, mystics and a free-speaking professor – but they were all too good for this world.

A number of the writers in this collection would not describe themselves as writers at all: they include film-makers, booksellers, sculptors and development consultants, though the majority are professional travel writers. All have agreed to donate their royalties (ten percent of the cover price) to buy schoolbooks for children in the Islamic world whose education has been interrupted by recent wars.

BARNABY ROGERSON *and* ROSE BARING

Here and Now

His Name Means Enlightened White Eagle

KEVIN GOULD

H IS GRANDFATHER had been shot for wearing Western trousers instead of traditional baggy şalvar. Granddad had had two wives. One was dark, short, Arab hot and flashy-eye sexy. Her side of the family couldn't keep their temper and couldn't resist a knees-up. Bride number two was his mother's mother and had been won from the Northern Ottoman lands – Bulgaria, perhaps – or was it Albania? Somewhere, without doubt, where your lightly-drawn features and pale willowy frame would mark you out an exotic catch for a dashing, landed, southern gentleman, especially one who raises two fingers to anything wrong or ridiculous.

Münir – the grandson – talks of his childhood in Tarsus as if his father's father were not yet born. To Münir's supple mind, Anthony and Cleopatra had only recently 'frolicked' – a term he culled from a tourist brochure – in the Turkish baths next to the family home, and St Paul, another neighbour, had yet to get Damascus in his sights. In Münir's world the past is yet to happen and the present is only a reflection of your state of mind. As for the future, it is as clear as the hairs on the back of his hand, the dark, wiry tangle which he perfumes with rose-scented soap and, occasionally, Givenchy Gentleman.

'If you dare to believe . . . ' slowly, his broken-nosed baritone rumbles from deep within: 'We are the early ones. Here before the others and still there after the rest have left.' A bewilderingly vulnerable smile plays across his full lips. 'Where did we come from?' A vague hand is waved, conveying everywhere, anywhere, helplessness. The 'we' is not a grand/modest ego-driven device to avoid saying 'I', nor does it mean mankind in general. 'We' is not just the sufis, either. We can be you and me. He is a sufi of course – note the lower-case 's'. Capital 'S' Sufi he denounces as a modish, disposable brand to be collected and worn (or worn out) by spiritual-path daytrippers, or tarnished and traduced by the unelect. 'Call yourself a Sufi only if you are not one.' This is the only time you'll ever hear him even mention the word.

Münir flows from a long line of sufis, swimmers against the tide of their times one and all. He recalls their names with laughter or with tears coursing down his smooth-shaven olive jowls. This particular effendi with the sightless eyes who could see into your soul. That one whose idea of fun was to appear to his kids in the guise of a dove, whose daughter later became a dervish who could control your actions by thought-power. 'Only by the power of Love!' he roars when you wonder to what extent he's controlling your actions, too. And, for good measure, he reminds you to: 'Forget measure, forget reason, and most of all forget yourself.' Over grilled fish one lunchtime, he forgot himself completely and became hypnotised by the sea, seeing in the waves memories and ripples of the tiny enormous deeds performed by all the early ones when they too were out of their minds. Coming to, his eyes were green then grey then hazel brown and for days afterwards lit by needle-point phosphorescent flares.

So, naturally, he has your complete attention and you concentrate hard, so he tells you not to concentrate AT ALL but to surrender. And out of your mind you float on shafts of dusty sunlight through the Covered Bazaar and see God everywhere, especially in the quiet young man who falls into step and asks ever so politely if he can help you spend your money, which of course he can and does. So you are excoriated for loving your floatiness too much and get given stern tracts of Ibn al-Arabi to study. This is it! Real Sufi – sorry, sufi – stuff and you half-cram the dimly translated works of all sorts of saints into your half-clever mind. Inventing elaborate conceits to insert inane aphorisms into conversations with Münir, you attempt to discourse on your latest earth-shattering mystical discoveries. He only talks about football.

Sunday is when Münir plays football, alternately whirling around the five-a-side pitch past players forty or more years younger, and bellowing fire and bile at the hapless referee. Afterwards, over çay and simit, white cheese and sloppy tomatoes (he hasn't touched meat for years), he talks sport with the lads and is energised and fresh where they are spent. The meat-free thing came from an encounter with a quasi-Brahmin sect of Hindus who eschew all matters of the flesh, not to mention garlic and onions.

So. Is he a Hindu nowadays? His smirking, chic, monied friends quite like the idea that he's gone off his spiritual trolley, not that any of them have heard the call to prayer in years. Actually, he has decided that, spiritually speaking, he is freelance, and tells the story of Moses/Jesus/Mohammed – whoever – hearing the sound of lullaby from a field. Investigating, [name your prophet here] found a simple shepherd singing heavenwards. 'If you were here, I'd brush your beard . . . come, sweetheart, let me pick the lice from your hair and I'll wash your hot feet, too.'

'To whom speaketh you?' asks the prophet in best saintspeak.

'Why, to God!'

'That is no way to address the Almighty!'

And the holy man whips out his travel Torah/Bible/Qur'an and starts teaching the herdsman how to pray.

'Get out of the way!' booms a voice from Heaven. 'I was enjoying that!'

Every December Münir used to travel to Konya in central Anatolia, driving through freezing fog and hailstones. The resting place of Mevlana Rumi, the Pole of Love and father of the Whirling Dervishes, is a turquoise-tiled tomb in the centre of a town populated by unsmiling hollow-cheeked religious fundamentalists. Once a year they tolerate an influx of blissed-out mystic types who pay their respects at the tomb then do battle at the town hall to get tickets to the municipal sema ceremony. This takes place at Konya's sports hall and has turned increasingly into a glad-handing stop on the politican's election trail. No matter how balletic and beautiful the whirling, no matter how haunting the plaint of the ney flute ('People think it makes the sound of air. Really, the ney is the true sound of fire'), men in smart suits deliver turgid speeches to the TV cameras and Münir fumes. Were Rumi not whirling in the celestial sphere, he'd be spinning in his grave.

So, over time, the visits to Konya have become less, and the power of Love is accessed in less ritual, more freelance circumstances. Following him through the streets of Istanbul, Münir appears a pied piper, with shoe-shine boys, waiters and cabbies all swept along in his suite. He has no interest in training disciples – in fact rather sits at the feet of whoever speaks to his heart. His teachers have included: a spinster aunt who wore permanently a most intent, beautiful expression; a man drummed out of every sufi group for claiming that, like Mansur Hallaj, he was God, and who claimed not to have slept since '64, though no one knew if that meant his sixty-forth birthday or 1964; and a recently departed ex-brigadier with eyes like burning coals who could make the weather change just by wishing it.

Münir has always been careful however to avoid the type of miracle-producing charlatan that inhabits the fringes of sufism. He and his line are more than capable of conjuring apparitions out of thin air, but would only do so to illustrate how misleading are such practices and how they veil Truth. A recent visit found him instead quietly, respectfully recognising that the trees in his local park are souls sent to heal human hearts. On a bright blue day without a breath of wind, and when no one was looking, they all bowed towards him.

Sisters and Brothers

HORATIO CLARE

WHEN THEY CAME and sat at my table, that first night in Casablanca, I thought they were setting me up; within minutes of saying 'yes' to them I was in the back of a speeding car, wondering if I was going to die. But they weren't, and I didn't, and the things they taught me, in the week I spent with them, I shall never forget.

Through my European eyes the two young women looked familiar: they wore jeans and T-shirts, they drank and smoked and posed. It was Friday night and the more liberal citizens of Morocco's most modern city were at play. The country's entire political and religious spectrum walks Casablanca's white streets, and its people wear their convictions openly, almost defiantly. Everything from the call to prayer, to the car horns and the beat of the nightclubs seems especially loud. From a conservative's perspective, these two, Saida and Nawal, were fallen, drowning in infidel decadence, and they never dropped their confident, confrontational front for a moment.

They are a team. Saida is thirty, proud and fierce; she is their brains and strength. Nawal, five years younger, backs her up. Saida has two children by her former husband, a Turkish sea captain. She worked as a cook on his boats and ran a restaurant in Istanbul. They were in Rotterdam for a while, until he left her. Now she lives with her mother and children in one of Casablanca's eastern suburbs, and does whatever she must to provide for them. She is not a prostitute, but she is a champion hustler. Her dark hair has red tints, and she has battles on her tongue. She has no illusions about Europe's charms and no patience with Morocco's backwardness.

She saw me come into the bar near the port gates, sent Nawal to sit with me, then followed. In return for drinks I could dance with Nawal, they intimated. Lovely as she was, I did not want to dance with Nawal, I countered, but I was happy to buy a round. We talked, ate sardines, drank and laughed. Saida, seeing that I was not looking for titillation, changed tactics.

'You want to see our house? Meet our family?'

What chance has a European, in a week's snatched leave from the desk and job, of discovering anything more than a guide book knows about anywhere? The planet is paved with travel pieces; most of its inhabitants have seen you coming before you have left home. I had visited Morocco three times already, and never caught it unawares. How will we know the world if we do not put ourselves in its hands?

So, I said yes and we set off for the family flat, via my first car chase. On leaving the restaurant, Saida insulted a cab driver. His price was too high and she rejected it in a withering blast of Arabic which so diminished him that he felt compelled to pursue us. For a few minutes we fled, racing through red lights and charging across junctions. Fortunately, the Casablanca traffic is light at midnight, drivers watch out for each other and the policemen standing on corners have no radios.

Saida soon tired, called a halt and jumped out to confront our pursuer. I followed, but she bawled me back into the car before turning on the man and lashing him with more abuse. Smaller and slower than she, he was soon in retreat. Not content with seeing him off, Saida now set about smashing his pride into little pieces.

At first I could not understand her extraordinary vehemence, her insistence on complete victory in any confrontation, but in the following days I began to see that she could not afford to take a single backward step, ever. Magnanimity might be taken as weakness. Carving out survival and respect for herself and her family, in a society which until recently granted all men's words and whims divine and legal force, demanded unfaltering courage and an iron self-image. It also caused her huge frustration, and woe to the man who gave her cause to vent it. Her ready anger was a kicking, spitting creation of her experiences:

before the law was recently changed a woman could be 'repudiated' by her husband: abandoned at will, economically marooned, socially humiliated. The new Family Code places divorce in the hands of a court, forces men to pay maintenance and allows a woman to divorce her husband. None of these conditions had applied to Saida.

The taxi driver trounced, we then encountered the police. They were not concerned with our motoring offences: the sight of two Moroccan women in a late taxi with a tourist had given them all sorts of ideas and excuses. Saida got rid of the first two with a lot of charm and a packet of my cigarettes, the next two with mock-righteousness, and another packet. In ten minutes I learned to regard street cops the way most Casablancans do: grasping, treacherous, a law unto themselves.

We arrived at the family's flat, where we smoked, drank and fell asleep, bedding down head to toe like dominos on the low, wide bench which ran around the main room. The next morning Saida's mother showed me her home: three rooms and a section of staircase, invisibly divided from the territories of the flats above and below. The roof was similarly apportioned, as most places were: where we use walls and doors, urban Moroccans, splitting less space between more people, agree and honour imaginary boundaries. There was a television, a CD player, a gas stove and a tap. Everything except the TV was low down, near the floor. Like many of the older women I met, Saida's mother spent a lot of the time bending down. She had a bent back and hinged hips.

Over coffee, Saida established that I did not have a firm plan (I meant to go to Fez, and hoped to find time for a beach) and suggested a trip to meet her brother's family, near El Jadida, one hundred kilometres down the coast. I hesitated.

'You want to meet Moroccan peoples?' she demanded. 'So come!'

We eyed each other. The terms of the bargain were clear, if unspoken. I would finance an impromptu family holiday, which Saida would organise and run. We would entwine our agendas: she would show me the pleasure and novelty I sought, I would help her provide for her family and her friend. She would commandeer my spending power. As long as I trusted her to be judicious, and she resisted taking more than was right, it might work.

'You think I am mafia woman?'

'No . . .'

'So come!'

I scrapped my plans and thought of Chaucer that evening as we set off for the seaside. There was Saida, our leader, mother, sword and shield, and Nawal, dolled up in kohl and earrings. There were Saida's sons, Emir, nine, and Edem, eighteen months, and there was Latifa, a large, smiling woman who looked exactly like the nanny, sister-in-law and cook that she was. The women had abandoned jeans and t-shirts in favour of jellabas, cotton robes. They would no longer smoke cigarettes in public. On the way we bought some lamb from a roadside butcher and picked up Abdellah, Saida's brother, who sat on my lap, so that all of us, five adults and two children, squeezed into an elderly Mercedes taxi and still left the driver room to change gear, just. As the dark road unrolled ahead of us and Casablanca disappeared behind, I imagined us telling our stories in turn, like the pilgrims, and wished that I might collect them.

Before we went to her friends' farm by the sea, Saida explained, we would spend a night with her brother's family in town. Abdellah smiled and nodded. He spoke very little English and little French. Saida spoke some English, which she preferred to French, except when she was cross.

After an hour the Mercedes crossed a river and curled into the dark back streets of a town. The tarmac gave out, the road became a rough track between silent houses. We stopped. Abdellah shouted, summoning his wife, the sister of our cook. She welcomed us, with her two year-old daughter, and we invaded. We were joined by our cook's husband, Nagy Abdellah. This delightful man spoke excellent French, and became my friend and Arabic translator. Nagy Abdellah comes from a family of Berber farmers. He used to work in an engineering plant but it closed, after injuring one of his hands, leaving him unemployed. He helps his relatives with farming, when they need it, smokes *kif* and eats little. He walks, acts and holds himself with quiet dignity, as if he is naturally thin and abstemious, but it seems he has trained himself to do without.

'You are very welcome,' he said, as we settled down to mint tea.

'Thank you,' I said, 'It is wonderful to be here, in El Jadida.'

'Azemmour,' he said, quietly, 'It's very near El Jadida.'

Twenty kilometres, according to my guide book.

There were now ten of us, my duty-free whisky, Nagy Abdellah's *kif* and the cassette player. Everyone danced, in pairs, to amuse everyone else. Sharing one room, sitting around with our backs to its white walls, meant that scarcely a flicker of feeling among us went unnoticed. If baby Edem felt ignored, or his 'aunt' Nawal impatient to dance or his uncle Abdellah muzzily insulted or his British guest self-conscious, then we all knew, instantly. Everyone participated in everyone else's feelings. We watched each other's eyes, sensed each other's breaths. To be with people and have no table, no meal, no occasion nor common purpose between you, nothing to shield or distract you, is more revealing than any interview.

We were all shy and curious and entertained by the situation, but guest and host are easy roles and Saida's nonchalant domination allowed everyone to relax. She chided her brother for drinking too much, kept the children in line, rolled her eyes at Nawal's dancing (Nawal seemed born to take the floor and shake) and told me to sit up straight when I began to get too comfortable. She transformed the entire party into a group of conspiratorially grinning children, frowned, and seemed content.

After a couple of hours the cook quietly produced a platter covered in a huge, aromatic mound of couscous, lamb and hard boiled eggs. Now everyone was ravenous. A low table was assembled and we surrounded it, humming and swallowing with pleasure. First a bowl and kettle full of water were circulated, for washing hands, then bread was distributed, expertly torn so that each received a piece roughly proportional to his or her size, and then we ate.

The feast was stacked in a rough cone. It was exquisitely cooked and most delicious. You ate with your right hand only, taking food from the section of the cone which was in front of you. Saida occasionally prodded morsels in one direction or another, ensuring a fair distribution. It was good manners to move a piece of meat into your neighbour's segment: as guest, I was over served and became involved in a benign battle with Nagy Abdellah, who, though much hungrier than I and much more in need of food, repeatedly urged me, through mouthfuls of couscous: '*Mange! Mange!*'

'*Oui, je mange!*' I protested, '*Mangez-vous!*'

'*Mange!*' he replied, and we grinned over our bulging cheeks and working jaws.

When it was done, and the huge clay dish completely bare, we all sank back, eyes slightly glazed, and thanked the cook profusely. She blushed. More smoking and drinking followed.

I went to bed first, having been roundly embraced, danced with and welcomed, but was woken after a short sleep by terrible shouts and screams. Abdellah was furious with his wife – a gentle and sweet young woman – for no reason but that he was drunk, and Saida was furious with him. He tried to hit his wife. Nagy Abdellah and I threw ourselves on him. He seemed to calm down, but as soon as we released him, went for her again; again we intervened. Saida yelled, the children cried, his wife wailed and Abdellah roared. He produced a knife and waved it. We remonstrated. It took half an hour for peace to return, by which time everyone was thoroughly fed up. We took to our beds.

The next day divided down gender lines. Saida, Latifa the cook, Nawal and Emir went shopping; the young wife cleaned the house and kept an eye on the baby and the men, and the men watched television, listened to music and smoked *kif*. It was hot outside. Shattering white sunlight fell from a blaring blue sky. The men kept low down near the floor, moving as little as possible. With no exterior windows and the lights off, the room was dim shadowed, lit by the television. A couple of Abdellah's friends came round; soon the gloom eddied with blue smoke. The Moroccan tennis team were on the box: every point they won drew hisses of admiration, every one they lost hurt. My friends seemed to divide their country into two. Morocco at work, which they bemoaned as a near disaster – no jobs, no money, bad police, poverty, corruption – and Morocco at play: the food, the music, company, *kif* and sports; the life of the streets, the balmy, limpid evenings, the stunning beauty of its lights and colours, which delighted and beguiled them daily as much as it ever did any tourist, and of which they were intensely proud.

It was a strange, guilty pleasure to lie there, as if in a company of eternal students. Denied earning power by their unemployment, and spending power by their women, who shopped, haggled and hustled for them, the men played endless cassettes, lost themselves in television and devoted hours to the preparation, sharing and smoking of *kif*. They were gentle, funny and respectful with each other, in that red-eyed brotherhood of the routinely stoned, but became defensive, raucous and obstreperous when the women returned, fomenting spurious conflict as if to divert attention from their self indulgence and redundancy. *Kif* is a perfect opiate for the long-term unemployed. Left with nothing but each other, their daydreams and low grade TV, *kif* smokers can be happily entombed for weeks and months. The craving for sugar is kept at bay with mint tea, the hours collapse into each other until late evening and the meal. It is not surprising African governments are relaxed about *kif* and khat. Beyond the economic benefits, they mummify huge armies of the continent's poor.

Saida reappeared with the shopping, hot, tired and righteous, and kicked up a fuss. She chased everyone out of the living room, insisted on the proper sweeping and stowing of everything, demanded more money then issued some of it back to me, with instructions to go to the supermarket to stock up on alcohol. Abdellah and Nagy Abdellah would accompany me, but first I would change out of my shorts. Only children, tourists and fools wore shorts in town. Was I trying to shame her? We did as we were told, and set off, giggling.

Azemmour is one of a string of walled Atlantic towns, built and fortified by the Portuguese. Violet bougainvillaea pours over the top of the ramparts; at their foot a wide, shallow river reaches the sea. We swung along holding hands. I was surprised and awkward at first, but Moroccan men link up with their buddies, so why not me? It is changing now among the modern, northern young, but until recently men and women did not touch in public. Holding hands with another man made me feel part of a brotherhood, and gave rise to an oddly innocent feeling of solidarity, like something between prep school boys. As we passed the communal water trough I was introduced to some of Abdellah's neighbours. The children already knew my name: the street was, literally, a closer community than any I had encountered. Then in the middle of town we came across a party of European tourists, who pretended not to see us. How stiff and self conscious they seemed! I bristled, senselessly. There is nothing like advancing an inch towards another culture to make you see the miles which separate yours from it. My companions were much more tolerant of these rich, distant strangers.

At the supermarket booze is issued from behind a special counter, as cigarettes are in Europe. Loaded like smugglers, clinking like pirates, we hauled bags of wine and beer back to the house, then on to the bus station and the ranks of Mercedes 'Grand Taxis'. To take seven adults, one a white foreigner, and two children in two taxis a few kilometres out of town required a detailed haggle, and Saida lost her temper. Soon she was insulting people's mothers (my Arabic was expanding in idiosyncratic directions), gangs of taxi drivers were taunting her, Abdellah was offering to fight one of them, our party were beseeching brother and sister to stop, the children were wailing, the sunset call to prayer was echoing out, unheeded, and I was beginning to wonder if my presence was doing more harm than good.

My skin and wallet were raising prices. The alcohol I provided had stoked last night's fight. As much as I wanted to be an ambassador for Europe, a respectful and beneficial guest, I also dreaded becoming a corrupting example of everything many Muslims say is wrong with the West and its influence. A vigorous man shepherded us to two friendly taxis. We left Azemmour, adrenalin subsiding, smoking celebratory cigarettes.

The farm was a few miles north of town, off the main road, down a sandy, tree-lined track. The fields were sand, the hedges were lines of high thorn, shielding low buildings walled in wood, mud and polythene, roofed in corrugated iron and thorn thatch. Breezes brushed through poplars and silver olive trees. We were greeted by friendly dogs, then staring children, then embracing adults. There were four men, three wives, four children and a matriarch, Aicha. This elderly woman was as low and broad as a small boat. She shook my hand with a powerful grip and her black eyes twinkled as she welcomed me.

The following days were luminous. Saida and Aicha decided and organised everything. The children hauled water from the well and helped out, wives cooked and cleaned. The men controlled the music (a cassette player running off a car battery), showed me the way through the fields and over the great sand dune to the endless beach – a strip of wild heaven where Africa and the Atlantic met in booming waves and coloured sprays – and challenged me to races and swimming matches. I began to see patterns, large and small. For instance, a favourite beach game involved sitting around a cone of sand with a twig in the top, taking turns to scrabble a little away, until the fall of the twig pointed out the loser. This mirrored the codes of the evening meal, where sensitivity to fairness and proportion were all. At the centre of everything was the group, not the individual. Our great wealth allows us to disregard our fellows in a way which was impossible here.

We lived close to the land. At dawn, Nagy Abdellah set snares for rabbits in the dunes. The names of animals, insects and trees were my first Arabic lessons; the correct use of a few words caused general delight. I gave Emir English coaching, and stupidly objected to Saida's disciplinary sanction, which involved seizing her son's arm and administering a Chinese burn.

'You know my son? I not know my son?'

'No . . . no – yes!'

I was lucky to escape a burn myself. And he was a beautifully bought-up boy.

The nights were rich with feasts, dances and parties, and loud with fights. Alcohol was not necessarily a cause. One night a teetotal male uncle struck his wife, because she objected to his plans for a second spouse. The wife was Aicha's daughter, and the old woman barrelled out into the night with a stout stick. Retribution delivered, they all came back to the main room, and sat with their backs to one another, both young women in tears, Aicha growling, the man skulking. The new family laws will eventually marginalise polygamy, which will reduce domestic violence. What I saw was never vicious but it was frequent, and seemed to spring from a mismatch between traditional and actual roles. Abdellah would be rude to his wife, in the manner of a petty tyrant, but then his sister, daily earning and underlining her dominance, would leap in, and soon men and women would be slapping and shouting. The men were vulnerable to the facts and the women's tongues. It always ended in tears, but though Moroccan women have decades of battles to fight, with enlightened legislation, and as long as there is no lurch back into conservatism, they will surely triumph: the strength and nous of Saida and her sisters will change their world, and ours. They are the key to a secure, prosperous and open-hearted Morocco; never mind symbolic handshakes with half-friendly despots: we desperately need just and tolerant Islamic societies, and Morocco is closer to that than most.

The men took me aside, one afternoon; the two Abdellahs, two uncles, and a younger man, Mohammed. What did I think of the war? Why were Muslims being killed in Iraq? What did the British people think? We talked about America, about oil and Saddam Hussein. Our feelings were broadly similar, until we came to Israel and Palestine. Although I was in sympathy with their positions, it was immediately clear that I did not, could not feel the depths of their anger and anguish. The back streets of Gaza do not look unlike the back streets of Azemmour. Historians might mock Arab attempts at unity, but in a simple and absolute sense, the Palestinians are my friends' brothers, and as they see it, our ally's allies are killing them. Al Quaeda has already killed Moroccans, and recruited Moroccans to kill for it: of all its mixed messages, there is no question which does most damage here, in a country with a history of good relations with Judaism. When we turned away from the subject, much later, they were still shaking their heads.

There were also moments of great peace. Saida and Nawal appeared on the beach and even tried the sea. I found my place – one night someone remarked on my improving table manners the instant before I reached out and, sin of sins, used a touch of my left hand. Saida froze in horror. A storm of laughter broke. It was more fun being the clown than the bank.

My final lesson was saved for the last day. Our goodbyes were all said, our presents exchanged and Saida had made sure I understood that the taxi driver wanted three hundred dirhams – about twenty pounds. She repeated it: she knew I had over-prepared, drawing seven hundred from the bank. As we drove away she gave me a strange, mixed look; partly an adult seeing off a naïve, over-confident child; partly a card-sharp bidding farewell to an amusing sucker; partly envy, and partly something else, something that might just have included, I wished, a grain of respect.

Arriving at the airport I opened my wallet and found just two hundred dirham notes. I was furious, vehement, enraged. How could she? After everything – a thief! But as the taxi driver drove away grumbling, I found myself smiling. I had sounded just like Saida, raving away, and I had got a great deal. With a few more weeks I might even have begun to understand something of the true nature of my own culture's God of Gods: the market.

Mr F.

FRASER HARRISON

THIS MAN HAS NOTHING. He stands before me with nothing to his name but the clothes he's wearing.

Actually, even that's not true. Some of his clothes have just been given to him and he has no name; at least not one that the authorities will necessarily accept. He landed on British soil without a passport or ID of any kind and has no means of proving what his real name is, no means of proving where he came from or how he got here. He is no one and owns nothing. He is an asylum seeker.

As a single man claiming to have left Afghanistan in fear of his life, he has been detained by the immigration authorities while his case is considered. I have been appointed his lawyer and we sit in a small room while he tells me his story. He has been supplied with a tweed jacket and a v-necked sweater, which lend him the air of a businessman on his way to a round of golf before Sunday lunch. However, I notice that he has disdained socks although it is November and I can see a brown, hairily-fringed ankle showing above his sandal.

My client – Mr F. – is forty-five, but like many Afghans looks older than his English equivalent. His hair is short and greying, his moustache is thick but brindled with grey, and several teeth are missing from his genial smile. As he speaks to me he folds his arms across his broad chest, looking me in the eye as he tells me the story of his life. I do not understand a word because he is speaking in Dari, but I smile and nod, hoping to lay the foundations of trust.

Through an interpreter he tells me he is from a town in the west of Afghanistan not far from the border with Iran. He is not an educated man, but as a child he was sent to the mosque by his father where the mullah taught him to read and write a little. I have already noticed that his signature is a florid affair, his name written right to left and encompassed within a bold circle.

He tells me that in the days when the *mujahadin* held power in his part of the country he owned two shops which sold household goods, pots and pans, kettles and so forth. They were profitable and allowed him and his family to live quite well, but then one day the local warlord threatened to close them down unless he paid protection money. To make sure he got the message the warlord beat him and threw his stock onto the street. Mr F. paid up.

Not long after that the Taliban began to take power in Afghanistan. They attacked his town and a bomb landed directly on his house. When he came back from his shop he found that his home had been completely destroyed. He met a friend and asked him, 'Where is my family?' He told him they were under the rubble. Mr F. fainted. When he regained consciousness he saw that his neighbours had dragged out the bodies. There were five of them: his father, his mother, his wife, his two sons.

He tells me the names of his two sons and weeps.

Finally he recovers his composure and apologises for not being able to remember the exact year: his memory has been affected by the things that have happened to him.

As if he has not lost enough, he has lost his memory.

Mr F. has nothing. He is indeed a poor, bare, forked animal, a naked figure exposed to the pitiless bureaucratic elements.

Like many asylum seekers he has spent the last of his money on his journey to the UK. He has arrived with empty pockets. This is no metaphor. His pockets are literally empty. He has no money, no possessions. And this is a man who was affluent by the standards of his community, for he had sufficient wealth to pay off the warlords and keep his business going. But now he is poor in a way that is outside our notions of poverty. He has no cash, not even a stray coin in the lining of his coat. He has no savings, no pension, no earnings. Nor has he any resources. He cannot arrange an overdraft, far less resort to plastic credit. Furthermore, he is financially impotent because, as an asylum seeker, he is forbidden to work or do business or engage in any form of money-making, including begging. He is condemned to be the object of the state's charity.

It is hard to believe but there are many asylum seekers whose financial state is still more dire than Mr F.'s. Some have reached this country with less than nothing in that they have debts, the single unwanted possession they could not shed. A Chinese client whose journey was organised by the Snakeheads or gang masters will owe them years of future labour. He may become a virtual slave, never earning enough to keep pace with the interest on his loan, far less reduce the principal. If the client is a woman who has been trafficked from Eastern Europe she will see no more of England and English money than the room where she is locked up until no further use to the sex industry. In this respect at least Mr F. can be called fortunate, because his father-in-law was able to finance his journey.

His poverty entitles him to be given £3 to spend, but without his being consulted the money has been converted into a phone card. He shows it to me, turning it over and over. It is useless to him. No one in his family in Afghanistan has a phone. He knows no one in England whom he might ring.

As well as his futile phone card he will have been issued with a so-called 'destitution pack': two disposable razors, two hotel-style bars of soap, a hotel-size bottle of shampoo, a miniature toothbrush and tube of toothpaste like the ones distributed as complimentary gifts by airlines. He is entitled to two sets of brand-new underwear, one to wear, one to wash. These are his possessions.

No, he has one possession that is indisputably his own: his worry beads which are purple and strung on a piece of silk with a long tassel. As I speak to him about refugee law and the Byzantine ramifications of asylum seeking, he sits back in his chair, listening carefully, and appears to draw comfort from the beads' steady rotation through his hand. Their rhythmic clicking must be one of the few familiar sensations that he has brought to the strange world of his new country, though, paradoxically, it marks him unmistakeably as a stranger. Whenever I tell him I am going to do something for him – write a letter on his behalf, fill in a form, make a phone call – he halts his beads for a moment, places his hand on his heart and bows his head. The interpreter volunteers that it is a gesture of thanks.

Mr F. tells me that once the Taliban gained control of his city they too demanded protection money. When he refused they confiscated one of his shops, but gave him a receipt declaring that no Taliban was to demand anything further from him because he had paid his 'fine'.

If the Taliban robbed him, it is nothing to the dispossession he has undergone by turning himself into an asylum seeker. He is only beginning to discover the extent of his poverty.

Once he leaves this interview room and the services of our interpreter he will be silenced: he cannot understand what is said, what he hears, what he overhears, what he reads (his reading is in any case very poor) and he cannot make himself understood, except by sign language. He may be lucky enough to find another Afghan to talk to, but if he is the only Dari-speaker in the place he will be alone, at least in this respect. Silent and isolated, he will struggle to make sense of what is happening to him and the welter of legal advice I have just delivered. Silence is a separate prison, a gaol within a gaol. Nor is the presence of compatriots always companionable. His fellow Afghan might be a Taliban sympathiser, or a member of the Hisb-e-Islami with whom his family has traditionally been at war, or loyal to the Mujahadin who robbed him. Mutual suspicion may well impose silence on the only two people among the four hundred who speak the same language.

Mr F. shows fewer signs of anxiety than many of our clients. When my advice is beyond his comprehension – and who amongst us can claim fully to grasp the Kafkaesque convolutions of our asylum system? – he smiles and tells me his destiny is in the hands of God.

When the Taliban were ousted and the Karzai government came to power, Mr F.'s part of the country became the fiefdom of a Northern Alliance commander, who accused him of collaborating with the Taliban and giving them material support. He said that if Mr F. wanted to avoid being arrested he should pay him the same amount he had given to the Taliban, a kind of pre-emptive ransom. Mr F. defied him and went to

Kabul to complain. He was convinced that Karzai himself had no idea that local commanders were terrorising people, but he failed to find anyone willing to listen to him and was forced to return home empty-handed.

The local commander immediately came to his house to punish him, boasting that Karzai was impotent outside Kabul and could do nothing to protect him. To prove his point he attacked him with a sickle and inflicted a terrible laceration on his chest. Mr F. pulls up his shirt to show me. His brown skin is ridged by a ragged six-inch purple scar, which has been crudely stitched. I make a note, but Mr F. is not satisfied: he invites me to feel it. I demur, but he reaches over and takes my hand, guiding my finger along the length of his wound as if I were doubting Thomas. He smiles, glad to have won my faith, and invites the interpreter to follow suit.

I ask him for the name of this bloodthirsty commander, but he refuses to give it to me. He says the man will murder the rest of his family if he finds out that his name has been given to the UK authorities.

Mr F. has not lost his nationality in the technical sense, but for the time being he has lost something of his national identity. He is not yet, and may never be, an *emigré* Afghan, and so far he has no aspirations to be British. Like many Afghan asylum seekers, he does not want to stay in the UK but wants to return home as soon as things get better there. He loves Afghanistan. He has remarried and wants to be with his second wife and his daughters. He only left them most unwillingly under severe duress. He had no dreams of a better, richer life abroad; how could life be better anywhere without his family? He had been a relatively rich man before his flight; why exchange a good business, despite all its problems, for penury? It had been the agent's idea, not his, to come to Britain, a country of which he has the haziest picture. Indeed, when he landed in Aberdeen he had to be told that Scotland was part of the UK. Still less did he plan to come here in order to milk the system or sponge off benefits, as the *Daily Mail* would have us believe were his true motives. He has no idea what the 'system' is. He understands charity, because it is one of the pillars of Islam and he is grateful for what he has been given since his arrival, but he has no conception of 'benefits'. His mind is not on what the UK can offer, but on what he has left behind in his own country: his family, his brothers, his business, his world.

He does not yet realise it, but in the eyes of the British, his new neighbours, he is identifiable as an asylum seeker first and, by a long distance, an Afghan second. On the street he will most probably be labelled a 'Paki', the generic subcategory of all brown people, whatever their immigration status and origin. He certainly does not realise that he has been, and until the imminent general election will continue to be, the subject of innumerable public opinion surveys designed to measure our increasing hostility to him. He has no idea that by fleeing the lawlessness of his own country he has turned himself into a kind of outlaw in this one, and he will be amazed to discover that merely by being a Muslim he is perceived by the British to be a threat to their security.

Mr F. tells me that the commander imprisoned him in the basement of a house with four other men. Above, on the ground floor, there was a small hole with a lid, which was lifted to let them in and out. On the few occasions when they were taken up from the basement they were hobbled with chains round their feet and hands. Apart from a candle, the basement had no light and the only ventilation came through a little grille in the wall. The men were forced to use a bucket as their toilet. The floor of the basement, which they had to lie on, was bare earth and damp.

When I ask him for the location of the house he apologises and refuses again; this time he says that neither Karzai nor the UN could save his family from the commander.

He has a second wife and two young children at home. No, not at home; he no longer has a home. After his first wife died he married her cousin, and she gave him two daughters. He has no way of finding out if they are safe, or even alive. They have no telephone. He cannot write, and if he could there would be no postal service to deliver his letter. Nor would it be safe to write, for the letter might be opened and used against his family. Now that he has left the country, they may be punished for his departure, or harassed because they have no one to protect them. He tells me he prays for them, and hopes they are in the care of his father-in-law, who lives in a town well away from the commander's influence. They are the second family he has lost.

He weeps again.

Imagine losing your children. It is unimaginable. The death of a child is often counted the most tragic thing that can happen to a parent. Mr F.'s second family are not dead, but the price of their safety is his absence. He had become the very thing every father dreads: a danger to his children. So far from being his family's protector and provider, he had become their enemy. To protect them he had to orphan his children and desert his wife. For their sake he had to engineer his own death. Imagine the grief that he must be suffering.

His loss extends still further, for the rest of his family, brothers, cousins, uncles, aunts, are also lost to him, as well as the whole communal network that used to form his world. He is now a singular being, unsupported by a community, history or culture that he understands. He has acquired individuality, something that we prize in the developed world, but to him it will feel like alienation. He has no concept of autonomy in the Western sense. Autonomy is the founding principle of democracy – one person, one vote and in liberal philosophy self-determination is the basis of human rights. The individual's autonomy is held to be sacred and must be protected against the tyrannies of state, religion and social custom. Mr F. has claimed the protection of our liberal values, as is his right according to international law, but in doing so he has unwittingly left himself unprotected in a new way: for the first time in his life he must live in society as an isolated individual – safe, but alone.

After keeping Mr F. for a week in his basement prison the commander had him transferred to Kabul and delivered into the hands of the national security department. Mr F. discovered that he had been accused of spying for the Taliban. He was tortured to reveal information about his surviving contacts. At the same time his guards told him they would let him out if he paid a ransom. They used to come at night to beat him and give him electric shocks. A wire was attached to his genitals and another was put into his nose. They did this to him for a month; as result he can no longer sleep properly and he still shakes.

I have spoken to many torture victims. In some cases their eyes tell you they have been to a terrible place and have not returned. They remain remote, still imprisoned in the place and time of their torture. Looking into their eyes you seem to peer down a very long tunnel, at the end of which lies a tormented darkness. Jean Amery, the Auschwitz survivor, wrote, 'anyone who has been tortured remains tortured . . . Anyone who has suffered torture never again will be able to be at ease in the world . . . Faith in humanity, already cracked by the first slap in the face, then demolished by torture, is never acquired again.' And yet I have also met torture victims who seem to possess an extraordinary resilience that makes them capable of coming back, damaged of course, but not broken. Mr F. appears to be one of the latter. I cannot comment on his faith in humanity, our acquaintance has been too brief, but the fact that he turned himself into an asylum seeker suggests that he believed that what was done to him was a local aberration that would not be repeated elsewhere. Nor has his faith in his fellow Afghans been destroyed by his experiences, for he wants to go home when circumstances allow it. I ask him why he chose to come to the United Kingdom, and he says, 'The agent brought me here. He said it would be safe.'

The Red Cross came to visit him in prison and gave him a blanket. They demanded that he be taken to hospital for tests because his eyesight had been affected by the beatings he had taken and he could no longer walk straight. He was peeing blood. When he came back from hospital the guards took his new blanket off him.

Finally, his father-in-law managed to visit him and burst into tears when he saw him. He promised he would sell Mr F.'s remaining shop to raise the money necessary for his 'bail'. One afternoon Mr F. was handcuffed, blindfolded and put into the back of a van. He was taken for a long journey beyond the city and then pushed out. He heard the van drive away, leaving him still handcuffed and blindfolded. Some hours later his father-in-law arrived and freed him. Mr F. told him that he wanted to go home, but his father-in-law said it was too dangerous and, in any case, he had already paid an agent a large sum to take him out of the country immediately. He tells me he has not seen any of his family apart from his father-in-law for more than a year.

I dare not tell him that if he is accepted as a refugee he would have the right to bring them here. Despite his ordeal, there is no guarantee that his claim will be accepted or even believed, because his credibility is one of his many losses. As long as he is an asylum seeker his truthfulness will be denied and attacked by the Home Office in whose hands his fate lies. He must labour under the legal principle that 'he who asserts must prove', and as a man who has nothing his assertions are, by definition, his only evidence; he has no proof except his word. If like Mr F. you flee your country taking nothing with you – no papers, records, documents, passport, birth or marriage certificate, no newspaper cuttings – your integrity will be your only credential. As a result the Home Office are left with a simple but devastating weapon: they can respond to whatever you claim by saying you are a liar, and you can no more refute them than you can absolve yourself. The question of credibility dominates the majority of asylum appeals, and the Home Office proceeds from the base assumption that all asylum claims are, to use the Daily Mail's favourite vilification, bogus ('sham, fictitious, spurious'). He does not realise it yet, but Mr F. has joined the ranks of the bogus: the death of his first family, extortion by the Taliban, torture, the loss of his second family – the British government will say he made it all up.

Mr F. left Afghanistan the day after he was released from prison, embarking on a journey by bus, train, boat and lorry that brought him at last to a dockside where he was arrested. He had to be told by the police that he was in the UK.

I have never been to Afghanistan and have no idea what the country-side round his village looks like. The TV pictures from the days of the war in 2002 showed us jagged mountains and stony, dusty plains coloured every variety of brown. There has been no time to ask him, but for all I know Mr F. lived in a green valley, surrounded by the orchards and market gardens for which Afghanistan was famous before the Taliban destroyed them. As yet he has not added up the precise account of his loss; however, one day in the near future he will realise that what was his familiar landscape, the topography of home, has been lost to him, possibly forever. Those of us who have not endured exile cannot understand the meaning of such deprivation. I try to imagine myself as an exile in Afghanistan: no matter how spectacular the mountains of my new landscape might be, they would be no consolation for never again seeing the Pembrokeshire coast or the marshes of north Norfolk. If confined to Afghanistan, I would never see salt water again. Mr F. has lost his family, never mind his mountains, but even if I were deprived of nothing more than the sea my grief would be acute and lifelong.

When the interview is over I stand up, but Mr F. remains seated. He indicates that he still has something to say. 'I'm sure you believe in God,' the interpreter relays to me. 'May God bless you and take care of you.' I smile a little queasily and thank him, but do not tell him that I am a non-believer. I bid him goodbye, reassuring him that we will meet tomorrow when his interview with the Home Office is due to take place. He bows his head repeatedly, placing his hand on his heart.

Mr F. has not lost everything, after all. His faith appears to be intact, and if I interpret his last remark correctly it is helping him to sustain his capacity for trust, a miraculous preservation given his history. Just as miraculously, he has retained his dignity, which is no small matter; indeed, you could say it is the whole man. The dictionary defines dignity, first, as 'a composed and serious manner', and, secondly, as 'the state of being worthy of honour or respect'. Mr F. has shown remarkable composure throughout our interview, a sign of his courage, but he has tempered his inevitable seriousness with flashes of affability that must have been his everyday manner when he was younger.

Dignity of the second kind is a far bigger concept. The opening words of the Universal Declaration of Human Rights (1948) state that 'recognition of the inherent dignity of all members of the human family is the foundation of freedom, justice and peace in the world'. Nearly two decades later the International Covenant on Civil and Political Rights (1966) identified dignity as the very source of rights. Its preamble declares that the states which are party to the Covenant recognise that 'these rights derive from the inherent dignity of the human person.' Successive regimes in Afghanistan did their best to impress on Mr F. that he was unworthy of respect and therefore not entitled to his rights, yet a stubborn evaluation of his own worth prevailed within him and left his dignity, in the first dictionary sense, undiminished, if battered. Now that he is in Britain our asylum-seeking system is the latest agent to besiege his dignity. It seems unlikely to succeed. A man who has survived torture and the Taliban and is still capable of asking God's blessing on another man is not going to be humbled by our Immigration Service. It may refuse him; in its wisdom it may even decide to return him to Afghanistan and extreme peril; but let us hope it will not break his spirit.

Youssou N'Dour

MARK HUDSON

D AKAR'S MARCHE SANDAGA shows only as a small triangle on the map of the Senegalese capital, but every time I come here this great hive of commerce seems to have expanded another few blocks. And you can feel the buzz, the intensity of the place minutes before you actually reach it. The women squatting with their merchandise along the kerbsides become more numerous, the number of hawkers and loiterers crowding the pavements larger with every passing step. And as you move into the lanes around the market building itself you can practically see the tension boiling in the air. Everyone seems to be looking around wild-eyed – though apparently indifferent to the occasional spectacularly glamorous woman sauntering through the throng – so that it's difficult to tell who's buying, who's selling and who's just standing, watching and waiting.

This is where every Youssou N'Dour cassette begins its life. Boys head out into the streets with trayfuls of cassettes. Everyone who can stump up the equivalent of £1.20 buys it as a matter of course, and within hours N'Dour's extraordinary, golden voice and his music's throbbing, rattling rhythms are blaring from every taxi and market stall in the city. Because everybody here wants to know what 'Youssou' has done next.

As the heaving rush hour traffic begins to build, N'Dour stands amid the tranquility of the courtyard of Dakar's Grand Mosque – only half a mile from the Marche Sandaga – a picture of serene composure in his coat of many colours. While the patchwork gown is of the sort worn by itinerant Senegalese mystics as a sign of poverty and humility, it will come as a surprise to no one familiar with N'Dour and his work that his is a couture version put together by a local designer. It's not that he's a dandy or particularly in thrall to vulgar ideas of glamour. But since he played his first British concert twenty years ago, he's made a career out of reinventing and interpreting African tradition, and of balancing the desires and expectations of Western and African audiences: the millions of Westerners who bought his hit '7 Seconds' with Neneh Cherry, the nit-picking world music enthusiasts and the people on the Dakar bus. Indeed he's made a lot more than just a career out of it.

Hailed as the man who would give African music a Bob Marley-style commercial breakthrough, he survived the collapse of that expectation despite being twice dropped by Western majors. He's made a vast amount of music, from the sublime to the atrocious, and is now not only probably the most famous and influential man in Senegal, he's Africa's most famous musician and the single most significant figure to emerge from the whole world music phenomenon.

Indeed, he's become a figurehead for Africa as a whole, tirelessly promoting the idea that there's more to this vast continent than corruption, AIDS and genocide, and establishing a reputation as wise, humane, and above all *sensible*.

Yet all the signs are that N'Dour is about to show a very different face to the world. The mystic's gown and the choice of mosque as photo location aren't mere exotic props. N'Dour's forthcoming release, 'Egypt', is an album of Islamic praise songs, and he has refused to play in the USA since the beginning of the Iraq war. While he has always worn his religion very lightly, the last time we met in November 2002, just after the release of his previous album, the highly regarded 'Nothing's in Vain', he was already talking about the current project, arranged 'by someone raised in my own religion, which is Islam' – all said with a certain bullishness that seemed to draw a very clear line, between *you* and *us*.

I first interviewed N'Dour in 1988, backstage at Wembley Stadium as he was about to go on stage with Sting, Springsteen, Peter Gabriel and Tracy Chapman on the first date of an epic international tour to promote Amnesty International. It was the most important moment of his career to date, and having blagged my way through several layers of security I'd blundered into the middle of it. Anyone else would have had the impertinent hack booted straight back into the audience, but N'Dour simply shrugged, sat down and got on with it.

Yet as I listened to him holding calmly forth about the need to protect freedom of speech internationally – while deftly side-stepping questions about human rights in Senegal – I found myself wondering, Does he actually mean any of this? In the Western African *griot* tradition to which N'Dour belongs – and which he has endlessly, startlingly reinvented – the artist speaks not for himself, but on behalf of the community as a whole. I must now have interviewed him at least ten times, and while he is always friendly, even jovial in a blokish high-fiving way (his English having got better as my French gets worse) he tends to be infuriatingly circumspect and diplomatic. At times I've felt that I've pushed ever deeper into what makes him tick. At others I've wondered if I've recorded one sentence that reveals who he really is.

As I drive from Dakar airport, after arriving at two in the morning, I find myself thinking back to something he said last time we met – eighteen months ago, when September 11 was still raw in the mind – that, of course, 'when you see a lot of people dying it's terrible, *but . . .*' – and it was that last word that had made me uneasy – 'if people don't help poor countries there will not be peace.'

From the perspective of the well-fed West, the connection between the blasting of the Two Towers and the struggles of the Wretched of the Earth may not be so apparent. But if you were one of the millions without a job, out in Dakar's sprawling poor suburbs – where to be poor, black and Muslim seem naturally to go together – how could you resist feeling a slight satisfaction that for once the all-powerful West was getting it (never mind that Bin Laden himself is a spoilt rich kid)?

With the highest birthrate in the world Senegal has a vast mush-rooming youthful population (of around twelve million), and while Dakar is a regional economic centre, poverty and unemployment are endemic. Senegal is considered one of the most stable of Islamic countries, with only a marginal fundamentalist presence, but that's exactly what they used to say about Egypt and Morocco. Of the series of oppositions that make up the popular Senegalese worldview – between rich and poor, Muslim and non-Muslim – none is more potent than that between the black man and the *toubab* – the white. And whether N'Dour himself subscribes to this way of seeing things, he understands it all too well. Because while he may now be a multimillionaire, the world of Dakar's *quartiers populaires* is where he comes from.

Yet as I drive around town the next day, past the once elegant, now rather crumbling administrative buildings, the walls scrawled with the images of the leaders of the sufi brotherhoods (popular mystical orders seeking salvation through a particular saint or holy man) that dominate Senegalese Islam, the building sites where work always seems at a lull, it's difficult to feel much of a threat. Dakar always has been hustly as hell, with vast numbers of people with nothing to do, but it's a basically amiable place. This doesn't feel like a society that's about to explode.

When we finally meet N'Dour at his studio out near the Pointe des Almadies, the westernmost point of the African continent, he's in a relaxed and expansive mood.

'This album began as a purely personal project,' he says. 'Six years ago during Ramadan, I was listening to the radio. There was deep Islamic music in Arabic for older people to listen to, and there was rap for the young people. But there wasn't anything in between – anything that answered the way I was feeling. And when I started to think about what I could do I remembered that I used to hear a lot of Egyptian radio when I was young, and my father was a great fan of Oum Kalsoum.'

A muezzin's daughter from the Egyptian provinces, Kalsoum is supposedly the most played artist of the twentieth century. Her austere, majestically yearning voice, steeped in the cadences of the Muslim liturgy, was both the defining sound of the heroic age of Arab national-ism and an excellent example of how the sacred pervades every aspect of artistic expression in Islamic society.

'To me her voice is magic – the quality of space in the arrangements. I wanted to see if I could achieve that with my own voice, and bring together north and west African traditions.'

Working with Egyptian composer and arranger Fathy Salama, N'Dour visited Cairo, and after much coming and going the album 'Egypt' was written and recorded – a fascinating work that pits N'Dour's invocatory *griot* singing against elements of sufi chanting, the magnificent droning microtonality of Arab classical music against Western harmonics and the benefits of multi-tracking. Certainly it is completely unlike anything N'Dour has done before – a world away even from 2000's semi-traditional 'Nothing's in Vain'. Yet it sat on a shelf for five years.

'I thought it was just private spiritual music for me and my family to listen to together. Then I played it to my manager, and my record company Nonesuch heard it, and they wanted to put it out right away. But for me it was too close to September 11. I didn't want it to be seen as a response to that. It's a very personal record. I didn't want it to be touched by politics.'

None the less, N'Dour is quoted in the album's notes as saying that 'Islam has been badly used by a certain ideology'. I wonder if he means Bush's demonisation or Bin Laden's Wahabbist ultra-orthodoxy.

'I'm not at a high level of Islam,' he says, tactfully withdrawing. 'I'm a modern Muslim. I pray, and if I have a question, I ask someone who is more educated in the religion than me. But for me bringing religion into politics is wrong, and it shouldn't be necessary to kill even one person in the cause of Islam.'

While 'Egypt' certainly represents a reassertion of faith in N'Dour's own life ('I'm forty-four. I have six kids. I have to think about important things.'), it is far from pan-Islamic in its application, being sung entirely in Senegal's lingua franca, Wolof, and in praise of the founders and leaders of Senegal's sufi brotherhoods, figures who are largely unknown outside Senegal. Popular mystical or sufi orders, based around particular holy men or 'saints', are common throughout the Islamic world, but they have acquired a particular importance in Senegal – most notably through Sheikh Ahmadou Bamba (1850–1927), founder of N'Dour's own Mouride Brotherhood. Yet N'Dour refers to all of them, including the founders of other brotherhoods, as Our Guides.

'The Islamic religion is one. But the way it is formed in different parts of the world is different. People really live Islam here. You can hear that even in our pop music. Our Guides have helped us to be real Muslims, while keeping our culture. That combination makes things very different here. If you see that very few Senegalese people are fundamentalist, I think that's due to the influence of Our Guides.'

Bamba's cryptic, veiled image can be seen everywhere in Dakar – peering from wall paintings, from talismanic stickers on taxi dashboards – while the packed minibuses that wend their way endlessly through the sprawling suburbs are daubed with the names of holy cities deep in the arid interior – Tivaouane, headquarters of the Tijani brotherhood, and Touba, the Mouride 'Mecca', where the tallest minaret in sub-Saharan Africa rises into the shimmering sky over Bamba's tomb.

Islam has had a presence in this part of Africa since the twelfth century but well into the nineteenth century the traditional order was still based in animist belief. Then as the old Wolof kingdoms began to collapse under the pressure of French expansion, vast numbers of people gathered themselves around Bamba, a Qur'anic teacher to whom miraculous powers were attributed. Nervous of this unpredictable phenomenon, the French exiled Bamba twice. But though he is often hailed in modern Senegal as a leader of anti-colonial resistance, he seems to have come to a pragmatic understanding with the French, preaching salvation through work – which aided the development of groundnuts as a cash crop – and submission to a spiritual guide, a philosophy which has given his descendants, the caliphs of the order, both enormous wealth and crucial political influence. And to the orthodox fundamentalist it's all the most utter heresy. Bringing Bin Laden here would be like taking Ian Paisley to the Mexican Day of the Dead.

'We believe there are different ways to get to the same place,' says N'Dour. 'On this album I sing for the leaders of all the different brotherhoods. In Senegal, we believe that our riches lie in diversity.'

This may sound like something culled from a seminar on multiculturalism, but it's borne out by Mohammed Jamal Dia, deputy imam at the Grand Mosque, who explains that in areas with substantial Christian populations, the different religious communities co-operate in the building of each others' places of worship. Rose-tinted or not –

and there have been isolated incidents of Christian-Muslim tension recently – this chimes broadly with Senegal's tolerant, pragmatic way of doing things. While there have been nasty moments since independence in 1960, most notably a brutal independence struggle in the southern Casamance region, by and large Senegalese democracy has worked. The first president, Leopold Senghor – a Christian, as N'Dour points out, backed by the Mouride Brotherhood – was the first African leader to stand down voluntarily, and his party recently ceded power after peaceful elections.

So, going back to that word 'but', what precisely was N'Dour driving at?

'Six years ago, the world seemed to be moving in a positive direction, with new ideas and declarations about diversity, the environment, human rights. Then America seemed to have moved away from that, to be ignoring the others. But since September 11, people have talked a lot. I'm not condoning terrorism, but you have to think about the world as a whole and create a balance.'

And what could be more reasonable than that? Indeed, N'Dour is now ready to play America again.

'I'm not against the American people, just the system – the Bush system.'

'There's no way you're going to photograph Youssou in front of the Arc de Triomphe!' says N'Dour's PR. He's in Paris to promote the new album, and the parade of petitioners, conspirators and hopeful musicians that wait at his Dakar door has been replaced by endless back-to-back interviews – yesterday the French, today the Poles and the Germans. There simply isn't time for the ten minute walk necessary to shoot this icon of modern African culture in front of that bombastic monument to imperial ambition. And in any case, the PR is sure – wrongly as it turns out – that N'Dour just won't do it.

Until recently the name Senegal signified almost nothing in the English-speaking world, but to France Senegal was the first of the colonies – the first black African territory reached by sea from Europe. The inhabitants of the four main towns were granted French citizenship, giving rise to a sense of special Senegalese identity. As one respected former BBC corrspondent in Dakar put it to me, 'The Senegalese would never admit it, but they consider themselves the most civilised Africans.' The first president Leopold Senghor is considered one of the twentieth century's finest lyric poets in French, and crucial breakthroughs in African literature, cinema and the visual arts all took place in Senegal.

Yet N'Dour grew up remote from these developments in the Medina, the city's original Native Quarter. A mechanic's son, he is descended on his mother's side from a line of *griots*, traditional praise singers. Listening to his grandparents, he learnt the arcane phraseology, the ancestral praise names, the alliterative rhythm and rhetoric he would later use to sway a crowd, to instill in them a profound sense of their own value and identity. N'Dour made his name giving traditional culture back to the youth of the *quartiers populaires*, filtering it through influences from latin music, funk, soul and jazz, and saying, 'This is you!' He wasn't the first to do it, but he took it further, made it sexier, more vital and more relevant than anyone else.

Having started singing at circumcision ceremonies before his voice had even broken, inducted into the Star Band, then the country's top group at the age of sixteen, N'Dour seems to have known almost from the beginning that he was not an ordinary person, would not lead the humdrum life of the common herd.

'I was the eldest child, and my father was very against me singing. No one in our family had been educated, and he wanted me to be a doctor or a lawyer. But eventually he agreed to let me sing with the Star Band, and from that moment I knew I was going to do a lot of things.'

Yet beneath this apparently superhuman confidence you can still occasionally detect a trace of the insecurity of the person from the wrong side of the tracks – the boy from the Medina looking out on the world of the *toubab*, the white man, to which he can never accede.

'When I was growing up, most people around me felt very far from the people who were governing the country. And when I started playing music, it was only in the Medina and the other *quartiers populaires* that people appreciated it. For a long time the top people didn't regard what I do as music at all. It was only when people abroad started talking about my music that it was accepted by the elite at home.'

By 1982, at the age of twenty-three, N'Dour had his own group, *Le Super Etoile de Dakar*, and was in sole control of his own business affairs. As other groups emerged who tackled social issues such as corruption and unemployment, N'Dour expanded his subject matter to include apartheid and sahelian drought – expanding the role of the *griot* from simple icon of cultural identity to social critic and political commentator. Having achieved an unassailable position at home, he began looking further afield. But while many of his West African rivals – such as Salif Keita and Baaba Maal – sought new careers on Paris's immigrant scene, N'Dour's destiny took him on a very different route.

'I respect French culture, but I never felt Paris was the place for me to develop. There's been too much between us in the past. When I first played in Paris, it was mostly Senegalese who came to see me, but in London the crowd was eighty per cent British, and people were coming to talk to me in a way I hadn't experienced before – people like Peter Gabriel.'

With Gabriel's support N'Dour was soon an important figure in the nascent world music scene, signing to Virgin amid a tremendous fanfare of publicity and expectation. He was dropped after two poor-selling albums, but re-signed to Sony, and just as hopes of that vital crossover hit had all but evaporated, he released '7 Seconds', a duet with Swedish/American soulstress Neneh Cherry that became one of the biggest selling records of the 1990s. The day he stepped off the plane in Dakar with that gold disc was a pivotal moment in Senegalese history. N'Dour was now unreachable, his status beyond what could be achieved by anyone else. He set about developing Senegal's music industry, building studios and cassette plants that doubled the industry's capacity, while increasing his own financial stake. Meanwhile, he was again dropped by his record label, when his next album 'Joko' – an all too blatant attempt to appeal to the people who bought '7 Seconds' – flopped in 2000.

The Western media should by any normal yardstick have lost interest in N'Dour long ago, yet he had stored up an amazing backlog of goodwill, and his next album, the semi-traditional 'Nothing's in Vain' was accorded a rapturous critical welcome simply because it represented something close to a return to form. N'Dour's rivals for the crown of African music had long since faded away, dying – like Fela Kuti and Franco – or simply running out of creative steam – like Salif Keita and Baaba Maal. But N'Dour was still there on the world stage, fighting, developing new ideas.

Yet while he can't now be ignored by the West and is rich even by Western standards, he must still understand how most of his country-men feel faced by the fact that it is the West – the white man – that not only has everything, but seems to own this world.

'It is very hard to accept. When we see the prosperity of the West, we think, "Look at that, man! They've got *everything*!" But our elders say, "Why did God create the *toubab*? To make things a little easier." Because the *toubabs* bring a lot of things in terms of infrastructure. They can give a lot. And we believe that in the next world, maybe, the situation is going to be reversed.'

Yet beside such magnificent fatalistic acceptance, he must some-times wish he could have done it all without having to rely, to some extent at least, on the magnanimity of the West.

'If you come from Africa with your economic poverty and your cultural riches, and you meet someone like Peter Gabriel or a person from a big record company, and they tell you that what you are doing is marvellous, that makes you feel powerful. Even if you don't know who they are, if they tell you that you think you are *down here*, but really you are *up here*, that gives you more confidence than if someone from Africa said that. Maybe that's not right – but it's the reality!'

Back in Dakar, it's two days before the *magal*, the great pilgrimage to the holy city of Touba. Within hours there won't be a single taxi left in the city. Our car radio is playing non-stop Mouride music – mystically inflected voices, wheezing synthesizers and clattering percussion – and all of it pop. Even cheeky young divas such as Ndeye Kasse and Tity – the country's Britneys and Kylies – record songs for the great mystics, dedicating their cassettes to their spiritual guides. Even singers who aren't Mourides sing for the leaders of the order, just as N'Dour sings the praises of the founders of the other brotherhoods on 'Egypt'.

N'Dour has never succumbed to the lure of haute couture and gold bathtaps. He hasn't put himself in hock to politicians, as many African musicians have done. He hasn't become a monstrous caricature – as Fela Kuti did with his dope and his thirty-seven wives. He did build himself a splendid modern house, but found it too big and grand, and now houses his offices there. He has his own record company which licenses material to the American Nonesuch label, and while he has been helped by a great many people, he is to all intents and purposes as independent of any external force as he could be. As we amble over the dusty headland above the sea near his house, he exchanges pleasantries with passers-by and joins in with a kids' football game. As our photographer, who's dealt with many celebrities, says, 'You'd think he was the headmaster of the local school.'

'I sometimes feel I'm a number of different people,' he says. 'It feels like the biggest part of me is here for other people. But I can't give everything. I have to have something that is only for me. I have to protect my family and have a life with them that is completely private.

'When I step outside these barriers, I'm a different person – working with a lot of different people, giving my name to a lot of things that I lead from a distance. But I'm not an open person. My relationship with God and my religion is something I don't want anyone else to know about.'

Nonetheless he's managed to share something of that relationship on his new album, without railing against the West – without, in fact, involving the West at all. 'Egypt' isn't so much a statement of pan-Islamic commitment as a love letter to the Senegalese people, celebrating the community of feeling between their many shades of belief. Senegal may be a far from perfect society, yet its people seem to have found a way, by and large, of living with their differences. And it's satisfying to observe that, having put so much energy into trying to second guess the interests of Western and African audiences, N'Dour has produced his most interesting music in years with this, his most personal project to date.

First published in *Observer Music Monthly*

Tea in the Pre-Sahara

JASPER WINN

ATE IN THE AFTERNOON Batchot arrives on his mule. He comes
in from the mountain side of the tent. I try to extrapolate from the
trajectories of people arriving at the little dip what they've been doing.
Batchot, I guess, has been at his garden, an hour's ride away, over by the
spring caves. If so, he's spent the day roping buckets up from the deep
well, and then dribbling water over the tattered sprouts of maize, and
down the runnels between the struggling potato plants, and marooning
the almond and fig trees in pools of turgid, sloppy mud.

'My family' has no interest in growing things. Nor even much interest
in eating vegetables. They raise sheep and camels and goats for meat. And
that, and soured milk and melted butter and couscous is what they want
to live on. Vegetables, whether brought in the souks or traded from the
other Ait Atta families, are for when there is no meat. Which is far too
often. Especially this year when they, and I, have stayed down on the arid
plains of the pre-Sahara, rather than taking the family's animals up to the
grassy *agudals* of the High Central Atlas Mountains.

It's still hot and, as Batchot hobbles his mule and ducks under the
tent's hanging wall and into the gloom of the men's area, the dogs
remain stretched out in the dark shade under the sheep-pen wall, their
flopped-out tongues twitching and dripping saliva into the dust. Batchot
lies out full-length against the pile of rugs next to me, and shouts at
Touda for tea. She is in her working clothes, with bloomer-like leggings
sticking out from under the tucked-up skirts, and cheap plastic sandals
on her feet. Her lacy, black over-robe has a hem ripped and tattered from
the ankle-height thorns she walks through each day in search of *afsar* to

burn and *adolfsa* for the camels to eat, or as she drives out the goats to graze. Two strings of seed pearls – one bought by me for her in the souk in Marrakesh – hang around her neck. A safety pin holds her bodice closed, and a small pair of blacksmith-made tweezers and a large needle hang from the pin. Her green headscarf has slipped back from her forehead, showing a small halo of dark hair. Her chin has no tattoos, unlike some other girls in the clan, but there is a faint shadow of *kohl* smudged around her eyes. The henna on her fingernails has nearly grown out over the weeks since it was painted on, and there is a blush of buttery rouge on her cheeks.

She shovels glowing embers from the women's fire into the pottery fire bowl and brings it round to our side of the tent, stooping under the drooping undulations of the dark brown goat – and camel hair – strips. She and Batchot joke over who's going to make the tea. The answer is inevitable; they are bored.

It's my duty to be entertaining. It's one coin in the currency with which I pay the family, and the wider clan, for having accepting me into the introverted, xenophobic world of the Ait Atta tribes. So I perform comic routines, with all they hold of pathos, idiocy and slapstick. The earliest jokes were based on Ishu, or Idir, or even the women in the family, getting me to do something, anything – with the camels, perhaps, or the bad tempered-billy goat – in the knowledge that I would get it wrong, in the way that a small child gets the adult world wrong. This crude, but gentle, laughing at my idiocy morphed into a more subtle joke, though only between Ishu or Touda, the cunning father and the clever daughter, who would wait until some point of abject misery in my life with them – when cold, tired and sluiced by wet sleet on a pass, perhaps, or as I trudged hour after hour through blinding sun and burning sand, or after a sleepless night running down and herding in lost camels – and to demand of me; 'Yusf, *ifoulki?*' And through gritted teeth, or from a parched throat I had to summon up an enthusiastic '*Ifoulki! IFOULKI!!*' assuring them that things just couldn't be better.

My tea-making is always comic. It might be my finest turn. I go through the actions with precision, each memorised from having watched many hundreds of times, each movement perfectly copied and practised on numerous occasions too. I'm like a television cook in a land without television; the same flamboyant gestures, the slick practised manipulating of the hardware, the easy aside to those watching. Though this being tea-making there is a certain solemn reverence of course, but from me – the *aroumi*, Bou Aserdun, Yusf, whomever I am at this point – buffoonery is allowable. So Batchot and Touda watch, ready to be entertained or amazed. They are undemanding as to which gallery I play to.

I push myself to a sitting position and shuffle closer to the *kanoun*. The heat off the coals feels scarcely greater than the dry, aridity of the air flooding in from around the edge of the tent, and it brings the water to a giggling, hissing boil in minutes. I open the glass basket. Flip open the tea box. I heft out the heavy cone of sugar, wrapped in its sheet of indigo blue paper, from the grubby tea bag.

The kettle has boiled. I shake out acrid twists of green gunpowder tea from the battered Menara box into my palm, and then sow them in the small, globular, green teapot. 'Eeh, Yusf! *Hak.*' Touda, like a magician's assistant hands me a plastic bag of days-old, bruised, limp mint. Mint, so integral to tea in the rest of Morocco, is a luxury here, bought in affluence in the souk; and like many luxuries, it is perhaps not really enjoyed for itself, but only for what it says about wealth and generosity at that moment in time. I'm fairly sure that the family doesn't much enjoy the mint for itself. Myself, I hate its taste of heated-up, just-spat-out toothpaste and saliva.

Still, I take out a bunch of sprigs and dribble water over them, bending clear of the rug to let the water drain into the dust, then twist them between my two clutching fists as if wringing their necks in revenge for their taste. I crush them into the pot, fingering any stray leaves and stalks tightly in through its mouth. Then I take out the broken piece of heavy car-door handle – found by a roadside somewhere years ago, which is now the sugar hammer and a family heirloom. Cradling the sugar cone in my hand I knap it with sharp blows along one edge to flake off sharp, quartzy arrowheads of sweetness. They too are pushed into the pot. I pour hot water from the kettle into the pot and it bubbles down into the miniature green jungle of mint, and over the shrinking icebergs of sugar.

Then I pull out the glasses, each from its own compartment in the circular, woven rush basket, with its tears and rips patched with tags of leathery vinyl cut from the seats of another – or the same – wrecked car. Nestling within the nine divisions are five good glasses, one broken rimmed glass, and two small mysterious packages wrapped in torn sheets of newspaper. A tube of medicinal ointment, as squeezed-out and nozzle-blocked as a child's Airfix cement, rattles in the broken glass. As I order four glasses on the brass tray in front of me, Batchot and Touda look on in eager anticipation of a punch line. Here in this tent, with this audience, I have the compelling watchability of Buster Keaton. Anything can happen. Yet I am totally serious; I am making tea to the best of my ability. Even, perhaps, and justifiably, proud of myself and my easy mastering of this complex ritual.

A chicken peeks in under the tent wall, and seeing little movement stalks in, with each step tapping its beak to the ground as if moving on three legs. Touda tosses a pebble at it, hissing; '*Gush, Gush! GUSH!*' even as I pump the bellows. Air rushes out of the nozzle deep into the embers, which flare and roar, and then burn so hot that they are silent and almost without light. The pot, filled with tea and mint and sugar, sighs and hisses and pubbles and putters on top of the *kanoun* whilst I polish the glasses with the torn-off strip of cloth, before setting each one back onto the tray with a rounded 'tock' so they form a crescent around the edge.

I pick up the teapot. Even with the cloth folded, folded and folded again, the handle burns through to my skin as I lift the pot high above the tray. A stream of tea falls into a glass in a steaming, splattering acrid yellow braid like a horse pissing on a cold day. I almost fill the glass, then flick the lid of the pot back on its wire hinge, and pour that glassful back into the pot. And then pour out a further glassful and return that to the pot. And again. And again. Mixing the tea and sugar and mint, working them into each other in rough alchemy.

The golden liquid grows stronger. I pour out a third of a glass, and from then on the glasses must be kept accurate track of as I raise the hot liquid to my lips and take a sip. It's already far too sweet for me; I chip off more sugar and press it down into the stewed mash of mint. Then pour the liquid back and forth through itself more times, until fully mixed and ready to pour into the glasses a layer at a time. So, pouring out and cutting off the flow of tea, from one glass to the next in a waving and dipping of the hand, as if conducting a largo. Back and forth from glass to glass, from left to right.

Batchot and Touda have their eyes fixed on the glasses. I cram more, more sugar into the pot and flood it with water, setting it to heat on the *kanoun* for the next round. Then I hand out the tea, first to Batchot, then to Touda, holding them overhand around the rims with the tips of my scalded fingers. They lift them to their lips and sip slowly at the rims.

The punch line is delicious. The perfect comic-magic trick. I have brought sleight-of-hand to tea making, deftly handling the tools, the apparatus, mixing the ingredients to produce the unexpected. There was no room for deception, I was watched closely, my every move scrutinised. Both Touda and Batchot would have agreed that I had been making tea, and correctly. Yet, and here was the best bit, despite everything I'd somehow made something that just wasn't tea. Or not tea that you'd want to drink.

And what was funnier was that I, Yusf, couldn't tell this. I was drinking the tea with every sign of enjoyment. And the richest part of the joke was that the two of them would have to drink the tea, too, and as if they enjoyed it. And then drink all the further doses I mixed up, until the kettle was finally exhausted. And I knew this, and they knew I knew, but none of us could say anything of this.

We sat there in good fellowship.

The Girl from Gardez

ALBERTO CAIRO

SAMAR GUL never stands around staring into space. She's a girl of about twenty, tall and well-upholstered. Having lost a leg, she's here for prosthesis, lodged in the sleeping quarters because she comes from outside Kabul. She's accompanied by an uncle who talks a lot and smiles frequently, showing his few remaining teeth. Samar Gul neither talks nor smiles. Having a girl like her in the sleeping quarters guarantees security, cleanliness and smooth functioning. Every morning, at first light, she gets herself ready for the day and begins sweeping the courtyard. On crutches and hopping on one leg because her prosthesis is not yet ready. This is not a duty expected of our patients: we have staff to do it, but if they want to help so much the better. Samar Gul is a new experience for us. The day before yesterday she washed all the windows of the exercise room and the bathrooms; this morning she helped Zarminà tidy up the plaster room. In the evening she mends the children's clothes and those of her fellow female patients. Her achievements as a seamstress are rudimentary, with the colour of the clothes and the thread clashing wildly and the stitches clumsy. But at least the tear is mended, the button sewn back. At mealtimes she helps by handing out food to everyone, hiding her face from the cooks, who are male. Then she clears away the plates and cutlery and sweeps the floor.

Joking with Zia Gul, who is in charge of the cleaning, I told her that she could take a few days off, because Samar Gul was doing everything. She must have taken it badly, because she forbade Samar Gul to do any work at all. Suddenly unemployed, Samar Gul complained to her

53

prosthetist, Simá, who immediately found her a job in the workshop, cleaning the large sheets of plastic and filling the moulds with plaster. Sitting side by side, both of them Pashtuns, they did a lot of talking. Samar Gul unburdened herself, telling Simá her story.

Four months ago, in their efforts to capture some of the Taliban leaders, the government forces and the Americans bombed several villages in the Gardez province. Many houses were destroyed. Six members of Samar Gul's family were killed. The only survivors were herself and her younger sister. They now live with an uncle. She says that keeping herself occupied helps to stop her thinking. When she has nothing to do she sees the faces of her loved ones, hears their voices and wishes passionately that she were dead too. Her sister is not speaking to her: she cannot forgive Samar Gul for having saved her life by sending her out to draw water from the well just before the blast. 'It would have been better if we had all been killed,' she says disconsolately. She adds that night is the worst time. All the saddest thoughts crowd into her mind. She prays for the sun to rise so that she can banish them with work. Here she is relatively comfortable, but in two or three days she will have to return to the village.

Living in Kabul you imagine every corner of Afghanistan to be peaceful. You are wrong. In Kabul new restaurants and pizzerias are opening all the time with exotic foreign names such as Golden Lotus, The Great Wall and New York Restaurant, the cinemas show romantic Indian films containing songs and violence, you see mobile phones everywhere, the traffic is chaotic, much of the city is a building site, refugees have returned in their thousands. Life seems to be surging ahead triumphantly. But peace has not yet spread through the land.

And then there are the mines, waging constant war against everyone.

A group of soldiers from one of the many foreign peace-keeping contingents comes to pay us a visit. A few of the soldiers are women. Some of the Afghans take a moment or two to realize that they are in fact female and not beardless, effeminate boys. They gaze at them round-eyed. The soldiers hand out sweets. They are sincerely moved by what they see. They ask questions. What happened to this patient, what was that one suffering from. Zarminà tells them Samar Gul's story. The soldiers say nothing. They are clearly embarrassed. Samar Gul, as always, hides her face. I wonder what she is thinking about them.

Extracted from *Storie da Kabul*,
published in 2003 by Giulio Einaudi, Turin.
English translation © Avril Bardoni, 2004

Kelakua

ROBIN HANBURY-TENISON

I WANTED to spend forty days and forty nights alone and so I went to a place I knew deep in the Sahara to walk, to think and to write.

*　　*　　*

The camels arrive like an armada, sailing over the nearest dune, past the tree under which I lie waiting, and they hunker down. Fine beasts, fat and with proud humps, they are the best I have ever seen. Kelakua, my old friend, an experienced *méhariste* or camel man, gives a great shout of Tuareg greeting as we embrace. Mohamed Ixa, the Tuareg chief who has brought me here, drives away. I will not see or hear another vehicle for forty days.

We are in the remotest place on the dry surface of planet Earth: the epicentre of the Sahara Desert, which is about the same size as the United States of America. It is one of the hottest, driest and least forgiving environments. It is said the Tuareg, who live here, always save three dates when they are travelling; if all else fails, a man can survive on them for nine days, eating a skin one day, the flesh another and sucking the stone on the third. On the tenth day he will die, but by then he will almost certainly have walked to safety.

No one knows exactly where the Tuareg came from or when they arrived in the central Sahara. They are a Berber people, who consider themselves white, although their skin is burnt dark by the sun. Babies are born snow white. They have their own language, Tamachek, and their own script, Tifinagh, which is related to the ancient Libyan script and has been used for at least two thousand years. There are twenty-five consonants represented by lines and dots. The Hoggar Tuareg write from right to left, like Arabic, the Aïr ones vertically from the bottom up. Their defining attribute is the veil worn by the men but not the women. Traditionally dyed with indigo and made from Sudanese cotton, it gives them one of their popular names: the Blue Men of the Sahara. It has a complex role in their society and its origins remain obscure. Some say its use is hygienic, protecting the eyes from sun and sand and the face from dehydration, but this does not explain why women and children do not wear it; others maintain that its use is symbolic, protecting the wearer from the evil eye and concealing the mouth, which should never be exposed before women and strangers. It adds to their mystery, since one can travel for months with Tuareg companions and never see their faces.

The Tuareg are overtly exotic in their attitudes and physical presence. The period of their conquest by the French and final subjugation to the new, independent regimes and their fortitude in surviving an unprecedented series of droughts is a story not widely known. Now travellers at last have the chance to visit their homeland, some of the most ravishing and spiritually uplifting landscape on earth. The fact that the Tuareg have survived and are cautiously rediscovering their identity gives hope to other nomadic and pastoral societies.

There are probably well over one million Tuareg scattered over many Saharan countries. The largest population is where we are: in Niger, followed by Mali, Algeria and smaller numbers in several other places. Each of the half dozen main clans has a hereditary king or *amenokal*. Our clan is the Kel Aïr and I met their *amenokal* in Agadez in 1966. His modest castellated palace in the centre of the town had fifteen small dark windows facing the great mosque, with its characteristic wooden struts all the way up the yellow mud tower. He was a tall, elegant young man in snow white robes with a fine indigo turban and veil, called *tagulmust*, behind which I could see soft, friendly eyes as I shook his hand. The Tuareg all kicked off their sandals when he came into the hall and approached him bent double, holding out their clenched right fists before bowing over his extended hand.

*　　*　　*

Kelakua and I study my maps. I want to go way beyond where small groups of tourists are beginning to be taken to edge of the Ténéré Desert. Originally, we had planned to go up to the Djado plateau on the border with Libya and perhaps continue to Djanet in the Tassili n'Ajjer, where I made my first camel journey in 1962. That plan has had to be abandoned; recent troubles in the region mean my Tuareg companions would not be able to cross the frontier with me. So we agree to travel through the northern Aïr Mountains visiting remote wadis, dried up river beds. This is a part of the Sahara into which almost no one ever goes now. Used by the Tuareg during the rebellion in the late '80s and early '90s, it is now almost totally abandoned, except for a few nomads with their flocks. Kelakua is pleased. We will be going to places he has not been for fifty years, but he knows that there will be pasturage for his camels up there and occasional wells.

*   *   *

I'm sitting at my folding table looking out across the dunes, rocks and thorn trees of the wadi Tezirzek on the evening before we set off. Achmed, the only one of my companions who speaks French, has buck teeth and takes great care of me. We have travelled together twice before. Now he is cooking supper and talking quietly to some Tuareg men, who have strolled over from their camp. Our things are spread out on the sand and will be loaded on the camels tomorrow.

We will be traversing some of the least known, least visited and remotest countryside on earth. There is a slight danger of kidnap by rebels or murder by 'contrabandiers'.

Last year thirty-two tourists were captured in Algeria by the Salafist Group for Preaching and Combat. Algeria engaged three thousand civilian and five thousand military personnel to look for them but it was months before the hostages' cars were discovered where they were abandoned, booby trapped, and camouflaged under cardboard sheets and rocks; and although the authorities successfully freed many of the hostages, one German woman died of heat stroke while in captivity. The kidnappers were able to merge into the brisk trade in cigarette, drug, and gun-smuggling going on in the area, which includes traffic of over four hundred four-wheel-drive vehicles crossing the Algerian border each day. Over a decade of civil war in Algeria has seen moderate Muslims in conflict with self-proclaimed radical Islamists and by the end of 2003 over one hundred and fifty thousand civilians, terrorists and security forces had been killed. Algeria's terrorist groups continue to proliferate and on September 11, 2003, Nabil Sahwari, a leader within the GSPC, released a statement declaring that they operated 'under the direction of Mullah Omar and of the al-Qaeda organization of Usama bin Laden.'

*   *   *

But there are other factors that have drawn me here, not least the exciting possibility that I will discover some new rock art. Yesterday as I walked off by myself into the dunes for the first time I realised it was the silence that had brought me back to the desert. It is tangible. It is why everyone should spend some time in the real desert. It engenders humility. I know I shall be humbled as I enter the deep isolation of the northern Aïr. There, I will be among unimaginably barren mountains; I will feel dwarfed by my surroundings, isolated and entirely alone. I can't wait. As I sit in the darkness under my hanging lamp, while the Tuareg have a most animated gossip around the fire in front of me, the new moon rises to my left and all augurs well.

*   *   *

Socially, the Tuareg are marvellously relaxed yet elegant in their robes of strikingly contrasting colours. They saunter over to talk wherever they happen to find one, whatever one happens to be doing. Five gentlemen, one of whom was Kelakua, just appeared, confabulating loudly and heading towards my tree to talk, and they bring some tiny glasses of tea. It comes from China and is called 'Flecha' – the picture of a bow and arrow is much admired. Very sweet, with a bitter background and aftertaste, it is the most thirst quenching of all drinks.

The Tuareg have a remarkable way of shaking hands when meeting a stranger, or someone they haven't seen for a long time: a bare touch repeated again and again, maybe a dozen times, with a flourish and much accompanying talk and laughter as recognition dawns. It is a strangely intimate and affectionate gesture between old friends who have not met for a while.

I have always maintained that the most important person to have on an expedition is a local. I have travelled with the Tuareg often before. They are perfect, solicitous hosts. They do not intrude if you wish to be alone to think your own thoughts. They are far more interested in their own affairs than in yours. Once the outline of a plan has been agreed, they know exactly how to implement it. We can never compete with their millennia of adaptation to their particular environment; their practical and instinctive knowledge of the desert. As at home in what appears a featureless wasteland as urban man is in a great city, they are constantly recognising rocks, landscapes, the lay of the land and so are almost never lost. They would die rather than let anything happen to me.

On my early travels with Tuareg I was always in a hurry. As I searched frantically for the elusive rock paintings of the Tassili n'Ajjer, the strange rock carvings of the Tibesti mountains of Chad, and on my first trip to the Aïr mountains, all in the early '60s, I can remember feeling frustrated at the pace. I was always asking 'How far? How long?' I found my Tuareg companions' own lack of interest in the art of their ancestors and predecessors disappointing. Now that I am older and have nothing to prove, I find their rhythm and attitude infinitely reassuring. Each day has its tempo, which is dictated by the needs of the camels, our grotesquely gorgeous companions, upon whom we depend for our survival.

*   *   *

Kelakua's camels are gentle, willing creatures. I no longer see their expressions as supercilious, but as concern to do the right thing. They allow the greatest indignities to be performed on them with barely a complaint: such as having the nose held up and all our slops poured down the throat. They seldom wander far off at night, like other camels I have known, and when fetched in the morning hunker down willingly to be loaded. If something feels uncomfortable, they will mention it by making a hideous open-mouthed groan, but I have yet to see one come close to biting.

Yesterday Aberog suddenly sat down with me on board. Apparently, something was rubbing his back. Solicitously, Kelakua gathered some soft, sweet-smelling shrub that looked a bit like Hare's Ears, and packed it into the place. They use the same shrub as padding when loading the camels in the morning.

I have been riding in the Toubou woman's saddle. Kelakua leads, with me attached to his camel and the rest of our string strung out behind. I said I felt like his new bride that he had just bought for many camels and was now taking home. This became a standing joke on the rare occasions when we met nomad relations of his along the way. Although one of the most inhospitable places on earth, the Tuareg are perfectly at home here and, because of that, I feel perfectly content too. I would not want to go somewhere where no one can feel at home. The rocks are so big and strange in the moonlight, making weird shapes in silhouette.

*   *   *

The four Tuareg, sharing the shade, are crouched round their bowl eating. The camels have been unloaded and are lying down some way away, while their baggage is carefully strewn near us. Except for Aberog, who hobbled back to us, stood for a while beside my table and then sat down right beside me. Perhaps he is lonely.

Kelakua has just given me a strange little sausage, which he has been making for some time, pounding and grinding things together with his pestle and mortar. He tells me it is made of Tuareg cheese, millet and dates, which are ground whole, stones and all. The taste of the 'sausage' is not too bad, although it does have a lot of sand in it, which grates my teeth. Harder to take is the look of it: the shape and texture of a fresh turd. Due to being rolled repeatedly between Kelakua's palms, it is slightly slimy and smells faintly of sweat. It has been made with such evident care for me and is presented with such solicitude for my welfare that there is no question of my not eating it.

*   *   *

We are, by any normal standards, living extremely hard. We are in one of the most barren places on earth where, when the wind blows, sand moves everywhere with it. We are walking or riding our camels up to twenty miles a day and sleeping at night on a thin mat on the hard ground; and in the same sleeping bag and the same sweaty clothes. Yet I feel wonderful. Always, on an expedition, there are irritations. I have none. I have put myself in the hands of experts who know exactly what they are doing and who are, themselves, patently happy to be doing it.

For example, there is Kelakua's 'dawn chorus'. If you imagine the noisiest and most revolting hawk and spit you have ever heard in an Arab street market and then increase it by a factor of ten, you will have some idea of what my friend does with his nose and throat each morning. From deep inside him I can hear the gobbet of phlegm being resurrected until it is finally ejected with a last alliance of throat, voice box, neck and head, to land on the sand some distance away. Now, this could be maddening, especially if the experience were being shared with others who found it offensive. It was also worrying at first, as I thought there might be something seriously wrong with him. To try and help, I sacrificed three of my precious Strepsil lozenges (honey and lemon flavour), which I had brought against the almost inevitable cold I usually catch in the desert. He accepted graciously, but nothing changed.

As I lie in my sleeping bag waiting for the sun to rise at 6.45 a.m. and take the first chill off the ground, I look forward to my *mehariste's* accompaniment, as he gets up first and blows the embers of last night's fire alight.

* * *

Today Kelakua suggested that I should go with him to fetch the camels and leave the boys to rest after their long walk in the night. They had had to spend several hours searching far down the wadi when the camels wandered off. I teased them that they had been looking for the legendary lone Tuareg girls said to inhabit this region.

I felt proud to be trusted to share such an important job, and so the two old men set off together and I earned my spurs as a chamelier. It is not so different from driving cattle, just much gentler. Everything Kelakua does with his camels is gentle. He always lets them finish what they are eating. He comes up behind them and softly places his hand on their rump, slowly sliding it across to the tail. They respond to this rather intimate gesture. I led the young white riding camel with a soft back. We have met no one for two weeks.

*   *   *

I walk faster than the camels. Round a corner, I saw about a hundred goats spread out along the wadi. Soon I noticed some activity behind a tree and I saw a very pretty girl in a flowered dress with her goats clustered around her. She started when she saw me, but walked on past. When I said 'Salaam aleikum' she cast her eyes down and did not reply. Achmed says she is about seventeen. She and her sister live here all year long, near the two wells at the mouth of the wadi. Their father tends the family's camels away in the mountains and their mother looks after the sheep elsewhere.

I stopped in a patch of shade to write and wait for the others to catch up. When they came on me, invisible behind a rock, Kelakua was upset for a moment, saying that the camels might have been startled and run away on seeing me, but they hardly turned their heads. I watched him intercept the girl. Shyly, and with her eyes still cast down, she had paid no attention and concentrated on her goats as our three lusty boys walked past her. When Kelakua called out to her, she dropped her stick and walked over to him. They did an extra long 'finger touching' handshake, maybe seven or eight times, and then had a long chat. We carried on.

*   *   *

This evening I went for a late night stroll along the sandy wadi in the moonlight. Meeting Kelakua returning from checking his camels made me realise that, robed and turbaned, a tall Tuareg looks like an ancient magician. As we met, Kelakua held out his arms and embraced me. With a huge grin he then held his arms up in the air, a gesture we share, having so little common language, and said 'Greboun, Temet, T'in Galene, In Azaoua – all this is Kelakua's country. I know it all and have been everywhere!' He was bursting with pride and happiness. He later told me that he had not been in most of the places we were to visit for fifty years, having last travelled there as a boy of fifteen. He never hesitated or made the slightest mistake with his navigation.

*   *   *

The design of the 'padding' sacks for the baggage camels is very clever. Everything is loaded on top of these, fore and aft of the hump, tied together. Each is a whole soft leather goatskin filled with dried balls of camels' dung. They act like ball bearings to match the contours of the camel's back and so avoid rubbing. The dried dung does not disintegrate to dust, as one would expect, but stays rock hard.

The camels shake their heads up and down to get rid of the flies on their noses. Sometimes, when following in line, one will shove his nose right under the tail of the one in front and have a good rub. This gets rid of the flies for a moment, but camels' bums being what they are, it only attracts more flies at once.

Every time we meet, even if Kelakua has only been to check his camels, he will greet me with 'Salaam aleikum!' and a handshake. I reply in kind and add my only Tamachek phrase: 'Surufahit, wérésenakh Tamachek'. This means 'I'm so sorry, but I don't speak Tamachek' and that always raises a smile or, being Tuareg, more often a whoop of joy.

For the first week or so, I carried a GPS in one of my pockets and constantly monitored our progress. I soon found that Kelakua's navigation is so accurate that this was a waste of time. When in mountainous country, he takes into account the contours of the land and with his local knowledge chooses a far better route than any machine can. On the flat I found that his orientation was spot on every time, and so I put it away, except to record the exact location of any interesting rock art I found. Now I carry a slim volume of desert poetry in my pocket, which I read when I stop and try to learn bits off by heart.

Midday. Achmed has just brought me four freshly grilled pieces of goat's kidney on a skewer. I defy any restaurant in London or Paris to beat this for flavour.

*   *   *

A very large white eagle with black edges to its wings has just flown silently over us as we saddle up the camels. Kelakua says that this represents very good luck to the Tuareg. Achmed starts to sing an impromptu song in French. 'Each day Monsieur Robin gets up and says, "On y va." We don't know where we are going, but Aberog leads the way.' I had been proud of my camel's name, which I assumed meant he was special, but I learned today that it simply means 'greyish'. The legendary camels of the Aïr Tuareg are white. Mine is off-white, but he is strong and good-natured.

* * *

I walked for a quarter of an hour up the rocky Zeline wadi to the famous guelta. This is a proper one. Deep in a rocky fissure, it must be wonderful to swim in when full and fresh. Now it is less than half full and a bit unappetising, with a good deal of dubious stuff floating in it. But this is the water we will be living on for the next few days. Rain is only expected every two years or so. Last year there was no water here at Zeline, or at Taghajit or Tamjit, and so we could not have made this journey. If there is none for a second year, then things get serious. This happened in 1974 and 1984. Kelakua and many others had to go to Djanet and Tamanrasset to find work, and many camels died.

* * *

Tamachek is an odd language. Through muffled ears it sounds like English. I can't understand a word, but the boys chat away animatedly all the time and it seems as though they are discussing world affairs or the latest football results. In fact I am persuaded that their subjects are really much more mundane matters to do with camp life. Half asleep, I could have sworn I heard one of them say just now, 'Growing up in the Scottish countryside, of course'. It was just my imagination, but such verbal illusions are not brought about by Arabic. Nor are there the accompanying gutturals and aspirants one associates with that language. Those are left to Kelakua hawking in the background. Nor is there any trace of European sounding words, like French, Spanish or German. It is just a pleasant, faintly familiar background murmur, which accompanies the music of the spheres.

* * *

It is 6.30 a.m. and already everyone is up, the camels have been checked and are grazing nearby and we are having breakfast. It looks like we are going to cover a lot of ground today.

Kelakua

At dawn the glorious sickle moon and the morning star are side by side in a duck egg sky with an ochre mountainous skyline. This turns through pale tangerine to blue grey as the light strengthens.

Nothing is wasted as we travel. All our dregs: tea-leaves, stew, washing up water, all is gently poured down favoured camels' throats in the morning. It is a pleasure to watch Kelakua approach his personal white camel, Abzaw, who clearly loves him, with the tin can of slops. The camel extends his neck with a sweet expression, almost opens his mouth like a bird in the nest, but actually Kelakua does it gently with his left hand, and the sloppy liquid is poured down the animal's throat. There is no objection of any sort. Kelakua's son is doing the same to his camel.

Sometimes unexpected little delicacies are pressed on me. Obscure bits of goat are passed over as they emerge from the cooking over the fire. I have just been given a milky dish of dates, millet, goat's cheese, all stirred into some dried milk and water. This was followed by another of Kelakua's little turds, which I am getting quite to enjoy, if it wasn't for the look of them, and the sand.

* * *

I sit and wait for my companions on the top of a small hill; looking back they appear over a ridge and approach slowly. As I watch, a sandstorm develops in the desert behind them and moves this way. Gradually it overtakes them and they disappear in a cloud of swirling sand. They just plod on, emerging again briefly through the fog and then vanishing again as the storm hits me. I put my head down and wait for it to pass. Then I cut across to rejoin them and to reassure them that I have not managed to get lost. Kelakua navigates accurately and confidently in a die straight line.

* * *

Today has been a fairy story. Like all Tuareg I have known, Kelakua has seemed extraordinarily unselective when I have visited good prehistoric sites, like Iouelene, with him. He makes equally enthusiastic sounds when we find crude stick men and camels as when what I consider great art appears. I was, therefore, not overly hopeful this evening when he said he remembered seeing some good pictures near here as a child, which he didn't think anyone else knew about. However, as one of my little fantasies about this trip has been that I might find something new and interesting, I have been encouraging him.

The place is the wadi Sumat, about ten kilometres north of Tesseroukane, the next water site to which we are heading. That is near Mamanet, one of the major known rock art sites of the Aïr. David Coulson recommended I go there. The wadi Sumat is a delightful spot with lots of vegetation in a fine setting with good views.

At 4 p.m. Kelakua and I, the two old men, set off together up the wider wadi on the right, the real wadi Sumat. There were lots of engravings on rocks on both sides of the valley and, among the more recent graffiti, there were some nice old animals. I was quite pleased after an hour and a half and so suggested we turn for home. But Kelakua insisted that we went on a bit further. This was unexpected, as I find that Tuareg men usually soon become quite bored as I search enthusiastically. And so I went along, and around the very next corner we came on it: a big rock with two mother and baby giraffes, which were just catching the setting sun. There was no question but that these were the real McCoy. They are not as big as the famous giraffes at Dabous, being only about a quarter life size, but I would swear they are of the same era and style. The head of the main mother is somewhat defaced, and it may be she was engraved over an earlier antelope or oryx, as there appear to be horns coming out of her head. The ensemble is exquisite and just as Kelakua remembered it. I was thrilled, as much for him as for myself. I told him to recommend them to future tourists, if any were ever to come this way.

They should be seen, I believe, as we found them: in the light of the setting sun. I was very happy and ready to return to our camp, but Kelakua, whose energy constantly amazes me, as he is my age, sixty-seven, insisted we crossed the wide wadi to look at something on the other side. Sure enough, there was another mother and child giraffe. It was larger than the others and well done, but a little too 'Disney' for my taste. We hurried back in the dark, ecstatic.

*   *   *

One evening I talked with Kelakua and Achmed about the recent history of their people. The Amenokol, the king of their clan, the one whom I had met in Agadez when he was a young man, is still their titular ruler and much liked, although he is not a full blooded Tuareg. They decided long ago that the best way to break the cycle of feuding and fighting which had crippled their society for generations was to appoint an Amenokol from outside. And it seems to have worked. The descendants of the original Amenokol, including the present one, are the central population of Agadez. They speak a dialect of Hausa, but are accepted as Tuareg.

The Tuareg of the Adrar des Iforas, based at Kidal, have never accepted foreign rule. They are now a wild and unruly bunch, by all accounts, living largely from smuggling. The direct route from Kidal to In Salah is today much too dangerous. The Algerians use planes to bomb anyone who tries to smuggle goods that way. So, to reach Ouargla and In Salah, which is the main outlet for smuggled goods, they cross Niger and the Aïr Mountains, enter Algeria by the northern desert and circle back to In Salah. It is a hell of a long way round and many people have died. The predominant cargo is cigarettes, which constitute today the biggest single source of smuggling in the world, exceeding heroin and cocaine. The reason appears to be that Philip Morris dump stock in West Africa where it is bought at rock bottom prices by smugglers, who, if they reach Algeria or Libya, can resell for four or five times the cost price. One successful journey can spell retirement, or perhaps new weaponry for a whole rebel division.

*   *   *

Kelakua tells me that the tree I am lying under has leaves which, if ground up with a pestle and mortar, will heal wounds. He says that there are cures in the desert for everything if you know what to use.

In my whole life I have never felt safer, more wrapped in friendship.

These extracts taken from Robin Hanbury-Tenison's new autobiography, *Worlds Within: Reflections in the Sand*. Signed copies can be obtained from Robin's website: www.cabilla.co.uk

The Blind Maulawi

JAMES FERGUSSON

IN THE AUTUMN OF 2002, when the memory of 9/11 and the subsequent US assault on the Taliban was still fresh, I revisited Afghanistan with my friend Mir, a young Pashtun whom I had first met while working as a journalist in the north of the country in 1997. Mir had been my 'fixer' then, but his involvement with me and other western journalists eventually led to serious trouble for him and his family. When he was forced to flee, I agreed – hesitantly – to help him gain asylum in the UK. He has been living in East London ever since. How he and his family survived there became the subject of my book *Kandahar Cockney*. What follows is adapted from that book.

One of the purposes of the 2002 trip was to investigate whether post-Taliban Afghanistan was safe enough for Mir to return to permanently. The answer in the end was a pretty emphatic no. Even now, in January 2005, President Hamid Karzai has still not succeeded in breaking the grip of the regional warlords. His remit does not run convincingly beyond the capital, and his cabinet, even after the election, remains riven by ethnic rivalry.

Post-war societies tend to be led either by military psychopaths or political deadbeats. This is a natural consequence of 'brain-drain': in times of civil war, most sensible people, including the ablest administrators, emigrate. And the longer the war, the likelier they are to settle and stay abroad when the war ends. After twenty years of war in Afghanistan, therefore, the lunatics really had taken over the asylum.

And yet Mir and I were not entirely depressed by what we found in 2002. Not all able Afghans had turned their backs on their benighted country. Here and there among the ruins of war were people of serious quality, people unquestionably endowed with the ability to lead and inspire ordinary men. I met no one more inspiring than a blind *maulawi* (the word means 'religious scholar') called Qari Barakatullah Salim.

The *maulawi*, I soon discovered, is famous in Afghanistan for his astounding singing voice. Qur'an-recitation is a highly developed art-form in the Islamic world. The honorific 'Qari' means 'Reciter'. I heard him lead the evening prayers on a couple of occasions, and for the first time understood why he was so revered. His voice – an eerie, high-pitched tremolo – made the hairs stand up on the back of my neck. He turned out to be the fourteen-times world champion at Qur'an recitation.

A week or so later in another Afghan city, I spotted the *maulawi* on television. He was standing next to Hamid Karzai on a dais in Kabul's main sports stadium, before a huge and silent crowd. It was National Liberation Day and the *maulawi* had been brought in to lead them all in a prayer of thanksgiving. It was then that I realised he was more than just a famous singer: he was a national institution. This hadn't been clear to me when I met him. His manner was so easy and approachable, his sense of humour so roguish. He simply didn't behave like the famous usually do.

As a man of relatively moderate Islamic views he was sacked by the Taliban from his job running a network of religious schools. Yet he was able to persuade them to let him continue teaching at the school he ran from his home. Even more amazingly, given the Taliban's views on the matter, he was allowed to teach girls at his school. That is the mark of a man of probity, and a measure of his enormous charm.

To me he is the perfect symbol of the new Afghanistan. He is able to 'speak' Taliban, to relate to their traditional values, while simultaneously espousing more modern ones.

He is in favour of education for women, for instance, as well as their right to work. And while the Taliban notoriously loathed and rejected technology, the *maulawi* loves it, and even argues that the Qur'an en-visioned computers. He is, by Afghan standards, a moderniser. With men like him in charge of his people's spiritual well-being, I know there is hope for the country. Should he get to hear about this book project (or better still, have it read out to him), I send him my warmest salaams.

*   *   *

On our second night in Kabul, Mir and I moved to the house of a rich Pashtun businessman called Nasratullah, an old friend of Mir's father with whom we stayed for the next four nights. Nasratullah lived communally with an entourage of more than twenty men: a brother, nephews, business advisers, guards, even a sort of court jester. On our first evening we sat in a big circle on the carpeted veranda, overlooking a courtyard garden where a small swimming pool had been filled in and laid to lawn. The pool's aluminium steps were still fixed in place, leading nowhere. A cherry tree stood where the deep end had been, with a fat-tailed sheep tethered to it, endlessly circling on a cruelly short rope.

We fielded questions about Lan-dan, but for once I was not the guest of honour. That accolade belonged to another visitor. His name was Qari Barakatullah Salim, a former teacher of Mir's. He and the other Afghans called him Hajji. Mir was overjoyed to see his mentor again and kissed his hands in respectful greeting. He was a gentle bear of a man, and completely blind. Whoever was sitting nearest him would guide his hands without fuss to the plate of food or the glass of tea at his feet. He had a habit of leaping up without warning and launching a projectile of expended *naswar*, the traditional green chewing tobacco beloved by Pashtuns, over the balcony into the garden, to howls of laughter if anyone was unfortunate enough to be walking by. He was a *maulawi*, a less senior religious figure than Mir's father, though evidently touched with the same ethereal spirit. He called me Mr Jeems.

'Go on, ask Hajji a question', Mir urged. 'Anything at all. He is "hafis": he knows the Qur'an by heart.'

And so began a long debate on everything from circumcision to life on other planets.

'If you turned all the trees on Earth into pens and all the seas into ink you would still not explain all the meanings of the Qur'an,' Hajji sighed, rocking on his haunches, his thick black glasses turned upwards to the darkening sky, a Muslim version of Stevie Wonder.

Nasratullah's little cook crept about with a giant tea-kettle and discreetly refilled our glasses. I asked if the Qur'an had predicted 9/11.

'The Qur'an tends not to speak in specifics but of things such as stars exploding millions of years ago that still give us life. However, it teaches that Allah granted us metal and machines and predicts that humans will use these gifts creatively, but also to destroy. In fact, whatever humans create, humans will also destroy.'

'Ashes to ashes, dust to dust,' I said poetically, thinking of the many tons of burned-out tanks that I had seen cast aside on the country's roadsides, their husks turning the same dun colour as the earth they were buried in, their turrets rusting and poking out like sinking dalek heads or the abandoned machinery of an invasion from outer space: heaps of alien metal returning to the ores and elements from which they were once struck. The resourceful Afghans made use of their old tank parts. Tank bodies had been pressed into service as buttresses for roads, as dams, as bridge supports. There were lintels and doorsteps and speed bumps crafted from sections of tank track and roadside café tables made out of sprocket wheels. But Mir wanted to know about the Bermuda Triangle.

'The Qur'an teaches us that Allah will always withhold certain matters from human knowledge. The Bermuda Triangle is one such thing,' the *maulawi* answered. 'But in my humble opinion it is a three-dimensional electro-magnetic column that extends infinitely into space and down as far as the earth's core. Mr Jeems, are you a Muslim?' he asked suddenly.

'No.'

'Why not?'

'Because – because I'm a Christian.'

'Ah, Christian,' he said thoughtfully, rocking back and forth. 'And would you like to become a Muslim?'

Nasratullah's entourage had fallen silent and were following this with interest.

'Come on, I'll teach you,' he went on. 'Say after me: Lah illahah illallahu Mohammeda rasulallah.'

And so I was catechised: There is no god but Allah and Mohammed is his Prophet.'

'Mubarak!' Nasratullah congratulated me when I had mastered it, to roars of laughter. A Muslim *feringhee*? Nothing could be funnier. Mir slapped me on the back as though I had successfully joined some secret brotherhood.

And yet there was a serious side to the *maulawi's* mischievous proselytising, a conviction common to all Afghans that Islam is superior to Christianity in every way. Although they technically accepted Christians as People of the Book – 'The Bible comes from Allah, no doubt about it. That is why we call it the Book of the Sky,' as the *maulawi* put it – at the same time they could not comprehend why they would not choose to convert. The heart of the argument was that Christianity was out of date. The Bible had been corrupted over the years, being at least six hundred years older than the Qur'an. Verses had been altered and chopped about by human hands. The text was not pure. By contrast the Qur'an had come directly from Allah via the Angel Gabriel and had never been tampered with. If Christians wanted the real Word of God, therefore, they needed to apply to the Qur'an.

'In the old days we used telephones that you had to wind up with a handle,' the *maulawi* said, holding up a mobile. 'Nowadays we have these. You don't use a wind-up telephone any more, do you?'

It was the same with Jesus, he explained. Like Moses and David he had been a Prophet of Allah all right, but Mohammed was the last Prophet – *like the last brick in a beautiful building,* he said – and so he was the one that seekers of truth should listen to. It was hard to disagree in the presence of twenty rapt men who rested their heads on their hands and nodded at everything the *maulawi* said.

After a huge dinner we were shown to our quarters, another cushioned and carpeted cell. The lights were out, and I was just falling asleep when Mir piped up, wanting to know if I had visited the Dome of the Rock in Al-Quds, the Arabic name for Jerusalem. I said that I had, albeit fifteen years ago.

'I really want to go and see it,' he said dreamily. 'I believe the rock floats.'

'No, Mir, rocks don't float.'

'Hajji says the rock floats. He says in olden times the people were so scared of the rock that they built a dome around it to keep it on earth.'

I flinched in the darkness and gently backtracked.

'I suppose it's possible that it floats. I can't put my hand on my heart and say for sure that it doesn't.'

This was true. There was a lattice fence around the base of the rock that made it impossible to look beneath it. Who was to say that it didn't permanently hover like some spectral asteroid? But Mir wasn't listening. His voice was slowing, already in dreamland.

'Can I go there? It's not in the Jewish sector, is it?'

'No, Mir, it's not in the Jewish sector.'

'That's good. I really want to go and see it.'

There was no escape from theology in Afghanistan, not even after lights out.

Adapted from *Kandahar Cockney: A Tale of Two Worlds*,
Harper Perennial £7.99

Thala Khair

BRIGID KEENAN

I HAVE LIVED with my diplomat husband in Muslim countries for more than ten years, and have met many extraordinary people of that faith, but my nominee for this book is Thala Khair.

As the daughter-in-law of a Syrian Defence Minister and the wife of a colonel in the Syrian Republican Guard, she doesn't sound like an obvious choice, but that's one reason I decided on her: she goes against all the stereotypes – of Syrians, and of women in the Arab world (except perhaps for marrying when she was almost a child).

I first came across Thala when my husband was posted to Damascus in the 1990s. She was the daughter of a couple we particularly liked in the social circle that surrounded the foreign ambassadors' 'groupies', I called them, and was famous for having married her soldier husband, at her own insistence, when she was only sixteen and he twenty-seven, as well as for her beauty. At the time we arrived she must have been about twenty-one, and had two toddlers; we often heard about her. We finally met at a dinner party given by the elegant chocolate tycoon Bassam Ghraoui (I never expected to find the best chocolates I have ever eaten in Syria, of all places, but there you are). I couldn't take my eyes off the young couple when they came into the room; they were golden somehow (is that why people talk about gilded youth?), she slender as a reed with long straight blonde hair, and he with the classical features of a young Greek god. I talked to Thala a few times after that and found her intelligent and thoughtful, as well as gentle and modest, though I couldn't claim to know her well.

Then, several years later, in 2003, the BBC asked me to go back to

Syria and help with a programme they were making on Damascus (as part of a series on Mark Twain's travels round the Mediterranean), and Thala popped into my mind as someone who should be in the film because she was so unlike what most people imagine a Syrian woman might be. I telephoned her and she agreed to take part, and we all rendez-vous'd in the Old City of Damascus. By now her husband had become a colonel in the Republican Guard and her father-in-law was Defence Minister of Syria, and so I imagined Thala might appear in a chauffeur-driven limo with a bodyguard; but she strolled through the souk alone, arrived on the dot, and played her part unfalteringly – she had to guide Irma Kurtz, the presenter of the programme, through the Great Mosque of Damascus, recounting its history. I was impressed again by her naturalness. (Thala had no idea that Irma was also Cosmopolitan's agony aunt until months later, when she was looking through the magazine and recognised her picture. She was so excited she sent me an email.)

After the filming we got talking and she told us that she had just bought one of the crumbling palaces in the Old City, and was planning to restore it. It was just round the corner, would we like to see it? Of course we would. We followed her through the narrow lanes of the old town and into her newly bought ruin, which was the house known as Beit Qwatli, one of the largest but most decrepit of all the old courtyard houses. (Indeed, when I was writing my book on the old houses of Damascus, the photographer, Tim Beddow, and I looked around the house and reluctantly decided that it was in such a bad state that there was no point in doing any pictures of it.) Thala took us round excitedly, proudly showing us places where the wall paintings were still intact, the mosaic or carved stonework still in place. She was planning to commission the German expert on Damascus, art historian Stefan Weber, to do a study on the house so that the daunting restoration work would be done as authentically as possible (no Saudi-style shiny marble for Thala), and, almost uniquely among the buyers of the old houses, she planned to use Beit Qwatli as a family home rather than turn it into a restaurant or hotel. She laughed that she was getting a lot of flak from friends and family who thought she was crazy to take on such an enormous project, and that she should have used the money to buy a more appropriate house for the family, squeezed up as they were in their apartment in the suburb of Mezzeh.

I regretted that we had left the house out of our book, and, since anyone who loves the old city of Damascus finds an instant place in my heart, I now looked at Thala with new admiration. And that was before I learned about the school she had started four years before for middle-to-low income families in Syria. I decided to find out more about this girl who could so easily have fallen back on her looks and become spoiled, but hadn't.

Thala's parents come from old Damascene Sunni Muslim families; indeed, her father is now dreaming of buying back his old family house in the old city, and restoring that. Her older sister works in tele-communications like their father, but also runs a group called Banna which persuades rich Syrian families to adopt poor families and help them by funding basic needs. Her younger sister is an artist who has moved to Kuwait with her husband. Thala herself is no slouch when it comes to painting.

Thala met her future husband at the Andaluz swimming pool in Damascus. This place is something of a curiosity: an old art deco sports club in the suburbs where Syrian middle-class families meet in the summer; her parents went there when they were young. She saw Manaf playing in a tennis tournament, knew that he knew her cousin, and wangled to meet him at her cousin's house. Syrian girls from good families are not allowed to be alone with young men for any length of time, certainly not out on dates together, but the couple courted at the cousin's house – 'My cousin would say, "Look I can't stay here all day, I have to go out and buy bread," so we were by ourselves for short spells.'

Soon, Manaf wanted to marry her and she wanted to marry him. 'I was at the French school, I was in a very "European" frame of mind, this was the last thing I could ever have imagined happening to me, but I knew I had to do it. I knew he would not wait for me, and so I had to go against everything my family wanted for me, and marry him.' Her parents were bitterly opposed to the idea – she was so young, still studying for her Baccalaureate exam – but in the end, faced with her determination, they gave in. Thala was married, left school and studied at home for her Bac, which she passed when she was nineteen and had just had her second baby. When this baby girl, Lamia, was three, Thala enrolled in the State University of New York which has a centre in Cyrpus – she checked into the college every three months, but did all her work by correspondence for three and half years. Looking after two small children meant that she did not graduate and still has one of her courses – on the land of Palestine – to finish. Now, two more children later, she is working on that course, and will graduate in New York this autumn.

A large number of Syrian women work in jobs outside their homes (the President's young British/Syrian wife is involved in several projects to help women and children achieve their potential), but I wondered how Manaf, her husband, felt about her many activities. 'He has been supportive all the way', she says. 'The house in old Damascus is my own personal project, but he is just as excited and interested in it as I am.'

Thala and two friends opened their school in 1999. 'Having done my studies at the French school, I realized that I had something that most of my generation here did not have: a more global "general knowledge" and languages' (Thala speaks four). In Syria, education is compulsory and free, but as in other countries, the State system is stretched, and classes are big. Thala and her friends wanted to open a school for people who could not afford the fees at foreign schools but wanted smaller classes and a wider education – as well as an Arabic one – for their children. The fees are seven hundred dollars per year.

As its name implies, The Little Village School started as a smallish project with one hundred and eighty pupils, but it has expanded vastly over the last six years and now teaches fifteen hundred, and should be changing its name to The Enormous Village School. Apart from the normal curriculum, the school involves itself in community projects. Litter awareness is my favourite, especially in Syria where plastic bags spoil the landscape everywhere. It takes pupils to concerts given by the Syrian Philharmonic Orchestra, where children are taught about listening to music and concert etiquette – no talking, and no clapping between movements – and it works with Syrian writers and painters on various projects: they are currently painting a huge mural on a wall at the school, for instance. This year the school was invited to take part in the Cairo International Child Film Festival. Like all schools in Syria, an hour a week is taken up with religious studies: Muslim pupils have their own lessons, and Christians, theirs. 'The lessons are taught mostly in a historical and philosophical context' says Thala, who believes that the wisest decision of Western, societies was separating religion from politics (a model that Syria follows too). Like all Syrians she is immensely proud of the fact that Muslims and Christians of all sects live harmoniously together in her country – 'I will never forget the image of veiled Muslim women in Damascus ululating the last Pope when he came here', she says. And she is sad, like many Syrians, that the centuries-old Jewish population were pressured by organisations outside the country to leave in the 1990s. 'I remember Jamil, an old Jewish man of eighty who told me that he hoped he could die before the day he left Syria'.

Thala herself prays five times a day and fasts during Ramadan, but she rarely attends the mosque, and she questions the interpretations of some of the teachings – on drinking alcohol for instance. 'My Islam is the Islam of tolerance and peace, it is the constant presence of the word 'mercy' in the Qur'an. My Islam is the Islam no sect represents. It is the simple message that was sent, with no additions and no confusing interpretations.

'Lately we Muslims have been talking about the glory of our past, forgetting that the key to it was the open mind that had a thirst for knowledge and was eager to think and create. We have such a wealth in our past and important lessons to learn, and what is holding us back is trying to relive a glory that existed in a different era and a different context.'

Strangely, Thala was brought up by her parents with exactly the same instruction as I was: SEIZE EVERY OPPORTUNITY! (For some unknown reason my father always used to say this to me in French – which he couldn't speak – '*Il faut saisir les occasions quand elles se presentent*', he would lecture me solemnly.)

Thala, now thirty, with four children, a busy husband, a hectic social life, parents and sisters to visit, the old house to restore, and the school to be responsible for, has clearly followed this advice, but she says she is still working on herself. 'I believe that there is always something to learn and something to give. If every single person *gave* in the area that they could give in, we would be living in a beautiful world. I don't want to be remembered for anything, but in the last minutes before I die, I would like to think that I have contributed to something.'

Wally

HENRIETTA MIERS

ARMS AROUND THE WHEEL, hunched forward and squinting into the blizzard that howls around the peaks. Madman that he is, this is how I think of him, wrapped in his shawl like a young girl in purdah, steering round those bends. Wally's all hung up on dying. 'Going time' he calls it. We die alone and sudden. He'd got a thing about life passing and growing old. He brings it up when we're on the road or throws it randomly into his ramblings through the night. 'Rich people in magazines die like poor people. The Sultan of Brunei he die one day. Age is like the river, it flows. Not backwards not possible. Life is like five minutes. I am young for six more years then old time.' He has a series of photographs of himself hidden inside his vehicle licence and insurance papers (expired years ago), locked away in the dashboard locker, each showing him a little older and each with his approximate age inscribed on the back (always in brackets as if unsure). 'We grow old,' he says, reminding himself of the inevitability of it all.

Wally is bewildered by the pace of other peoples' lives. 'Watch people no good people. Life is always hurry,' he says, baring his watch-less wrist with pride. Anything that marks the time makes him anxious. He has a habit of turning clocks to face the wall and when their ticking disturbs him he removes the batteries. The thought of seasons sobers him. 'I no ever know what season it is,' he tells me, and sometimes I believe him.

The road is time for stories, and Wally's stories are one long narrative with no end and pauses only to inhale. Over the years we've travelled together I've learnt his life story, starting from school. He'd been clever in drawing and languages, of which he speaks six. He was a class monitor, although the responsibility weighed heavily on him. Now and again like a mantra he chants his favourite lines from school, eyes fixed on the road and one hand solemnly planted across his chest, in awe of some imaginary teacher. 'Sir, respectfully I beg to say that I am suffering from fever and cannot come to school today. Therefore I request kindly grant me leave for three days, your obedient pupil Wally Ahmad.'

In tenth grade he decided to be a driver. Since then he's owned a series of jeeps, all called Ma Dost, which means 'my friend'. He prizes his 'outside' driver's days and nights, while his brothers have government jobs and 'inside' lives. His father was rich and parcelled out six houses to his six sons, of which Wally inherited the one with his mother in it. 'I am the littlest but the favourite', he says proudly. He also inherited land which he shows me with a sweep of his arm as we drive by. 'Look Henry, my land, my land, my land, my land, my land, STOP'. During the summer he drives tourists through the valleys and over some of the highest mountain passes in the world. He tells me that for three weeks he drove an old French queen who kept him constantly on his guard. 'All the time he say "Wally I come from behind", but I no want he come at all'. During the winter Ma Dost becomes a cargo jeep for locals to collect wood. He likes life this way. 'Tomorrow I die, today I am happy', he says.

With Wally there's always music on the road. Music changing time: he removes his key from the ignition, leans over, unlocks the dashboard compartment where he keeps his precious tape recorder, changes the tape, locks it up again and returns the key to the ignition, all with one hand on the wheel and one eye on the road. When we pass a mosque or school or hospital he turns the music off. This is one of his few rules, out of respect, he says. Off the road he packs his tape recorder and his tapes into his rucksack along with his Swiss Army knife and his sunglasses and his gloves which he calls hand socks. His most treasured possessions.

'Henry, no clutch, what you do?' he asks out of the blue, midway through a story. Then he shows me how to drive around those mountain bends with no clutch. 'Only three jeep drivers can do and I do best', he boasts. Next he shows me how to drive with no clutch *and* no brakes, which involves an emergency stop half way down an overhanging track with a hundred-foot drop to the river below. But not before carefully turning the music off first. He tells me he can drive with no accelerator – 'just some string in hand no pedal under foot'. He runs out of hashish and tells me he's no longer safe at the wheel and that the road is jumping before his eyes. Then he removes his arms from the wheel and flaps them up and down to illustrate.

A road trip through the mountains. Ma Dost collapses bit by bit, dropping its parts on the roadside like an animal shedding fur. On the first day the radiator hisses and bursts and Wally brakes to a halt. He opens the bonnet, peers into the steaming engine and announces 'Henry, I wants to cry'. We glue up the radiator with chewing gum and limp on, stopping every ten minutes to replenish it with water from the river until we come to a village where they doctor the holes. On the second day the axle snaps clean as we drive over a stream at three thousand metres, and Ma Dost sinks like a dying horse into the icy waters. We shiver and stamp our feet and blow warm breath into our cupped hands and tell each other stories until a passing jeep takes us to a village on the other side of the pass. The next day Wally returns to Ma Dost with a new axle and races back triumphant. 'Ma Dost has transplant. Now it no weak' (Ma Dost is never assigned a gender.) On the final day I find a haemorrhoid poking out of the front tyre, but when I show Wally he tells me we can't change it because we don't have a spare. We drive right through till dusk around the hairpin mountain bends. I wait for the tyre to explode and for Ma Dost to skid and roll us into the river below to join the ghosts of all the others who have tumbled off the road. 'I was surprised no puncture', Wally whispers as we hobble to our journey's end. He says it was because he prayed.

Evenings off the road. I hear a soft tap tap tap at my gate and Wally appears on my balcony with his shy smile and his shuffling gait. 'Today I come full', he says, which means he's found some wine. He travels the road with the wine strapped to the underbelly of Ma Dost and he crouches underneath to wrench it free with a spanner. Then the ramblings begin and we talk about friendship and religion and love and all sorts of things that cross our minds, pausing to watch the moon rise off the mountain, and then continue rambling beneath its light to dawn. 'Five minute friendships are no good. The road to friendship is long,' he tells me. Most things with Wally are measured by roads. We laugh from the wine and then Wally reminds us that life is short and we become melancholic and he says 'this is life what can we do?' He's obsessed with the here and now and reality of life. He doesn't like television ('opposite eyes') because it's not real life but just a story. Sometimes, if the wine is strong, I go inside to sleep. 'I sorry I talk too much', he says, and then turns his tape recorder on and I fall asleep to the sound of him humming softly through the night. In the morning he's gone and my balcony is strewn with his butts and the ghosts of his lonely thoughts.

We're having one of these evening ramblings. The town is full of Ismaili pilgrims who have come to pay homage to their spiritual leader, the Aga Khan, who is passing through the valley. I ask Wally if it's true Ismailis believe the Aga Khan is a God. 'How can he be God, Henry, he goes toilet?' he replies. This leads him on to explain the difference in beliefs between the Ismaili and the Sunni sects of Islam and his explanation ends somewhere in Paradise. I ask him if Muslims and Christians will meet in Paradise and for the first time since I've known Wally he's momentarily speechless. Then he gets all dramatic and like a dying hero on the stage he throws his arms palm up above his head, looks at the stars and cries, 'Where will they be in Paradise, often wonder I, my friends like Henry, where will they be?' Wally believes in an exclusively Islamic Paradise but I prefer to believe in a less judgemental end the other side where all religions meet. I wonder what we'd discuss, my Angel of the Road and I, once they've been dispersed, those earthly fears of growing old and 'going time', that chase him round the mountain roads and haunt him through the night.

The Street Philosopher and The Holy Fool

MARIUS KOCIEJOWSKI

> When I die, amid my bones will be found the gold your
> Friendship gave me
>
> *Arabic proverb*

T HE SYRIAN NOVELIST Rafik Schami writes that the citizens of an ancient city inherit the accumulated eccentricities of its past inhabitants and that this alone should account for why there are so many strange people in Damascus. Damascus is reputably the oldest of all cities – or at least the oldest continually inhabited one. I am not sure that this does not also explain a suffocating conformity, a rigid pattern whose every layer is a little harder and more brittle than the previous one. 'We lack democracy not only in our politics but in our lives,' a carpet seller told me. 'You may think my words are free and often I go against the opinions of many fellow Syrians, yes, but in the end you must remember mine is an Oriental mind and however much I might complain I will resign myself to this fate.' Still, given the number of fascinating people I would meet in Damascus, there can be little arguing with the novelist's words.

This was my return journey here.

I will pass over my first visit in silence. While the several misadventures I had to endure were of great interest to me, the world, if it were to be apprised of them, would say I fell among clichés. What made me return were matters of a gentler and less hackneyed nature. I had it in me to write a particular book. The fact that I failed to do so causes me no displeasure. Such plans as I had made were to be soon replaced by others, and almost immediately I began to ignore the map I brought with me, which I had so carefully plotted with red crosses.

A yellow cab blistered all over with rust took me to the district, on the slope of Mount Qasiyun, where I hoped to find Sulayman again. Salihiyya, now a suburb of Damascus but once upon a time a separate village, has been long associated with holy figures. There are many saints' tombs and residences of holy men. The most important tomb of all, on the main thoroughfare, Madares Assad al-Din, is that of the saint and mystic, Ibn al-'Arabi, 'the great master', arguably the most influential of all sufi teachers. If one were to seek a figure of comparable stature in Christianity it would probably have to be St Thomas Aquinas. Such is his importance that it is better to produce a thumbnail sketch than to even attempt a larger picture, for truly his works are close to unfathomable. If, for his sufi followers, he represents the height of mystical theory, for the orthodox Muslim he continues to present problems; there is and will always be much debate as to whether he was a monist or a pantheist. It is probably a measure of his greatness that neither label sticks to him, for his system, if that is a term he himself would allow, is based on the notion of the unity of being. Ibn al-'Arabi regarded the teaching of poetry above all the sciences, saying it is 'the archive of the Arabs' – his own verses are both mystical and erotic. He was born in Spain in 1165 and died in Damascus in 1240. Today pilgrims from all over the world visit his tomb, sit before it in silence, hoping to draw from it spiritual strength for themselves. If I stress his importance the reason is because Ibn al-'Arabi is a major spiritual element in the lives of my two main protagonists; it is in his writings that the idea of the 'holy fool', as a conduit for God's word, reaches its highest expression and it is there, too, that one finds much of appeal to the 'street philosopher', although human logic, in this most demandingly intelligent of figures, is not of prime importance.

A couple of minutes away from the mosque where Ibn al-'Arabi's tomb is, in the busy street market, Sulayman, perched behind his open suitcase of tattered volumes and old magazines, pointed me out to his companion. There was no show of surprise. A second could not have passed between my appearance and his recognising me. I heard him say the word *sha'ir*. The other looked up, all alert, like a dog at the mention of a bone.

'An English poet,' he cried, 'I have yet to meet one of those!'

Sulayman, meanwhile, remained a picture of perfect calm, dressed as I remember him from a year before, like some figure out of the *Arabian Nights* – in a pointed turban, collarless shirt and balloon trousers. Anywhere in the world he would have stopped people with his gaunt face, amazingly high cheekbones and piercing eyes. Sulayman was half Bedouin, the family on his father's side having originally come from Saudi Arabia. His mother, of whom I caught a glimpse once, as she vanished from the hallway of his family's house, was Damascene. What first drew me to Sulayman was his magical ability to communicate beyond the confines of spoken language. It didn't matter if he spoke not a word of English nor I Arabic, for he was a master of nuance. Also, he used his hands with the most graceful movements I had ever witnessed in a human being, such that even in his conversations with other Arabs the words themselves seemed but mere subsidiaries to the elaborate gestures that he would sometimes freeze for as long as ten or twenty seconds at a time. I had on that first occasion spent a whole hour with him, mostly in silence. All the while he wrote between the printed lines of a huge book he balanced on his knees, apparently copying out the text, and here he was, a year later, still doing so. The strangeness of that first meeting would later revisit me in dreams, and indeed were it not for Sulayman and the longing for *otherness* that he inspired in me I might not have returned to Syria.

Abed, his companion, glowered at me with a slightly crazed smile. A young man with beautiful green eyes, he had a strong yet strikingly gentle face, modishly unshaven, a slight turning down at the mouth suggestive of much pain. Although handsome there was also something physically clumsy, almost oafish about him. A woman will frequently despise her best features, desiring normality where she is most fetchingly unique, and if there was something of this in Abed this is not to say he was not physically masculine, only that his awkwardness was somehow feminine. These may be later impressions spread over early ones, true, but Abed made as immediate an impact on me as, say, a first reading of Dostoevsky's youthful characters, God-haunted and inwardly driven by their own scourge; later, he became for me rather more of an Oblomov figure. When I asked him how he was, Abed spoke of life's vicissisitudes, throwing in an extra syllable.

'A word I picked up from Oscar Wilde!'

I would have asked him from which work it came, but already he was telling me how he always strove for the most sophisticated word, and how, in order to reach into the soul of another people, one must always seek out their language's cutting edge. Also, he told me how much he liked the English sense of humour, without which the English would not be what they are. 'One must never smile when making a joke' – an English manual on acting had taught him this. 'One must listen carefully to other people.' A peculiar, elevated tone such as one finds in translations of Arabic tales, although a bit artificial on the page, gave his speech its peculiar charge. It was infiltrated by bits of English and American slang he picked up here and there. 'Cheesy, huh?' was one of his favourite expressions, by which means he would frequently send up his own poetic excesses.

'You come at a new dawn in my life.'

I watched for his sun to rise.

'Aren't you going to congratulate me? Will you not say to me, "Abed, this is good, I have arrived at precisely the right moment." I give you news of a great triumph and all I get in return is your silence.'

'What, then, shall we celebrate?'

'The girl I want to marry finds me acceptable.'

'Acceptable? Can you not hope for more?'

'She is sixteen – you may say *only* sixteen – but full in body and in mind.'

Abed made a sweeping gesture that managed somehow to convey both her physical and mental attributes.

'Her name is Ghufran, which in our language means "forgiveness". So you see, *forgiveness* will be my bride! I was in torment for eight years, but now that my family has found me a girl whom I like – a girl whom I will *love* – my anguish will be removed. Yesterday, a mediator brought me the good news and now I'm waiting to see whether her father will accept me.'

'Are we not being a little premature, then?'

'No, no!' Abed waved away the shadow my words made. 'You mustn't say anything negative. You will contaminate my hopes.'

'If her father approves, will you stop biting your nails?'

Abed's fingernails were chewed down almost completely to the flesh, so severely that I could see he was at pains to hide them, and immediately I regretted my question.

'Yes, and perhaps I will stop smoking too. Arnold Schwarzenegger used to smoke two cigars a day. Then he got married and now smokes only one.'

'Which means he's found only half the happiness he was looking for,' I replied. 'The balance is in his remaining cigar.'

'Ah, this is a poetical response!'

I assured him it was a mathematical one.

'You must forgive me asking you this, but what can a girl of sixteen who has never left home possibly know of life?'

'You have the usual Western prejudice against arranged marriages, even when so few of your own survive. Here, a girl of sixteen is ready for marriage. Anyway, there is a period during which time if one finds the other unacceptable the engagement can be broken without too much damage to either side. There may be two, even three such engagements before anything is decided. A man in his twenties will usually marry a girl of sixteen, a man in his thirties a woman in her twenties – '

'And if the woman is beyond being marriageable?'

'Then the man must be very old indeed.'

Abed smoked furiously, always lighting a new cigarette with the glowing stub of his previous one. Sulayman did not smoke at all. He seemed to be able to divine most of our conversation, adding comments in his strangely high-pitched voice, winding up each sentence with an impish smile. Abed would immediately translate, and Sulayman, mind-reader that he was, would correct him from time to time. I remarked Sulayman had lost no time in recognising me.

'That is because he is a sufi and because of their great mental discipline sufis are blessed with incredible memory.'

All the while, Sulayman was writing in his book, barely looking down at the page.

'Ibn al-'Arabi's *al-Futuhat al-Makkiya, The Mecca Revelations*,' Abed explained, 'the four great sufi books. Ibn al-'Arabi is the Ka'ba of saints, the one towards whom the hearts of all other saints are directed, and these books, his greatest achievement, are so complex that even religious scholars have trouble deciphering them. A single misunderstanding can lead one into heresy. Sulayman is copying out the text so as to remember it better.'

'To what order does Sulayman belong?'

'The Naqshbandi. The strange clothes he wears are not for the tourists but are of his particular sect. His guru is Sheikh Nazim.'

Sulayman showed me on the inside of the top of his suitcase a poster of sufi eminences. A white-bearded figure he pointed to was Sheikh Nazim. Sulayman repeated his name fondly several times.

Sheikh Muhammad Nazim 'Adil al-Haqqani is the spiritual world leader of the Naqshbandi sufi movement. A native of Cyprus, although he lives in London part of the year, he has sought to revive Islam in the face of much opposition from the secular Turkish government and for his efforts he has been gaoled many times. At one point the state brought one hundred and fourteen cases against him. A moderate, he steers a middle course which his followers describe as true Islam, that runs between the severity of the fundamentalists on one hand and the permissiveness of other groups on the other. His lineage goes back, on his father's side, to Jalal al-Qadir al-Jilani, founder of the Qadiriyya order, and, on his mother's side, to Jalal al-Din Rumi, poet and founder of the Mevlevi order.

'Sulayman's quest is for knowledge, the knowledge that comes from God and not from the reading of books, which is given by Him only to special people, sometimes with the help of St George.'

'Khidr' interjected Sulayman.

Khidr is one of the most mysterious figures in Islam and, if not exactly interchangeable with the Christian St George and with the Jewish

Elijah, may be said to share their characteristics to the extent that he puts on their spiritual clothes and even, on occasion, bears one or the other's name; as a figure of fecundity and renewal he may predate all three religions. There are hints of him even in the Gilgamesh epic and he is said to have accompanied Alexander the Great on his travels. Khidr is for Muslims what St George is for us, the patron saint of travellers; he is supposed to have drunk of the waters of immortality and is frequently invoked in the healing of the mentally deranged. One important detail which no sufi will allow one to forget is that Khidr, as opposed to the martyred St George, is still very much alive – madmen and mystics speak of their meetings with him in much the same way Christians will speak of meeting Jesus. Many sufis receive their initiation from him, through visions, and are thus directly connected to the highest source of mystical inspiration. 'The Green One', which is how his name translates, invites countless other analogies. I would suggest the figure who emerges from all three religious traditions is not an imagined saint, as Calvin described St George, but a saint of the imagination. I dare say Abed and Sulayman would protest at these words. Although I have little doubt our St George is based on a historical figure, there is no actual road that will lead to his bones. There is and will always be flesh on Khidr's bones.

Although he is never named in the Qur'an it is Khidr who, in the *sura* called The Cave, accompanies the prophet Moses on his journeys. Khidr tells Moses he will remain in his company but also warns him that his actions will seem so strange that finally the other will not be able to bear his company. Firstly, they board a ship in the hull of which Khidr proceeds to make a hole. Moses is shocked by what he believes will result in a wanton loss of life. Secondly, they come across a youth and, without any word of explanation, Khidr kills him. Again Moses protests. 'Did I not tell thee,' Khidr answers, 'that thou couldst not bear with me?' Finally, they go to a town and ask for food from the inhabitants who turn them away. They come across a dilapidated wall that Khidr restores. Moses asks why they should repair a wall belonging to people who refused them sustenance. Once again, he is rebuked. 'This is the parting between thee and me,' says Khidr, but before taking his leave he explains his actions, saying everything he did was not of his own choosing but an order from God. The ship that Khidr damaged was being pursued by a pirate king who would have taken it by force. The boy had good and decent parents whom, if given the chance, he would have driven out of their faith; God replaced the boy with another more pious. The wall belonged to orphan boys whose father was a righteous man. Later, the orphans would find beneath the wall a treasure the father had hidden for them and which God wanted them to have. I must confess there is much concerning the morality of this *sura* that continues to baffle me.

I asked Abed if he were a sufi as well.

'There are ninety-nine definitions of Allah, and it may be in one's destiny to get spiritual support through one of those names and also the knowledge concerning that name. Allah the Beautiful. No, I am an aesthete, although I consider myself a philosopher too.'

'Would you not describe this as a kind of fatalism?'

'If one is an aesthete, aestheticism is already in the blood. This is not fatalism. There are two kinds of fatalism. One is a gift from God – talent, for example. The other is that which comes through sustained effort. If my path is through aestheticism, philosophical enquiry, Sulayman's path is in his tireless efforts to reach the truth through hunger, silence – the five pillars of sufism.'

'In the quest for beauty can one not fall on the side of heresy? I asked. 'Is it not possible to love the things of this earth more than He who put them there?'

'Yes, if you worship human beauty which is not eternal, whereas God is beyond getting old. So what's left, one must ask, when beauty fades? This is a delicate point. When God wants to give you a great thing He will give you the respect of his creatures and, whatever your creed, you will appreciate His qualities. The Prophet Muhammad, peace be upon his name, is a present for all people. In sufism, people attribute their talent to God. Both knowledge and mercy are essential, as one without the other is useless and because knowledge on its own can be destructive. You need only think of atomic power, its uses and abuses. When God wants something to happen He will temporarily remove the sanity of the people, and when that thing He wishes to happen happens He returns to them their sanity. This is beyond human logic and power, and although seemingly an illusion is truth also. I will give you an example – if God wants you to marry a certain girl and her father is very materialistic and you are poor, He will temporarily wipe away the father's way of thinking so that he will agree to the marriage.'

'And how, Abed, does that pertain to you?'

Abed smiled from the bottom of his verbal transparencies.

'Sir Marius, I will address you from now on by this name.'

Sulayman, on the other hand, unable to manage the 'i-u-s' sound, always called me Marcie.

The following day I returned to Salihiyya.

'Sir Marius, stop where you are!'

Abed signalled to me like a railwayman flagging down an engine.

'At this distance you look thirty-five. Now, step back five paces. Yes, good, now you look thirty. This, you see, is our Arabic art of flattery.'

Sulayman immediately went for tea and when he returned his suitcase was closed up to become a table for our glasses. The bookshop was closing early that day. Abed and Sulayman would tell me the story of their lives . . .

By kind permission of Christopher Feeney of Sutton Publishing

Mustafa Akalay, King of the Realejo

MICHAEL JACOBS

I MET MUSTAFA AKALAY at a time in Spain of mounting neo-Moorish mania. The controversial celebrations marking the five centuries since the defeat of Moorish Granada in 1492 had just ended; and the country had been left with a massive hangover tinged by guilt towards its colonial and fanatically Christian past. Sanctioned by political correctness, Spaniards had begun reappraising their once much neglected Islamic heritage to the extent that flamenco was becoming fused with Moroccan music, Spanish chefs were obsessively trying to recreate 'hispano-moorish cuisine', and a burgeoning number of bars, restaurants and nightclubs were springing up with pseudo-Moorish names and pastiche decorations often best described as 'Califatal'.

This was the Spain that the Tangier-born Mustafa set out to conquer in the spring of 1993. Together with his Spanish wife Tita, with whom he had been living in Morocco for years, he crossed the Straits of Gibraltar to settle in Granada, the Andalucían town at the heart of this land busily reclaiming its Islamic roots.

At the time of their arrival, Granada was experiencing a phenomenon dubbed by some observers as the 'second coming of the Moors.' Refugee families from North Africa were slowly 'moving back' into the once exclusively Moorish district of the Albaicín, where they were being joined by growing numbers of new age Muslim converts headed by a former Beatles manager who had found his real self as Sheikh Abdalqadir al-Murabit. A muezzin had been famously secreted one night into the watch tower of the Alhambra; and plans were afoot to

94

crown the Albaicín with a mosque whose scale was intended to antagonize a Catholic Church still determined to celebrate the Christian victory over the Moors every January 2nd.

Mustafa was a Muslim settler with no such zealous intentions. He was a secularist and intellectual *bon viveur* who distanced himself from the mainstay of Granada's Islamic community by moving not to the Albaicín but to the similarly picturesque though once far less prettified Realejo, on the opposite side of the Alhambra hill. In the Middle Ages this had been the site of a Jewish ghetto, whose memory is recorded today in a statue of a turbaned man vulgarly known as the 'Moor Hailing a Taxi'. This had now turned into a district where families who had been resident here for generations happily mingled with a high percentage of the town's numerous pot-smoking idealists.

I was first introduced to Mustafa late at night in one of the terraced bars that take up the entire lower end of the Realejo's Campo del Príncipe, a large and sloping landscaped square with views looking up to the neo-Moorish monstrosity of the Hotel Alhambra Palace. Then in his late thirties, he was a man of cuddly appearance, with a Buddha-like belly that matched his outwardly calm and unhurried demeanour. He spoke in a slow declamatory fashion, occasionally reducing his eyes to slits when smiling, in a way suggestive of someone recalling some exquisite line of poetry or morsel of food.

He had only been in Granada for a few weeks but was already as familiar to the inhabitants of the Realejo as the taxi-hailing statue of the pseudo-Moor. Every morning, I soon discovered, he established his base in a popular breakfast institution called the Bar Las Flores, where, surrounded by gossiping groups of hippies and housewives, he sat immersed in his newspaper until approached by someone asking for his opinion on the latest news item from the Islamic world. The rest of his day seemed largely to be spent leisurely roaming the streets, stopping to greet people at all the Realejo's bars, and then disappearing off to other parts of the town, which I suspect he largely visited to pursue both his notorious passion for gossip and his uncanny gift for assimilating information even about the most ephemeral visitors to Granada. For all I knew he could have been a spy.

Mustafa Akalay, King of the Realejo

Only gradually did I find out more about him, and what he actually did, or rather was planning to do. One of eight children, he was the son of a humble craftsman who had risen to become royal carpenter to Hassan II. His eldest brother was said to be 'the official architect of Mecca', while his only sister was the founder of Tangier's first and short-lived fashion boutique. Mustafa, as an unemployed wanderer, was the black sheep of the family. His one quantifiable achievement to date was to have studied art history in Paris, where he had written a thesis about the Catalan architect Gaudí's little-known project for creating in Tangier a cathedral as provocatively huge in its dimensions as the planned mosque in the Albaicín. Mustafa had now set himself in Granada a far more ambitious task. In the Realejo he was renovating a restaurant on which he had placed hopes that were more literary than culinary.

I went to see this place shortly before its official re-opening. Known as the Tragaluz after its large skylight, it was situated on a near unvisited alley hidden away off the upper end of the Campo del Príncipe. Mustafa appeared unperturbed by the fact that this establishment, like the adjacent and perpetually closed Scherezade night club, had so far resisted all attempts to make it economically viable. 'Maiquel', he said, pointing to walls he intended giving over to 'important' artists, 'this is going to be the new intellectual heart of Granada. The best food in the city will be accompanied by the best conversation. This will be like the villa where Ibn Battutah regaled Golden Age Granada with tales of his travels.'

When I returned to Granada a few months later, the place was already functioning, and, more remarkably, still surviving. Its intellectual credentials were signalled by a couple of blurred photographs showing Mustafa in Paris in the company of the Spanish writer Juan Goytisolo and the Lebanese author of *Leo the African*, Amin Maalouf. But its main draw, to a regular clientele made up largely of my hedonistic, night-prowling circle of Realejo friends, was the cheapness and excellence of the cooking, which was prepared by Tita herself, and comprised an inspired mixture of Moroccan exoticism and the hearty simplicity typical of the cuisine of her native Cantabria.

Unfortunately, the red-haired and matronly Tita was also

responsible for the Tragaluz's ever more frequent moments of high tension. Telling me every time I saw her that she was feeling 'absolutely *fatal*', she had developed an alarming tendency to throw up her hands and eyes to the ceiling, and then storm off back into the kitchen, only to re-emerge shortly afterwards to scream or throw a plate at her husband. Mustafa reacted to this by continuing calmly to expound to his disconcerted clients his views on Goytisolo, Maalouf and other giants of his intellectual canon.

In principle Mustafa was the waiter; but his talents in the restaurant business lay elsewhere. Famously he made the best gin and tonics in Granada, for which he lovingly used the zest of a lemon to moisten the rim of the most capacious glass he could find. But his greatest asset, though not always appreciated as such by Tita, was his flair for public relations.

Giving me a bear hug whenever I entered the restaurant, and shouting out my name so that everyone could hear, he always immediately insisted that I go over to meet the latest 'important intellectual' who happened to be eating there that day. Interrupting the conversation of intense couples quietly enjoying their food, he would introduce me to them as 'the most important foreigner to have written on Spain since Washington Irving'. Other clients, impatiently waiting to be served, would see their dishes getting cold on the counter while Mustafa persisted with his obsession of turning the Tragaluz into one of the great literary meeting-places of modern times.

Surprisingly, he would succeed in this aim rather more than anyone had imagined. A major breakthrough came after securing the support of a charismatic local lawyer who had just founded an organization dedicated to raising further the awareness of Spain's Islamic heritage, *El Legado Andalusí*. Visiting academics, writers and dignitaries from all over the Islamic world began visiting the Tragaluz, and would sometimes be entertained by Mustafa reciting Arabic poetry to the accompaniment of a flamenco guitarist. Maalouf came on one occasion, as did the Moroccan author of the harrowing but probably vastly exaggerated childhood memoir *For Bread Alone*, Mohammed Choukri, who embarked here on a night of drunken oblivion.

But Spain's neo-Moorish boom would soon diminish in its intensity, tempered by growing recession and a new mania for things Cuban. *El Legado Andalusí*, which, in its heyday, had been promoted by a comic mascot named after Mustafa's son Nassim, moved out of its once palatial headquarters, and woke up to reality. Al-Qaeda cells succeeded 'sufis' in infiltrating the Albaicín; and the Tragaluz was forced to survive by reluctantly catering to tour groups and rowdy parties of American language students.

Mustafa, who had done more than anyone I know to further links between Granada and the Islamic world, was offered a job in local government organizing Moroccan cultural events. For a while he was in paradise. But the same Granadans who had once talked in the Tragaluz of how their hearts missed a beat every time they climbed up into the Alhambra, and who had formed a committee to stop the celebratory ringing of the town's bells on January 2nd, now revealed that their noble emotions were as superficial as neo-Moorish cladding. They surreptitiously gave away Mustafa's job to a Spaniard.

The perpetual optimism of the man who had once been the uncrowned king of the Realejo finally deserted him. 'Maiquel', he said when I last saw him, just before the Christmas of 2004, 'I shall soon be leaving Granada. I have no other choice.' Then a flicker of a smile brought back for a moment the Mustafa I had known before. 'But, unlike Boabdil', he added, 'I shall not be shedding a single tear.'

Siwa, the Sanussi and Tomorrow

EAMONN GEARON

> 'What can my enemies do to me?
> I have in my breast both my Heaven and my garden.
> If I travel they are with me, and they never leave me.
> Imprisonment for me is a religious retreat.
> To be slain for me is martyrdom,
> And to be exiled from my land is a spiritual journey.'
>
> *The Heaven of this World*, IBN TAYMIYYAH

WHEN MUHAMMAD first invited me into his two-room premises it was lit by a kerosene lantern. We sat on cushions in the room furthest from the road and the dust that was raised when a motor car or donkey cart passed by. This back room was Mohammed's private space, behind the shop, which was full of ovens for sale and bicycles for hire.

The lamp sat on the floor in the middle of the room, the thick orange hue battling the darkness as best it could. Although not a large room, the corners, upper and lower, felt distant and remained invisible and cold. The oasis had occasional electricity in those days, no more than two or three hours most nights. There was none during the daytime. And so there we sat, drinking black, sugar-thick mint tea, talking.

We had met first in the afternoon of the previous day, as I returned the bicycle I had hired from his younger brother earlier. The sun was warm, and I was hot after cycling hard along the rough dirt track that led me back from the Mount of the Dead. I was in a hurry to get back to my hotel before sunset and thought that I had probably made it with ten minutes to spare.

There was a faded orange curtain, decorated with flowers, which hung loosely across the entrance to the building. It kept a lot of mosquitoes out and let a little air in. Mohammed appeared from behind the curtain with a broad, natural smile on his face. It looked as though his smile was there before I arrived and would be there after I left. It wasn't imbecilic or forced, it was simply at home, and it belonged. I returned the gesture, suddenly cheered by this man's obvious joy, and we shook hands before I said thank you and went quickly to the roof of my hotel.

*   *   *

The oasis town of Siwa, Egypt, is the remotest human settlement in the country. The remoteness means that life there remained virtually unchanged for centuries. A farming community, it exists because of the water that comes from hundreds of seemingly miraculous springs. Siwan dates and olives are praised throughout the Middle East. Leave Siwa in any direction and you are soon aware of what nothingness there is without water.

The remoteness of Siwa made it the ideal place for the Sanussi in their early days, when needing a home base detached from city life. One of several sufi orders founded in the nineteenth century, the movement was created to lead the faithful back to a pure form of Islam, as well as for the more political purposes of resisting incursions from outsiders, especially Europeans. The order was founded in 1837 by Sidi Sayyid Muhammad ibn Ali ibn as-Sanussi el-Khettabi el-Hassani el-Idrissi el-Mehajiri who came from the Walad Sidi Abdalla tribe. He travelled the Sahara as an itinerant preacher, spreading his vision for the renewal of Islam. Sanussi believed that Islam had become polluted since its early days, the result of contact with a world that was itself corrupted. His vision was inspired, he said, by dreams he had in which the Prophet Muhammad spoke to him. To travel, to move, is a blessing central to sufism, and so Sayyid Muhammad as-Sanussi travelled.

Siyaha, the act of travelling, a forward movement or progress, stops men becoming complacent or too comfortable with their surroundings, with the world. Religious nomads, some sufi never stay in the same place for more than a matter of weeks, so determined are they to fight the complacency of a settled life. The sufi must follow a path, and a path must lead somewhere. If man stays still he will become stale and inflexible, attracted to routine instead of the path. Sufis are taught that to love what is fixed or permanent is a natural desire for man. It is just one more desire to be conquered. The sufi should also know that the idea of things being fixed, the safety of permanence, is a myth. Nothing remains but the journey. Siyaha is to journey, whether it involves physical or mental progress. Adapted to modern realities, siyaha now also means tourism.

Sayyid Muhammad as-Sanussi travelled to spread his message, teaching that the Qur'an should be one's sole guide in life. Alcohol and tobacco were proscribed, as were music and dancing, religious or otherwise. Anything that might be considered ostentatious became illegitimate. He travelled to Cairo and Mecca. In both cities his reformist, or returnist, message was viewed by the ulema, religious scholars, the guardians of tradition, as unorthodox, and he was forced to keep moving. Returning to the Sahara he established his first African *zawia* in Siwa. This *zawia*, a community of believers where scholarship and worship took place, was the first of many across the Sahara. The order's permanent home was soon established in Jaghabub, Siwa's sister oasis, today just across the Libyan border. The name of Sanussi and the *zawia* at Jaghabub eventually grew strong enough to rival even al-Azhar's reputation for learning.

The movement, with its message of purity, spread swiftly in the desert. Sanussi soon had a following among wandering Bedouin and oasis dwellers alike. Travelling camel routes that connected the oases, numerous small Sanussi cells positioned themselves along commercial routes, establishing meeting places in markets and by wells, wherever possible converts could be met. The message spread to Kufra, Borku, Wadai and distant Timbuktu. Sayyid Muhammad as-Sanussi was soon the most powerful sheikh in the North Africa, with religious domain over the vastness of the virtually empty Sahara. By promoting agriculture and commerce alongside religious instruction, they established law and kept order in the desert. Trans-Saharan trade prospered. Siyaha allowed the spread of the message, and the message was *jihad*.

An unfamiliarity with Islam may lead one who hears the word *jihad* to simply imagine a 'holy war' as one might think of the Crusades, wars of conquest and reconquest, taking the Holy Land back from the Saracen. As surely as *jihad* can mean fighting the enemy without, so must it also be understood as the fight against the enemy within; fighting the urge to sin, and through introspection trying to defeat evil. It is in this way that the believer wages *jihad* daily. To fight the good fight. Since September 11, 2001, I have thought a great deal about *jihad*, and my friend Muhammad whose example showed what it means to be a *jihadi*.

After my first, hurried meeting with Muhammad, I returned at leisure the next day and found him sitting in his back room, reading. He asked if I could help him compose a letter in English, a reply to one of his many foreign friends made in the process of hiring bicycles. He first taught himself English through coming into contact with the tourists, before commencing a distance learning degree to qualify as an English translator.

Muhammad is a remarkable young man, and I was lucky to have him as my friend when I lived in the oasis. A native Siwan, the only time he has spent outside of the oasis was to attend periodic meetings with his degree supervisor in Alexandria. In conversations about our respective backgrounds and upbringings, it transpired that Muhammad's whole world had always been the oasis. He had never been to the cinema and television had only just arrived in town. Unsurprisingly, therefore, he was unaware of the kind of cultural icons that loom large in Britain. The Beatles, Elvis Presley, Clint Eastwood, Mickey Mouse and Fawlty Towers were all as unknown to him as most big names in African popular culture are to me. And yet, Muhamad always conveyed an ease with the world outside Siwa that betrayed a wisdom that comes with security in one's owns beliefs.

Meeting in his back room, we spent many days and nights discussing a host of matters, lofty and inconsequential. We would meet, talk, eat, rest after lunch, hiding from the afternoon heat, and then we would talk some more. Brewing tea in turns, our mutual investigations into one another's ideas and opinions, against a backdrop of our respective cultural or religious roots, went on until the time seemed right to stop on any given night.

I was especially interested to learn what he thought about the changes which were coming to Siwa, changes that I wasn't happy about. Electricity is the example that most struck me. I was used to electricity, had grown up with it, whilst I had also enjoyed the fact that when I first came to the oasis it was without a regular supply. Lanterns and stars are beautiful, while bulbs and neon tubes are not. But the oasis is not a paying attraction for foreigners. It is a small but vibrant town that happens to be in the middle of the world's largest desert. The truth of this, perhaps, took me longer to realise than it should have.

Muhammad was right to be less concerned about this than I was. He understood the need to harness the opportunity, as the times were indeed changing. He was the first Siwan to learn to swim. After talking to outsiders with the knowledge he wanted, Muhammad borrowed some money from his father and went to Alexandria for a few days. He returned with a computer and after studying the manuals he was proud to introduce the internet to Siwa.

*   *   *

The festival of *siyaha* takes place in Siwa when wheat and baskets of fruit surround altars in English churches. As well as being a harvest festival, it is the time in the year when hundreds of the Sanussi brotherhood are welcomed to the oasis. From Morocco and Algeria they come, from neighbouring Libya and far off Syria, meeting each year at the same time. The festival takes place during the October full moon, and for three days and nights the faithful and the interested gather in the shadow of Jebel Dakhrour, a limestone mountain that marks the point where desert and oasis meet. From the top, one can look north across the unbroken miles of date palms, one million trees, and the salt lakes that live uncomfortably close to the fertile soil. To the south there is nothing green, but instead the dunes of the Great Sand Sea that stretch into the Sudan. For the Sanussi, *siyaha* is far more than a time to catch up with distant brethren. It is a time for reflection, a remembrance of their founder and his message. After prayer there is feasting. *Siyaha* is an outward action that attracts blessing, just as *jihad* can be an inner activity that equally attracts blessing if performed sincerely.

Siyaha and *jihad* are both progressive, they both deal with forward motion. *Siyaha* had brought me to a place that I could never find at home. *Jihad* for me was initially wrapped up in a struggle against change, a resistance to any physical changes that might affect my flimsy dream. Having found Siwa, I didn't think I could be happier anywhere else on earth, and I didn't want it to change. I failed to understand the unreal nature of such unimportant changes, whereas Muhammad was perfectly happy to stay at home, and wasn't afraid to open up to the arrival of the world at large.

*   *   *

The last time I left Siwa I had been living there for eighteen months. It was an ordinary early morning waiting for the bus to Cairo. The only people up were soon-to-be-fellow passengers, brought to the town square on donkey carts driven by friends, who went home after wishing the travellers a safe journey, God willing. And then Muhammad appeared, unexpectedly but completely in character: smiling his smile and carrying a parcel of food that had been prepared by a family member for my journey. I was happy to leave Siwa because I knew that all that was good about the place would be safe in Muhammad's hands.

'The nature of existence is that of a journey. Everything is based on movement. Electrons journey around the nucleus and the earth journeys through space. The first thing a child does after being born is to move. The whole of creation is a journey from Allah, to Allah, by Allah, and the highest benefit for man comes if he emulates it by journeying into the land.'

*   *   *

The leadership of the Sanussi order stayed in the Sanussi family even after Libyan independence. In 1951, Sayyid Muhammad as-Sanussi's grandson assumed the title of Idris I, King of the United Kingdom of

Libya. Muammar Gadaffi, who led the 1969 coup, was bo
Sanussi tribe, in a Sanussi village, educated in Sanussi *zawia*.
own order, the tomb of Sayyid Muhammad as-Sanussi's in Jagha
was destroyed, and his grave and the graves of his family desecrated.

GERALD MACLEAN

O UR LAST PARTING was regrettable. Mehmet was furious with us for leaving by bus for Diyarbekır and not letting him drive us in the Renault. We had insisted it was safer for *yabancı* tourists to travel by bus rather than private car on what was still a dangerous road, which he knew to be true. We had other reasons for needing to travel alone that were important at the time, but irrelevant now. They had nothing to do with Mehmet, who was taking our leaving Urfa by public transport to be a personal affront. It was as if, he kept indicating, we must have felt he had somehow failed in his hospitality and were refusing it now. Nothing could have been further from our thoughts or feelings, but I recall him acting inconsolably, waving with both arms as the bus pulled away while he plaintively and repeatedly yelled '*mektub*', followed each time by a string of vowels and plosives more emphatically expressive than before. I could not construe the syntax, but knew he was telling us that he would never write us another letter, and that we should not write any more to him.

We had first met Mehmet two years before, when Donna and I had come to Urfa with several aims besides visiting the sites of the ancient city where, it is said, Nimrod had tried to immolate Abraham by throwing him into a great fire. Among them was to investigate the breeding of purebred Arab horses along the Turkish border with Syria. We also wanted to see if we could find somewhere to have a ride. We were introduced to Mehmet through a student who wanted to practise his English and had picked us up outside the Ain Zeliha mosque, set on the famous lake where, it is said, the holy fish created by Allah when he extinguished the flames of Nimrod's fire till swim. Warned in Istanbul and Ankara to travel no further east than Urfa, and our wits about us even there, we had already disproved their fear wandering about the city and visiting most of the holy sites that were open to people like us. All the time we marvelled at the friendliness of everyone we met. Even the gangs of young boys, who from time to time stopped us on the street, were never menacing. The bolder ones would proudly take turns at offering us their right hands to shake while showing off their English: 'Hello, what is your name? Where are you from? What are you looking for?' Most often we were promptly escorted to the requested mosque or the nearest tea-shop, eliciting further questioning in remarkably good English.

And so it came about that we found ourselves one afternoon shortly after our arrival drinking tea in one of the shady gardens by the Birket Ibrahim and discussing numerous topics with a young man who had earlier introduced himself to us while we were admiring the fish. He had left school and hoped one day to study to become a professional translator for the United Nations. First, however, he had his army service to look forward to and that, for an educated Kurd, required special planning. 'In the army,' he explained, 'they will make me to stand many hours to guard over a silly thing, perhaps the door for the captain's private bathroom. But all the time in my mind I will recite the verbs of many languages.' We admired his plan for staying sane, and silently hoped they would never make him do anything worse than stand guard. 'But tell me, for this summer I have worked in the big hotel and they explained this to me about the bathrooms there; they are so big because in the West bathrooms are big. Why is this?' I cannot recall what either of us might have replied, but the conversation soon turned to horses and our friend told us that we needed to find Mehmet with the big yellow Renault taxi. 'He knows horses among the Arabs. Mehmet will show you where. He knows.'

Finding Mehmet the next day was easy, and he was happy we found him because he knew of a Dutch woman who wanted to make an overnight trip to Nemrut Daği; why did we not come along and share the costs? To which we were delighted to assent, the more so once we

lived in Turkey and knew enough Turkish to
we might possibly need – an ability which,
ity to charm everyone she met, made Rita an
e road. Since Mehmet spoke several different
ish, Rita's ability to speak better Turkish than
ncy in English made us a chatty crew. And so we
would remain throughout the overnight expedition to see, at sunset and
again at dawn, the monumental statuary on top of the tumulus at
Nemrut Dağı – all that remains of the great Commagene Empire.

On that first drive together, from the lowland city on the edge of the
vast Syrian plain, up across the snowline to the mountain top where the
road ends, I quickly learned two things about Mehmet. Unlike most
multilingual taxi-drivers we have come across, he did not want to
improve his almost non-existent English but to improve my Turkish.
Mehmet is an organic linguist. The father of a large family brought up
speaking the Arabic dialect of their mother, Mehmet was long practised
at teaching his sons to speak Turkish. He assessed my own elementary
abilities in that tongue instantly, and set about the task of improvement.
As we drove out of town the next day, he tackled expanding my
vocabulary by instigating a new form of 'I-Spy' in which he would point
out and name something, I would then repeat the word and search for it
in my pocket dictionary. I already knew '*inek*' and '*at*' for 'cow' and
'horse,' and had learned not to say '*eşek*' to mean a donkey without first
apologizing. From Mehmet, I learned Turkish for 'stork' and 'butterfly,'
and listening to him discovered the great pleasure to be found from
saying their names and feeling how the tongue imitates the languid
swoosh of the one and the rapid flapping of the other: *leylek, kelebek*.

I also learned that he knew a name for, and understood the properties
of, all the flora we encountered as we drove across diverse natural
habitats. Barely had we reached the edge of the snow when, with great
excitement, Mehmet pulled the car over and stopped. With all the
careful attention of a cat trailing some small game, he walked slowly
over a patch of snow that was still clinging to the mountain side, and
then suddenly pounced. '*Kenger!*' he proclaimed with delight, waving at
us to come over and see what he had found. There at his feet, just

showing through the thin layer of snow, were the green tips of a plant that was growing outwards from its root, flat and close against the rock. With great delicacy, Mehmet broke off a single shoot about five inches long, and showed us how a bead of white sap immediately began appearing at the tear. '*Kenger,*' he reminded us, and then, waving his right forefinger dramatically in the air, announced '*Çok iyi! Ilaç!*' before dipping his finger tip into the white sap, touching it to the tip of his tongue and grimacing broadly to mime the unpleasant taste. '*Kenger! Çok iyi. Ilaç, ilaç, midye için, ilaç, ilaç.*' With these words, he began rubbing his stomach and smiling broadly while offering the sample for us to try. We agreed that only a few drops of this bitter-tasting but admirably organic medicine which might well cure any stomach disorders. But we were also glad not to be suffering from any at the time.

Of Nemrut and the magnificent monuments to human vanity that can be seen there, others have written. You must go for yourself. Thanks to Mehmet, who had thoughtfully brought along cigarettes, bags of tea, sugar, coffee, pistachios, and a bottle of *rakı*, we dined merrily that night with the Kalashnikov-wielding guards who live at the top of Nemrut Dağı. We were later shown to rather rickety bunks for the hours between the end of the *rakı* and the coming of the dawn. Sunrise itself was rather spoiled by the sudden infestation of large numbers of aggressive and grumpy tourists who kept insisting that the four of us were in the way of someone's very important photograph and would have to move.

They had arrived tightly packed into minibuses that would have made slow time up the mountain, and must have left their hotel in Kahta at such an early hour that few could have slept very much. The journey up a bumpy road in the dark would have spoiled anyone's temper. That many of them were dressed and acted as if they were accustomed to travelling in style while staying at five-star hotels is perhaps more important than the fact that they were Italian, since in all fairness they might have come from anywhere. But there were too many of them, unsuitably dressed in wrinkled linen suits, too many women wearing full make-up and high-heels, not to provoke Rita, who was eventually moved to show her proficiency in what I believe was Neapolitan rather than Sicilian dialect. Her exposition continued for so long, in fact, that before it was over, she had started to win a few Italians over to her side. Rita's triumph came when the utter silence following her speech was finally broken by a muted exclamation of 'Bravo!' that rapidly produced some sporadic giggling from the crowd.

On the drive back, I failed to find *kenger* in my pocket dictionary, but confirmed that *ilaç* was indeed medicine. Mehmet took a detour and we stopped for ice-cream of the sort they make in Maraş.

Once back in Urfa, we started making plans to find some horses. Mehmet suggested that we head out to Harran – the village of ancient beehive houses from which, Genesis tells us, Abraham departed in his seventy-fifth year – and which we were keen to visit anyway, and take our lead from people he would talk to there. Perhaps we would spot some *asil araplar* along the way, but Mehmet had family connections in several of the villages in the area and we would pay some visits according to what the word was in Harran. Rita, *maalasef*, would not be joining us. She had finished her time in Urfa and was heading back West along the coast to Kaş where she had been living for several years.

But this is Mehmet's story, and it was while Donna and I were having a final dinner with Rita that Mehmet met Hisashi Shinohara. Hisashi had come alone, all the way from Tokyo, to visit the village of Soğmatar where ancient temples house statues and carvings of the sun god Samas and the moon god Şin, which many believe to be the same as certain antique deities once worshipped in Japan. About fifty kilometres from Harran along the Turkish side of the border with Syria, Soğmatar would be an ideal next stop in the search for horses, and we could visit the rock tombs of Şuayb along the way. The village of Soğmatar itself is set amidst seven hills right on the edge of a plain that seems to stretch endlessly south into Syria. The astrological cult of Septemism which developed here made a great deal of Soğmatar's seven hills, each of which features a temple. Even Islamic astrologers from the university at Harran – fabled to be the world's first university – once recognized the importance of the site, and for centuries allowed the Septemists to claim they were really Sabians, people of the book, whose religion was therefore to be permitted.

So next morning with Hisashi, who spoke neither Turkish nor

English but had a fabulous collection of cameras, we set off with Mehmet at the wheel and a map marked with approximate sites of villages where Mehmet had family ties. In Harran, our plan for seeking horses on the way to Soğmatar was approved. Along the way we spotted several decent examples of the *doru* or bay *seglavi* type with their excellent bone, considerable stamina, and their invaluable ability to keep weight on despite hard work and poor grazing. But it was in the village of Soğmatar itself, just as we were coming out of one of the most mysterious of all the local temples, that we were surprised by a display worthy of any equestrian fantasia staged for high-rolling tourists by some top-end North African resort hotel.

The Pangon cave, right in the middle of the village, was not known to archaeologists until 1971 when a French consul named Pangon found that it contained life-sized carvings of human figures and inscriptions from 150–200 CE. Barely had we adjusted to the strong light that greeted us as we emerged from the cave's entrance when alarming sounds and a storm of dust came billowing toward us from one end of the village. Because of the dust, Hisashi had packed his cameras away after capturing all of the statuary, so unfortunately he was not able to record any of the sights unfolding before us. Three mounted men, fully robed and waving their rifles in the air, were driving a herd of perhaps twenty fine-looking young bay and chestnut mares right across the village and out onto the plain where, kicking up their heels, the youngsters needed no further encouragement to spread out and gallop furiously off. Had word arrived about foreigners interested in horses? Were those young mares being removed from, or displayed for, our inspection? Were we being shown what we would never be allowed to buy? Mehmet, who knew we were not there to buy but to find out about breeding, had no idea. At the house where Mehmet enquired, we learned that the men were taking the mares into the desert as they do sometimes, so perhaps we had simply been extremely lucky to have been there in time for the show. Of course, if we returned after the horses were brought back, we would be welcome to see them more closely and talk with their owners, who might or might not be willing to sell. Meanwhile, since we had come such a long way in the heat, would we not care for something to drink?

From inside the house, a deep metal bowl of slowly melting ice was produced. Mehmet carefully instructed us how we must only sip a little at a time because it was so cold.

I have often thought of those moments, and the unlikeliness of ceremonially sipping at melting-ice water from a metal bowl on a very hot afternoon in a magical place that I had not known existed until that day. I would remember those polite sips often that night, while wondering whether the icy water had caused the unimaginably horrific stomach cramps that had started their attack soon after dark. Since I was the only one afflicted, this seemed most unlikely, but the pains lasted for several hours until I finally remembered '*Kenger! Ilaç!*' and reached for the sample that had been carefully preserved in a plastic bag.

We returned to Urfa two years later with our friend Rosemary, horse-woman extraordinary. We were planing to repeat and expand on our previous search into horse-breeding practices and set out to find Mehmet. He was drinking tea in the gardens near the Harran Hotel and, instantly excited to see us, greeted Rosemary with all the effusion suitable for a long-lost friend. We caught up on news. Mehmet had stopped smoking cigarettes, and his wife, Rabia, had given birth to a new son, *kuçuk* Mehmet, of whom he could not have spoken with greater delight. He had no photograph, but we would see tonight. Grinning broadly, Mehmet produced a pocket phone, '*Cep telefonumu, iyi!*' and proceeded to call home and announce there would be three more for supper. Mehmet, like Urfa, was clearly prospering in a modest way from GAP, the Great Anatolia Project, involving government plans for a dam that would irrigate the region again; on our way into town we had seen the new medical research facilities aimed at forestalling outbreaks of water-borne diseases, and noticed signs for the new Agricultural College of Harran University. There were still very few tourists from the West, and the increasing numbers of wealthy Iranians who came to visit the holy places came in their own luxury coaches, but the comings and goings of government ministers and businessmen of all sorts had kept Mehmet busily employed. So much so that the Renault had been rebuilt. 'Before,' Mehmet explained, 'I would have been most proud of this, but now I am most proud of *kuçuk* Mehmet,' and the grin returned.

At dinner that evening, *kuçuk* Mehmet proved to be as adorable as only the newly born can be, and slept contentedly on his father's lap while Rabia showed no signs of wear from having recently given birth, but moved about serving us all as lithe and energetic as ever. Rabia had carried her beauty through nearly two decades of marriage and five children, and wore her long braid of hair wrapped in a scarf around her shoulders, but kept her head otherwise uncovered here at home. Her Turkish is as bad as mine, and she is shy of using it. But we spoke again of how Mehmet had bought the first taxi with money saved from driving sheep into 'Arabistan', of how Rabia first heard he wished to marry from her aunt; of the wealth and wonders of living in a building in the city, and of the greater pleasures of taking the children to see their grandmother and sleeping again in a tent. Rabia could not help finding herself in stunned awe of Rosemary, who emerged as the star of the evening as she sat pronouncing the Turkish names of familiar house-hold items with a clear English accent. Mehmet had explained Rose-mary to Rabia before our arrival, but he rehearsed his tale once more before the older children as we sat at supper. Rosemary, he proclaimed, is evidently old and equally wise; she is a great and wealthy and powerful woman who owns extensive lands in England where she keeps more than thirty horses only for pleasure and has come to find fine horses here. We knew that whatever we said would be dismissed as false modesty, but we insisted nonetheless that she was just a farmer, a *çiftçi* who had a small *çiftlik* and some horses. We had travelled with Rose-mary in rural Anatolia many times before, and knew that keeping a riding stable on Dartmoor for summer visitors would never quite make sense. Misunderstanding over this matter we knew to be unavoidable, but there was no reason to dissemble since Rosemary was here to talk about horses and came armed with a formidable Turkish vocabulary for matters equine and equestrian, and just as extensive for natural history generally. We had not been surprised when Mehmet took to her instantly, or that he quickly developed a passionate interest in making her feel both comfortable and important wherever we ventured.

Over the next few days, we set out looking for horses and revisited

Soğmatar, where Mehmet gathered a variety of herbs for making medicinal infusions and engaged Rosemary in animated botanical explanations. We were sad to see that the statues inside the Pangon cave had been badly defaced. Mehmet explained that the local people were 'superstitious,' though it took a while to find that word in the dictionary since '*hurafatçı*' was, he insisted, not quite the word he wanted. So the destruction might have been not so much a matter of pious iconoclasm in conflict with older structures, but rather that someone locally had destroyed the statues to avoid drawing the unwanted attentions of superstitious people to the area. The rock carvings on the outdoor temple to Şin, that had so excited Hisashi when we visited before, were still intact, however, and we were relieved to find the other hilltop sites had not been vandalised.

As we were leaving Soğmatar, an eager young soldier beckoned us over for a chat about what we were doing. Life standing guard over the small military camp outside the village must have proven monotonous, and we could hardly avoid being a welcome distraction. By the time the young soldier had dutifully examined Mehmet's papers, I had fallen into conversation with some of his colleagues, who had clearly been watching our antics crawling around on the hilltop temples and disappearing into village caves. We agreed that the *çavus* – sergeant – who knew English should come out to join in the talk, especially about the large sack of various green herbs that we had collected for making healthful *tisanes*. I think we all knew there was nothing worth smoking or likely to get you high, but if there were something of interest growing locally, they wanted to know about it too. Mehmet seemed alarmed when Rosemary insisted on getting out of the car, which at rest had become stifling, since it breached his sense of decorum, I think. The young desk sergeant had learned his English during a two-year programme in New Jersey and was keen to talk about American football, but Rosemary soon took him in hand and asked to be informed about the two beautiful gazelles that were grazing by the soldiers' compound. Hearing Rosemary's use of the Turkish word '*ceylan*' (gazelle) he beamed and began explaining how they were preserving and indeed breeding desert gazelles to stop them being wiped out by local hunters: there was a fenced and patrolled compound stretching way into the desert, he explained. The army post here had been running the project for some time, and had already begun selling breeding stock and, he admitted under pressure, some of the men who were not true believers were, on occasion, treated to fresh venison, but this was seldom. We declined tea and took our leave. 'They could not have been more charming,' Rosemary observed as we drove away, our bag of botanical specimens intact and uninspected.

With possible and fortuitous misunderstandings still in mind, our quest after information about horse-breeding practices in the area often turned over certain terms and the different ways they needed to be translated for us by Mehmet. Among these terms is '*asil*', an Arabic loan word for purebred, that Mehmet preferred to '*safkan*', a modern Turkish word used in racing circles. One afternoon some days after our visit to Soğmatar, while visiting Mehmet's sister's cousin's aunt at her house near Şuayp, we were drinking goat's milk *ayran* when Mehmet announced that he had heard Benazir Bhutto had recently visited a special government breeding farm and taken some purebred specimens back for her palace. The place was called Ceylanpınar and was on the border with Syria, but we could drive there and back in a day, stopping at Kırlık to visit the *muhtar*, to whom Mehmet was related. All of this sounded like a splendid plan and was confirmed by various cousins, who gradually showed up as the afternoon wore on into the evening and *ayran* had been replaced by tea. By now we were fully acclimatised to these visits as Mehmet introduced us to and into the families to which he was related. We had learned to come prepared with two rolls of film that would be dedicated to multiple portraits of the various unmarried daughters and cousins, who would dress in their finest prospective wedding clothes for these occasions. Donna would usually be asked to dress up in the mother's wedding kit and jewellery too, and to pose alongside for these bridal portraits, which Mehmet would have printed and circulated. Very soon we noticed how quickly our cover stories about cameras and horses had spread before us, and I regularly fell into joking how I travelled with wives one and four, leaving two and three back in England to manage the farm. On the slow, dusty drives, I rehearsed the sounds of the words in my mind: this one is wife one and this one is four. And for full effect, I practised doing the numbers in Arabic too and getting them confused: '*bu wahad, hatha dört*.' The routine regularly raised a laugh from the men and older women, though some of the younger people seemed astonished and perplexed.

And so it was that we set out to find a government sponsored farm where pure breeding was going on, dutifully paying respects to the *muhtar* in Kırlık on the way with promises to stop by on the return journey. We had consulted the map and found Ceylanpınar poised at a major military and trade intersection between Turkey and Syria. As we turned off the main road, evidence that there was ample water in the area quickly explained why there was settlement here and why it was named '*pınar*', or source, in Turkish. Heading south we passed by extensive settlements of low houses set amidst plantations of trees, some of them olives, others clearly orange and pomegranate. Western suburbs seldom look so pleasant to live in. These, Mehmet told us, were settle-ment camps for refugees, but from where he knew not. Once the road into town widened and the arches over it began to appear, we became once more the only show in town and were soon pulled over to talk to some charming young men in uniforms. I had noticed that the scripts inside the arches into town had not been of the '*Ceylanpınar: Hoş Geldiniz*' variety but of the '*Emniyet*' and '*Güvenlik*' variety, words that shifted in my mind between 'safety' and 'reliability,' but really meant men in uniforms not always certain what they were doing. Mehmet, on such occasions, bravely asserted his authority by insisting on Rosemary's evident importance, of which she is assured by her age. Rosemary hates being called old in any language, but can be charming too when necessary. So we were sitting drinking tea in a shady courtyard outside the building of some *Güvenlik* and *Emniyet* chaps, and, having failed to learn anything about horses locally, had turned the conversation to other matters, such as other places we had visited in Turkey, when the big black motorcar showed up. Amidst a rattling of guards, a dapper colonel wearing dark sunglasses stepped from the car and joined us even as Mehmet, who had been sitting with us, took his position standing behind Rosemary's chair to ensure she remained seated. The colonel, whose name I fear I have forgotten, was never in any doubt that, unless we were genuine lunatics, we were what I said we were and not threats to security, and he extended an invitation from the *Kaimakam* to join him for lunch and a visit to the government farm.

At this point in the Ceylanpınar visit, we were separated from Mehmet, who travelled in a support vehicle and ate in the kitchens while we were whisked off to meet and to lunch with the *Kaimakam*. But before letting him go, it is worth insisting that Donna and I are still unclear whether Mehmet had known all along that the breeding programme at Ceylanpınar – as we should have figured out, in any case, from the name of the place and from recent experience – was, like that at Soğmatar, for gazelles. It was not until we had enjoyed a pre-prandial coffee and chat with the *Kaimakam* in his splendid office – into which we had been escorted with much of the dignity described by nineteenth-century European diplomats – that we learned fully about how the Turkish government and army were working together on such schemes to employ border patrols to guard breeding grounds for the desert gazelles. But after a jolly and ceremonious lunch (during which the colonel assured me that the border crossing under his governance had long been entirely trouble-free and that, despite his early years at Ankara College, he was content to be serving his country by protecting endangered species instead of killing men) we set off to see what horses there were scattered along and across the border. For this we found ourselves travelling in the leather luxury of the *Kaimakam*'s great black Lincoln, with the appropriate flags flying from front fenders and the windows dark against the glaring sunlight. With motorcycles before us, and several military personnel carriers behind us, we were quite a jolly crew as we passed along desert roads over into Syria. As we had suspected all along, the mares were all out in the desert, and any youngsters too, but back on the Turkish side we were introduced to a few useful riding horses kept for going around the farm.

On the drive back to Kırlık, Mehmet was exuberant. He had clearly eaten exceptionally well in the kitchens, and had met some army drivers who had recently patrolled routes into 'Arabistan' that he knew from the old days. In Kırlık we stopped for tea, and to arrange our return the next day, when there would be a photo-shoot and dancing. And we were to eat the old ewe who was still lying in the yard when we arrived back, just where she had been that morning when we had passed by, but who, as the sun passed slowly, was finally and swiftly dispatched by one of the young girls with a sharp knife. One of the *muhtar's* brothers, who ran a thriving general store in Viranşehir, had arrived already, to meet us and to butcher the carcass. He would be going back that evening to refrigerate some cuts and returning the next day with supplies and various cousins. He was hard to persuade that, despite where we came from, we did not require tinned milk in our tea, and that he should please bring no more on our behalf for the next day.

We returned from Urfa early next morning, having loaded the Renault to the springs with great quantities of fruit – melons from Diyarbekır and apricots from Malatya, sacks of olives and fresh vegetables from the market, bags of dried seeds and nuts that Mehmet rightly predicted would be a great hit with all the children. In Urfa we were staying at the Güvenlik Hotel, a clean business class hotel with private bathrooms, but had eaten the previous evening on the roof terrace at the more luxurious Harran Hotel across the road. So I would have soberly finished off three or four glasses of *rakı* the night before, and our marketing early next morning took on the magical ambiance that only the *rakı* buzz can provide, a mystery tour with Mehmet at the wheel.

And so the rest of that day progressed just as it was bound to do, with Mehmet in control of both the script and the direction – a sort of Prospero figure as Peter Greenaway imagines him in *Prospero's Books*. When we arrived in Kırlık, he gracefully insisted that we take up our seats on cushions set up for us on the shaded porch while he unloaded the car; given the numerous pairs of willing and able hands that eagerly offered their assistance, he managed this in one trip. Meanwhile the *muhtar* and his wife sat with us and insisted we drink a special con-coction that had been made for us. Since it was well known we liked *ayran* but did not like whitened tea, we clearly liked white coffee, and were ceremonially presented with cups of instant coffee powder dissolved in boiling goat's milk. It was still fairly early in the morning, so the temperature had not yet reached much above the high forties, yet the coffee drink managed to form a skin on its surface as fast as one could drink it off. We spoke of the *muhtar's* sons in Germany who sent cash sometimes, and of his other family on the other side of the road who managed the herd of cattle. We learned that his wife with the cattle would not be joining us today, but her sons and daughters would be appearing later.

As the day wore on, numerous people of all ages came by – girls and women came in from the desert with sheep and goats, while young men and old arrived in cars and trucks bringing with them sisters and daughters and the smells of diesel and goat. Mehmet knew them all and formally introduced us, sometimes in Turkish, sometimes in standard Arabic, and sometimes in what we came to recognise as the Arabic of his mother's family. We ate amply of different bits of the ewe cooked in a variety of ways and served in several courses with salads and breads and pickles. There were a great many earnest discussions interrupted by periods of sometimes inexplicable laughter while we drank countless glasses of tea and children swarmed about eating sunflower seeds and staring at us bewildered. The value of Rosemary's bride-price was carefully calculated at one point, and the rich *yabancı* widow with horses was declared the best but unaffordable match of the day. Later there was heated debate over where exactly Abraham had declared the borders to be that marked out areas for grazing rights, since if someone were to marry Rosemary, and she were to bring all her horses, the matter would require very careful scrutiny. One of the senior goatherds defended his position by breaking into a rhythmic chant that, Mehmet explained, was a list of names of the men of his family since Abraham who had grazed horses over this area with success, but confessed he himself could not afford another wife, however richly endowed she might be. Once the heat of the afternoon had passed, it was time for photographs, and later, while it was still light, the women took Rosemary and Donna off to milk a goat and some sheep while the men quarrelled over how to rig up the cassette player.

As if on cue, once they were finished with the last ewe, the milking party returned to the house and became caught up in a general movement onto the roof from which loud dance music had started emanating. The *muhtar's* house is the only building in Kırlık, and it commands the narrow road joining Urfa with Viranşehir along which there was a regular flow of local and longer-distance traffic. When dancing on the roof broke out that evening, cars and trucks slowed down to allow passengers to wave and shout while the friendliest drivers greeted us with their horns. The *muhtar* had forbidden the shooting of small arms, but some of the young men waved theirs in the air for exuberance.

Mehmet's achievement that day became uncannily lucid to me while I was trying to take nicely framed photographs of the line of dancers even while they moved about the roof top, hand in hand, to the incessant beat of a recording that might have been a concert by the great Emin Arbani. From the road, the horns of paused cars were hooting, and youths with large lungs were calling out cheerfully from opened windows. On the roof before me Donna was between twin sisters, laughing as they practised mutual shoulder shaking without missing the four-step beat with their feet, and young men were taking turns to break from the line and take centre stage while reeling to idiosyncratic beats that allowed them to wave their pistols in the air. I was worried that the light was fading and that I would need to override the automatic light meter on the camera, or risk the flash starting to spoil things, when I noticed Mehmet. He was between two of the younger girls, who had come nervously kitted out in their new, unfamiliar and slightly oversized wedding costumes, and was holding their hands and dancing with them while chattering away and wearing the same grin that animated his face while talking to his own children.

Looking for horses had by now involved us becoming part of Mehmet's world in ways we could not have anticipated. One day he took us to a village near Siverek where people speak the Kurdish dialect known as *za-za* and an old friend of ours from Adrasan was living and teaching. After lunch in the school, we were joined by sundry of the local dignitaries and promenaded about the village. We all stopped to eat ripe mulberries from the trees and exclaimed how fresh the air was up here, and how rich the soil. While strolling by an irrigation canal, Mehmet and I reached the limits of our ability to talk and, for the first time, he became genuinely exasperated with me when I refused to agree that it was good to kill a snake that was eating a frog, and I still fear I might have said something offensive. Later, our friend Suleiman, who had missed the early part of the discussion anyway, wisely offered no comment, but if there were a reason to prefer the frog over the snake, the *korba* over the *yılan*, I never quite grasped it. As a result I tried to say something about nature and whether we could fully understand divine intent, and I probably said something that made it clear I was an *allasız kaplumbağa*, a godless turtle, who did not understand what he was saying. Looking back, I think Mehmet was starting to become upset that we would soon be leaving, and was looking for ways to express his displeasure. On the drive back to Urfa he told a pithy tale about a *yılan* and a *korba* that he knew none of us would understand, and then laughed at his own punch line to indicate all was now well between us.

And so came about the painful morning when we bid farewell to Rabia and *küçük* Mehmet and the other children and I again assured Mehmet that we did want to be dropped at the bus station for the trip to Diyarbekır. We had a schedule involving a flight back to Istanbul from Van in less than three weeks, and before that we had arranged to meet with other friends who would contrive for us to travel without drawing undue attention to ourselves. Mehmet knew full well that he was licensed only a certain distance beyond Urfa, and that his journey home alone from Diyarbekır would involve him paying numerous fines and being constantly delayed at the checkpoints. On our previous bus trip, Donna and I had talked briefly with the passengers of a private taxi who had already been delayed at a checkpoint for over two hours before we arrived. Rita had told us to travel this road by bus and in the daytime, and we had seen she was right.

Mehmet has written on two or three occasions since and I have from time to time persuaded friends who can write in Turkish to help me draft letters back. I trust he receives and understands them. Even as I write this, Donna and I are planning our return to Urfa, telling ourselves that we really must continue our quest for *asil araplar*. But if I look up from the desk I am offered other reasons, for there, on the wall above the lamp, hangs a photograph that I took one extremely hot and humid afternoon in Kırlık. It shows a group of people posed on a shaded porch, retiring from the sun. On the right, two small boys in brightly striped

T-shirts stand before their velvet-clad smiling mother, each proudly holding pieces of fruit brought that morning from the Urfa market. The taller, older one is staring straight into the camera, defiantly gripping his apple lest someone might be thinking of taking it away from him. His smaller brother has already begun chewing on his cucumber which he holds before him with both hands, for all the world like a clarinet player taking a pause to gaze in wonder at Rosemary who is sitting on his right hand. On the left of the photograph another pair of brothers are sitting and grinning for the camera. The *muhtar's* brother has changed into his best pink shirt and finest baggy *şalvar* trousers, a fine cotton scarf wrapped jauntily on his head. The *muhtar* himself has opted for a European look, white shirt and silky gray trousers; his broad smile displays two gold teeth and he is leaning to the left to rub shoulders with Donna who has been dressed up in a bridal scarf and a blue silk robe over a long black gown embroidered in gold filigree. In the foreground sit the *muhtar's* twin daughters, one each before my two 'wives,' modest in full-length long-sleeved black gowns and almost indistinguishable but for the differently coloured headbands that hold their hair back behind their ears to show their stunningly beautiful faces.

And right in the centre sits Mehmet without whom none of us would have met. Although he appears calm and poised, his slightly crooked grin tells me he is about to break out into full-scale laughter. But in the moment that the shutter opened, his eyes are staring straight through the camera and telling me to come back.

Memories

A Muslim from Palestine

GHADA KARMI

ALL THE WORLD'S MAJOR CONFLICTS,' my father was fond of saying, 'have religion as their basis. And the most intractable of them [the one between Israel and the Arabs] will never be solved without understanding that.' When you pressed him further, which, as he grew older and became increasingly irate at the apparent obtuseness of his listeners one was less inclined to do, he would expand on this thesis. It was not a simple conflict of Judaism versus Islam, but rather it was a Judaeo-Christian West pitted against the Islamic world. 'Because all Christians are also Jews,' he would explain. 'How could they avoid it? Jesus was a Jew, Mary was a Jew, and the twelve apostles were Jews. The Scriptures were written by Jews.' He pointed to the Old Testament as the motivating force underlying all Western aggression towards the rest of the world. The Chosen People concept, which comes from the Hebrew Bible and first referred to the Jews, was taken up by the Christian colonisers of the Americas, of Australasia, the Far and Near East and so forth. They conquered these lands with a conviction of an innate superiority and a God-given right to do whatever they wished to other, lesser breeds of humanity. He particularly saw this supremacist ideology in the Balfour Declaration of 1917 that ushered in the handover of Palestine to that other 'Chosen People', the Jewish forefathers with whom Christian Britain identified, in total disregard of the wishes of the inferior, 'non-chosen' natives. It was the same notion that converted the Arab lands of the Muslim Ottoman Empire into Western colonies and client states after 1918. The inhumanities practised every day against those who are neither Jews nor Christians, from

Afghanistan to Palestine to Guantanamo Bay, are evidence that the same ideology persists today.

I got to know my father when he was eighty-eight. He was by then living alone in Amman, my mother having died two years earlier. I don't mean of course that my father and I had never met before. Indeed, except for several short periods of absence during my childhood we were all together until I left for university at the age of eighteen. Though I never lived with my parents again, I saw them often and followed the progress of their lives until they left London for Amman in 1989. But in all those years I did not know who my father really was. I saw him as just that: my father – a man who was always reading and buying books, fighting with my mother over space for his ever expanding library, (more than five thousand books), and usually closeted with his writing in the small room that was his study in our modest, suburban London home. I knew the main facts of his life, of course, but they never added up to a picture of who he was. What did these amount to? He joined the BBC Arabic Service in 1948, soon after our forced departure from Palestine. Within a short time, he rose to prominence there, interviewing eminent Arab personalities, many of whom came to our house, and travelling to meet kings and leaders in the Arab world. We accepted all this as natural and I was surprised when a school friend, to whom I was describing one such incident, once accused me of fibbing.

In 1952 he started to record a weekly literary programme for the BBC, whose name roughly translates as, 'A Saying upon a Saying,' (Arabic: qawlun 'ala qawl). Listeners wrote in, requesting the authorship of some poem or verse and the occasion on which it was written. He would respond to each query, which might sometimes be very obscure, with a richly documented and entertaining answer. It was a novel idea, and soon the programme became must-listening all over the Arab world, eagerly awaited each week. My father's fame for this alone was such that once, when I was facing a difficult immigration officer at Casablanca airport, he suddenly asked me if I was related to one Hasan Karmi. 'His daughter,' I said. The man's face lit up. 'Why didn't you say so before? Please tell him from me and all the people of Morocco that we love and esteem him. May God preserve him.' And he let me pass with smiles and handshakes.

Such was the programme's popularity that when my father retired in 1968, the BBC retained him for a further twenty years. He went in to record it once a week as he had always done, rather like an Arab Alistair Cooke. When it finally came off the air, he was eighty-two years old and it had been the longest running programme in the history of the Arabic Service. Subsequently, all its recordings were compiled and published in fifteen volumes. All this time, he was engaged on another project, I suppose the other great enterprise of his life: his dictionaries. While we were at school, or later at university, he sat in his study each night – after the day job, so to speak – working quietly on his first English-Arabic dictionary, *Al-Manar* (the lighthouse). Published in 1971 by Longmans/Librairie du Liban, it was the first of fifteen that were to be compiled over the next three decades. The last was published in 2001, when he was ninety-six. Of these, nine were English-Arabic dictionaries of varying sizes; three were Arabic-English and three others, Arabic-Arabic. He wrote them, he said, to promote an exact understanding of Arabic through English and vice versa. He always complained that Arabs did not use their language with exactitude and so showed the same failing with other languages. This largely arises from the existence of two forms of Arabic, the literary, for reading and writing, and the cruder and less grammatical colloquial for speech. In this form terms are used imprecisely, so that the same word can mean several things. For example, *rijl* or *ijr*, can denote leg, thigh, foot or ankle, and likewise, *eed*, can mean arm, upper arm, forearm or hand, *tifl*, can mean baby, infant, toddler or child and so on. Arab children first learn the colloquial form and then progress to written Arabic in school. Because language is so crucial to the development of thought, Arabs, he said, are thus handicapped from the start. Precise language leads to precise thinking, and its lack in childhood can lead to a lifelong inability to think clearly. This contributes in his view to the Arabs' current poor performance in scientific and intellectual fields – so different from that of their great ancestors during the age of classical Islam.

It was his fascination with language, I think, that made me so aware of the nuances and subtleties of English – and so repelled by the current vulgar abuse of this beautiful language. 'Look at the way an English word can change its meaning entirely with only the slightest of adjustments,' he would say, 'as in: "few men" and "a few men"' or the difference between, "attractive" and "not unattractive" or "I like him" and "I do not dislike him".' In our house, we were always surrounded by dictionaries of all sorts. My father would come down periodically from his study to the kitchen, where my mother was cooking, and bombard her with questions about what such and such a word meant to her – he might also do the same to some hapless visitor, who had popped in just for a chat. She complained that, while fast asleep at night, he would trace words on her back, as if still writing in his study. We took all this as part of how he was, a foible, not much different from the abstruse discussions he insisted on having about philosophy or religion. If people did not respond as he thought fit, or showed no interest – which was hardly surprising, since most people don't expect a social visit to turn into a seminar – he dismissed them as fools. He read widely on philosophy and religion, and in my mind's eye I can still see the books on his shelves – Plato, Descartes, John Stuart Mill, Wittgenstein, not to speak of the numerous Arabic works on similar themes – which I never thought to open.

Strange to recall that, throughout all this time, as our father gathered fame throughout the Arab world as a foremost savant and intellectual, a linguist and lexicographer, we children were unaware of him as anything of the sort. Not because we thought the opposite, but rather it was a matter that existed in the background of our lives, as something that he did, like a hobby which he enjoyed. It didn't impinge on our lives and I, who had strong intellectual pursuits myself, thought little about it. In fact, I rather deprecated the way that he did not integrate into English society, had scarcely any English friends and had never joined any literary group or club. Granted that my mother, who had resisted coming to England and saw herself as still living in Palestine, though London was her home for forty years, didn't help. But I thought he could have done better than follow her lead. He worked alone and I think we all left him to it. Perhaps all children of remarkable parents react in this way. They want to see them as ordinary folk and find it difficult to be objective about who they are, rather in the same way that children cannot imagine their parents having sex. We understood the fact of my father's prominence, but it went no further than that. None of us read what he wrote, nor were particularly engaged in his ideas beyond hearing them repeatedly propounded to our Arab friends at the traditional gatherings where the men talk politics and the women gossip about their and other people's husbands.

If I had paused to think at the time what a long way my father had come, how far he had travelled from his modest origins in the Palestine of the Ottoman Empire to the considerable status he attained while in London, I would have marvelled at it. There was little in his background, except perhaps his father's religious knowledge, which could possibly have prepared him for his later achievements. He was born in a small town called Tulkarm in what is now known as the occupied West Bank. It was 1905 and Ottoman rule was in decline. His father, Sheikh Said, was a relatively learned man, educated in Islamic jurisprudence at Cairo's Al Azhar academy. But for all that, Tulkarm was essentially a large village and its people farmers and peasants. Dependent on agriculture, they underwent intermittent times of hardship and poverty. Once in 1914, when a locust infestation devastated Tulkarm's farms, he and his siblings nearly starved. Because he was bright, his father took him to school in Damascus, since only a limited education was to be had at home. He did well there and returned to Palestine to join the English College in Jerusalem. By then the British Mandate had replaced Ottoman rule in Palestine and my father saw that the future lay with learning what he could about the English. But his youth, from 1925 onwards, was over-shadowed by the growing Jewish encroachment on the country and the increasing Zionist threat to turn it into a Jewish state. Unlike other young Palestinian men, he joined no political movement, but single-mindedly pursued his study of English and mathematics. This enviable ability to focus on one goal was to result later in the production of his dictionaries, which nothing, from retirement to my mother's lethal final illness, interrupted.

His studies at the English College and his contact with British Mandate officials when he became a school inspector kindled a keen interest in English as a language and not just as a vehicle for dealing with the authorities. He began to compare it to Arabic and thought they had striking similarities. Idly, he drew up a five-hundred-word list of Arabic against English, and it was this that would later grow into his first dictionary. A love-hate relationship with the British developed over the period of the British Mandate: here was a people whose language and literature he admired, but the same people were blatantly facilitating the Zionist takeover of his country. He was sent on twelve-month courses in London twice, in 1937 and 1945, each time as a British government scholar, and that cemented the relationship. Perhaps, therefore, it was no surprise that he accepted a job in England in 1948, where we followed him, despite having been offered several others in the Arab world. He is convinced that his choice was the right one, because his life in London gave him a clarity of vision about the Arab world and its language that would have been impossible had he stayed there. 'Yes,' I said, 'maybe, but it also meant that you dragged an unwilling wife along with you and made us grow up in a society not our own.' It is an old accusation that he refutes with what are to me, sophistries. 'If I'd let you stay in Jordan, you and your sister would have been married off to some Bedouin.' Or, 'Look at the education you had in England. How could you have got that in the Arab world?' and so on.

It was only in 1993 that I started to see my father as a person. It happened during my regular visits to him, which, after my mother's death, I felt to be a duty. He refused to return to England because, he said, to leave her grave unvisited (she was buried in a cemetery just outside Amman) would be disloyal to her memory. There was little to do in Amman on my visits, so we would discuss his ideas at length. And so I began to discover that this monolith, my father, was in reality a complex and original thinker whose ideas I had never properly examined. I remember asking him for the first time if he believed in God. This was against the background of yet another vicious Israeli attack on Palestinian refugees. Can there be a personal deity who cares about us and, if so, what should one make of him? My father had been brought up in a religious Muslim environment and, though I had never seen him pray or fast, he admired Islam, often quoted the Qur'an and abstained from alcohol and all forms of pig meat. I also slightly thought that his great age might have conferred a wisdom on him, which could help me in my perennial and often anguished quest for meaning. He said, 'No, there is no such thing. But there is an intelligence that fashions the universe and we cannot know it. It is like a giant maze. Just when we think we've found the way, it eludes us. What we solve only unearths more puzzles. That's how it'll always be.'

'But humans have believed in a God of some sort who has a personal relationship with them since history began,' I said. 'Are they all wrong?'

'No. They discern what I am describing but give it different shapes and names to try and understand it. Why do they think it's a personal god? Well, that's part of being human, like talking or walking on two legs, nothing more.'

He continued to revise his ideas well into his nineties. While he could still read, he was, as ever, immersed in philosophy, religion and social theory. It was at this time that he began to take a political interests in Islam. Returning to the East after decades spent abroad, he began to feel there really was a Western onslaught on Islam and that Arabs were not just imagining it. Worse still, neither they nor the majority of other Muslims understood the essence of their own religion and so could not defend it. He elaborated his thesis of the Seven Principles, not to be confused with the Five Pillars, of Islam in a long essay called 'Islam: what it is' (Published in English by ISESCO, Morocco: Rabat, 2003). Islam's central message is universalist (Arabs are not mentioned once in the Qur'an), inclusive, egalitarian (no chosenness, no racism), and intensely concerned with social justice. He holds that the notion of today's welfare state derives, even if unconsciously, from this precedent. Islam's other essential aspects are what he calls 'reciprocity' – the mutual acknowledgement of rights – and *taqwa*, a word difficult to translate adequately but roughly meaning God-fearing, not overstepping the boundaries, acting with propriety. With *taqwa*, for example, the bombing of Hiroshima could not have taken place. Likewise, ignoring the principle of reciprocity resulted in the imposition of European Jews on the Palestinians when Israel was created, as if only they had rights in Palestine. Were these principles to be taught in schools, they would help raise a more moral generation which could not grow up to perpetrate the injustices and atrocities we still live with.

In the last few years, he has become obsessed with what he terms Judaeo-Christian hegemony over the world. He harps constantly on America's disregard for law and decency, its brazen support for an equally lawless and arrogant Israel, and its responsibility for so many of the world's ills. The notion of chosenness, which explains the whole of history's Western-made turmoil, is to him now a 'theory of everything'. No counter-argument shifts it and almost every world event is made to fit his theory. 'What, even global warming?' I once teased him. He ignored me and rattled on, 'America is Protestant and its people, like the Jews, are Chosen. Their covenant is with God, and their mission is appointed by Him alone. They are above our man-made law.' When I gave him a copy of Clifford Longley's *Chosen People*, he pounced on it as a vindication of his theories. And indeed Longley discusses this question in similar terms. He traces the concept of chosenness to its Old Testament roots and analyses its influence over Protestant England and America from the time of the Reformation until the present day. The English and later the Americans' view of themselves was based on an identification with the ancient Israelites, 'Chosen People', selected by God for His purposes, and so their presence is 'fundamental to the human race on this planet'. Like my father, Longley believes that religion is a vital, if unconscious, force that still influences the attitudes and behaviour of these two dominant nations, which have so changed the world's political map. Discounting the role of religious motivation as a determinant of secular policies, simply on the grounds that a majority of Protestants are now non-believers, ignores the power of inherited ideas in mapping a cultural trajectory, which becomes self-generating. The argument is so cogent and persuasive that I have found myself beginning to believe it.

It saddens me that at the end of his life – he is ninety-nine years old and should be one hundred when this book is published – my father's fine mind, still lucid and marvellously coherent, has been taken over by this obsession, to the exclusion of nearly all his other ideas. His bitterness and anger at what he views as the monstrous injustice of a world system dominated by the 'Judaeo-Christian West' comes across in repetitive tirades meant more for himself than his listeners. His Arab friends react variously: to some, his message appears to be quite simplistic, that 'Jews control the world', and they humour or secretly agree with him; to others, he is either irritating or boring, but they tolerate him because of his age and standing. I too have lost my temper with him many times. But I think I understand and it fills me with pity. For years, my father spoke little about his Palestinian past and the events of 1948, as if he had forgotten or never minded much in the first place. Perhaps for a while, his intellectual preoccupations had compensated for the loss of his homeland. But it caught up with him in the end, finding expression I believe in this elaborate, vehement theorising – in reality, a surrogate for the pain, grief and anger he has held in for most of his life, and a way of making sense to himself of a cruel destiny he had never sought.

IG

TIM MACKINTOSH-SMITH

> I am a treasure: hidden I was beneath
> This talisman of dust ...
>
> <div align="right">ABU HAMID AL-GHAZALI, <i>tr.</i> Martin Lings</div>

IN THE BACKGROUND, an Indo-Saracenic portico flanked by a pavilion. The photo hasn't caught the true colour of the columns, a washed-out sky blue; and it's just missed a girl, flitting behind the columns in peacock silk. In the foreground, a lawn, recently clipped by the gardener and his boy, of a perfection rare in the lawns of Uttar Pradesh. Here, on that type of long-armed reclining chair called a Bombay Fornicator, sits a bearded middle-aged man in narrow white trousers and a waisted black frock-coat. The waist is a little too tight: we've just had an Id lunch of *payah*, a cousin of *osso bucco*, sprinkled with shredded ginger and drizzled with the juice of miniature tangerines. It simmered for two whole days, and its aroma hangs inside in the high gloomy rooms of Saman Zar, the house 'where jasmine buds abound', lingering among dark teak and portraits of men in uniforms and tall turbans. The man in my portrait, the master of Saman Zar, is the very model of an old-school Muslim gentleman. He is a member of the Communist Party of India (Marxist). He is a Dead Head. He doesn't recline; he sits on the edge of the chair, right hand clenched into a fist, smiling quizzically at the grass.

In five months in India I took fewer photographs than most people take in five days. I'm glad I took this one. From Delhi to Kerala I met many remarkable Muslims: Khwajah Hasan, head of the Nizami *pirzadahs* (shrine guardians); dervish trance-dancers; a shrine guardian who whacked me with peacock feathers; Bibi Ayishah of Cannanore, as far as I know the only sultana in her own right on the planet. Of these, and many others, the most remarkable was that smiling man with the clenched fist – Dr IG Khan, Reader in History at Aligarh Muslim University.

I should explain here that it wasn't IG who took me to Aligarh, but IB – Ibn Battutah, the fourteenth-century Moroccan traveller and master of disasters. One of his finest messes happened near Aligarh when he was abducted by insurgents rebelling against his master, the Sultan of Delhi. He charmed his way out of captivity but took a week to get to safety – seven nightmare days of fear, hunger and disorientation. It was his frightful wanderings through the Doab, the plain between the Ganges and the Yamuna on which Aligarh lies, that I went to investigate. At first, seen from a bus on the Grand Trunk Road, it seemed an innocent, even a tedious landscape. I would come to know it better, to feel the threat that hung over it, invisible but pungent like the pollen from the mustard fields; to sense a darkness deeper than shadow in its tree-hung lanes and mango groves. When I left I realized the threat was an illusion, brought on by my attempt to revisit Ibn Battutah's nightmare. A year later it would seem real again.

Aligarh wasn't only a relief from the apparent tedium of its sur-roundings; it was a magical place. Picture a *djinn*, commanded to build academe in the dusty Doab. A quick look in the pattern-book – Oxbridge; turn chapels into mosques, Gothic into Mughal; throw in a château here, a Dutch gable there; plant palms around the quadrangles and – hey presto! – you have Aligarh Muslim University. I loved it at first sight, from the top of the bridge over the railway where you first glimpse its dreaming minarets; loved its old-fashionedness, its kindness, even its decay. Where else but in AMU Publications Department could you pick up a critical edition of the Indian part of al-Idrisi's *Nuzhat al-mushtaq* at the 1950s publication price (Rs 4), albeit eaten by half a century of the invisible worm – and, despite all protests, be given a twenty-five percent discount?

IG, as I've hinted, was no less fascinating a fusion than Aligarh itself. He lived in the squirearchical splendour of Saman Zar; he had a passion for horses, could discourse on thoroughbred pedigrees and Derby winners, and was President of the University Riding Club with its spacious stables and generous supply of bicycle-borne *syces*, pedalling behind the mounts of young latter-day *nawabs*. He was also President of the Union of Aligarh Cycle-Rickshawmen. Mostly farmers from the sticks, these were men who, before IG, had been little more than slaves – to inherited debt, to the 'rickshaw sharks' who owned the source of their so-called livelihood, to the machines on which they toiled and even slept. IG had founded their union, and it gave them a measure of freedom and self-esteem. This was no champagne- (or perhaps sherbet-) socialist gesture: he'd poured *lakhs* of his own rupees into the organization, and knew hundreds of the men by name. He had also funded a medical trust for the needy of the city, whatever their occupation or lack of it. There were few among the poor of Aligarh who didn't know IG's name, or rather those impersonal initials that stood for it. To them, Muslim or Hindu, he was IG-*sahib*, or more often IG-*bhai* – our brother IG.

His generosity went far, and it included the stranger who turned up looking for a long-dead traveller, to whom he gave vast helpings of time, knowledge and *payah*. But in small ways IG could be ungenerous. A fellow don with whom he had a very minor tiff was pronounced 'absolutely bonkers'. Those who had the impertinence to delay the progress of his car – the drivers of bullock-carts, even a bridegroom in a wedding procession – were called far worse things, and to their faces. To my ears Hindi is the language of vituperation *par excellence*, and IG could eff and blind like the best of them.

It was on a day-trip to Agra that I first witnessed this side of him, and that he introduced me to his cassette collection. The journey began with Qur'anic recitation, progressed through devotional *qawwalis* sung by Murli (and drowned in a flash-flood of abuse as we hit our first Agra traffic jam), passed into Miles Davis and ended with the Grateful Dead. Listed like that it sounds, to say the least, eclectic. But the backing-track to our jaunt had an unexpected unity. It came from IG's utter involvement in each performance: whether he was jiving to *qawwalis* or kool jazz, whether he was commenting on Surat al-Baqarah or the career of Jerry Garcia, he did it with a passion so absorbing that at times he was a danger to other road-users. And it was passion in its various other manifestations that gave a strange logic to an equally eclectic man: passion for horses and history, passion against bullock-carts and rickshaw sharks; perhaps most important, compassion for the individuals who had no justice.

He fascinated me. But if he was forthright about others – from the Hindu nationalist Bharatiya Janata Party who were then running India and 'saffronizing' the universities ('I tell you, they pull palmists off the nearest station platform and give them lectureships! Bloody fascists!') to the 'arsehole' who'd had the temerity to break down and block the road – he was less vocal about himself. Over the weeks we spent together I picked up some fragments of personal history. His ancestors were Pathans, part of that human river that had once flowed into India from the north and left so rich a sediment of energy and talent; his more recent forebears, the ones in tall turbans, had been in the service of the Nawab of Rampur. His own career had been shaped successively by AMU, the London School of Oriental and African Studies and by Duke University. 'Actually I was one of Duke's biggest failure stories,' he admitted, with a rueful wiggle of his head. 'I took off for a whole month to follow the Grateful Dead on a concert tour.'

'So you were a real Dead Head!'

IG grinned. 'I still am.'

On other objects of devotion he was more reticent. Walking in the gardens of Saman Zar one day, he let drop that his *pir*, his Sufi master, was the thirteenth-century Sheikh Sabir, a disciple of the great Baba Farid. That was all; but his eyes, shining with the memory of a man dead seven hundred years, said more. He then began to speak about his living teacher at Aligarh, Professor Irfan Habib, the grand old Marxist of Indian history. He talked about him often, and with so intense an admiration that it suggested another *pir*-disciple relationship, a secular one.

One evening I tried to draw IG out on this apparent duality of devotion. He'd been telling me how he'd arranged loans for eighty rickshawmen to buy their own machines. Three years later he came back from London with a doctorate – and a debt of two hundred thousand rupees. 'They'd sold their rickshaws and buggered off to Budaun to pay off the money-lenders. How can you blame them? I just paid up.'

'Did you – do you – help them as a Muslim, or as a socialist?'

He shrugged. 'I don't know. I suppose as a socialist. But hmm . . . there's probably a sufistic element to it all too.' He looked as if the question hadn't ever crossed his mind.

I tried to pursue the line, wondered aloud if Islam, with its *zakat* tax that slowly eroded hoarded wealth, might be seen as anti-capitalist. I wasn't so much interested in the answer as in *his* answer.

'I suppose you're right.' He smiled that quizzical, almost diffident smile. Looking at the photo now, I wonder if there was a sufistic element to that, too; and to those self-concealing initials, IG. Ahmad Abd al-Haqq, most famous of the Sabiri sheikhs, said that self-effacement was the prerequisite of being a sufi: the individual must dissolve himself in the divine as mud dissolves in water. And even if he drinks an ocean of divine secrets, he should reveal nothing.

IG was killed on 14 February 2003. He was abducted, said the letter from his colleagues, and found, bludgeoned and shot in the head, near Akrabad, in that innocent-seeming landscape of mustard fields and mango groves. They went on strike, the dons and rickshawmen and poor of Aligarh in their thousands, and brought the Grand Trunk Road to a halt. (The irony of it, to commemorate thus a man who could rage at a single bullock-cart blockage!)

Why was he killed, this man who had done so much good? Looking at his portrait today – the smile, the fist – I wonder if IG would have wanted anyone to know; whether he even knew himself. I'm glad I took the picture, even if it only shows the talisman of dust that hid Iqbal Ghani Khan.

A Conversation Paid for in Postage Stamps

TAHIR SHAH

HICHAM HARRASS lives in a one-room shack he built himself on the westernmost edge of Casablanca. The walls are made from third-hand breeze blocks and the roof is laid with rusting tin. His home does not have an address, but it does have a number. It is number 2043. All around it there's a jumble of other shacks, each with their number daubed on the wall in dripping red paint. If you turned up at the *bidonville*, the shantytown, you'd have no hope in finding Hicham's place in the maze of alleyways. But ask for him by name, and every man, woman and smallest child will jab a finger towards his door.

I met Hicham because of his passion for postage stamps. Our house is half a mile from the Atlantic. Its gardens are an oasis of date palms and mimosa trees, and are surrounded on all sides by the shantytown. When we first moved into the house I must admit I was anxious. We had no idea how our neighbours would greet us, whether they could get used to a family of foreigners living in their midst.

One morning during our first week in Casablanca, there was a tap at the door. I went to open it, and found an elderly man standing in the frame. His skin was the colour of roasted almonds. He had a long shiny face with a scrub of white beard at the end of his chin. He wore a frayed black and white wool *djellaba*, and old yellow *baboush* slippers on his feet. Before I could ask how I could help him, the man extended a hand, smiled, said his name was Hicham, and that he collected postage stamps

'Do you have any to spare?' he enquired politely. 'I could pay you a money for them, a few dirhams.'

I thought for a moment.

'We haven't received any mail yet,' I replied. 'We've just arrived.'

Hicham's smile melted. I told him to come back in a week.

'Will you forget?' he asked.

I promised not to.

A week later Hicham was at the door again. I had collected five British stamps, all bearing the Queen's head. I handed them over, and a remarkable friendship began. After that I collected all the stamps on my letters and gave them to Hicham. He was a proud man and insisted on paying me, although he had almost no money at all. I didn't want to offend him by refusing payment, and so we came up with a solution. We agreed to meet at his home at the same time each week. I would pass over the postage stamps and, in return, he could tell me about his life.

Hicham Harrass was born in a village three days' walk from the southern city of Agadir. His father was a farmer, with half an acre of dusty land. Along with five brothers and a sister, he grew up in a house made from jetsam, gleaned from the Atlantic waves. When Hicham was seven years old, a *sehura*, a witch, came to the house and declared that he would drop dead within the next cycle of the moon. The only way to avoid such a fate, she said, was for Hicham's parents to give the boy away to someone they didn't know. The family was very upset but, believing the witch's prediction would come true, they gave him to the next man who came into the village. Fortunately for Hicham, that man was a trader, called Ayman.

'He needed a boy to help him', said Hicham, 'and so I travelled around Morocco with him and his cart, buying and selling scrap metal as we went. On the long journeys between small towns he taught me,' Hicham continued. 'He taught me about life, and how to live it.'

I asked what he meant.

The old man's wife flustered over with more mint tea.

'Ayman taught me to be selfless,' he said. 'That means giving more to the people you meet than you take from them. And it means walking softly on the Earth.'

As the years had passed, Ayman and the young Hicham crisscrossed the Kingdom. They travelled from Agadir to Essaouira, from Marrakesh to Fez, from Tangier to Casablanca, always on the donkey cart piled high with scrap metal.

'We visited places that aren't on any maps,' said Hicham. 'It was adventure. Real adventure. You can't understand what it was like – it was like waking from a dream! Every mile that we travelled, Ayman would talk. Every mile was a lesson.'

'He taught me about honour, and to tell the truth,' the old man said one afternoon, as we sat in the shade of his home. 'It's because of Ayman that I cannot lie. Truth is the backbone of my life. It's my religion.'

'But Islam is your religion,' I said.

'It's the same thing,' said Hicham. 'Islam *is* Truth. It's the truth to believe in yourself, in those around you, and in God.'

Almost every week for a year, Hicham and I met and talked and talked, in conversation paid for in postage stamps. There are so many memorable conversations in my head, but few have ever been quite so revealing as those with Hicham. Over the months, I found myself grasping the basics of what must surely be *real* Islam.

One afternoon, Hicham invited me in, served me a ubiquitous glass of steaming mint tea, and said:

'You are young, your eyes are wide open, your mind is clear. But you must take care to understand.'

'To understand what?'

'To understand the right Path.'

Hicham called out the door to his wife, who was chatting to a neighbour in the street. He apologised.

'I'm sorry,' he said, 'she forgets the duty of honouring a guest with food.'

I asked about the Path.

'To understand the right Path,' Hicham said, stroking his tuft of beard, 'you must understand what it is not. It's easy. It's a lesson in life. Islam is not complicated, or cruel, or unfair. Anyone who cannot describe it in the most simplistic way is telling falsehoods. He's telling lies. He's as bad as the fanatics.'

I asked about the fanatics – about al-Qaeda, and other radical groups. Hicham rubbed his eyes.

'They pretend that what they are doing is in the name of Allah, but it's in the name of Satan,' he said very softly. 'They are hijacking our religion. Open your eyes and see it for yourself! Islam teaches tolerance and modesty. It doesn't tell people to fly passenger jets into skyscrapers, or to strap plastic explosives to their waists and to slaughter innocent women and children. These people must be stopped.'

The next week, I handed over a fresh crop of postage stamps. As always, the old man spent a few moments poring over them, commenting on each one. His favourites were from England, but 'not those silly ones with the Queen,' he would say. 'I like the big, more unusual ones. They hint at the society, the tradition.'

I steered the conversation away from postage stamps, and onto the problems of the world. I asked Hicham how Islam could stop al-Qaeda. He didn't say anything at first; he was too busy sorting through the stamps.

'I'll tell you,' he said at length. 'You have to starve them of publicity. That's what to do. Don't report their misdeeds. Ignore them. Pretend they don't exist.'

'Won't that just make them wilder for publicity?'

Hicham laughed. He laughed and he laughed until his old sagging cheeks were the colour of dark beetroot.

'Of course it would,' he said. 'But it doesn't matter how angry they get, so long as we rise up tall and spread the truth about Islam. We must tell people the facts, the *real* facts. That's what I'm saying.'

'What are the real facts?'

'Tell them that Islam doesn't order women to veil,' he said. 'The tradition was copied from the Christians of Byzantium. And tell them that Islam doesn't say you cannot drink wine – it just says you can't become intoxicated. And,' Hicham went on, his voice rising in volume, 'you can tell them that Islam says that all Muslims are equal. We are brothers. That means an *imam* or a religious scholar is equal to us. He can't tell us what to do!'

Three weeks ago I flew to London for a few days, leaving my wife and the children at our oasis in the shantytown. On the evening I returned to Casablanca, there was a knock at the door.

'That will be Hicham,' I said to my wife, 'he'll be wondering where I have been.'

I opened the door, expecting to see the old man's face. But it wasn't him. It was his wife, Khadija. She was crying.

'My husband died three days ago,' she said. 'He told me if anything ever happened to him, that I should give you this.'

The old woman was holding a box. She held it out towards me. I thanked her. A moment later she was gone. I went inside to my desk, turned on the lamp, and opened the box. In it were Hicham's stamp albums. I sat down in the dim light. I was sad to have lost a wise friend, but at the same time I was happy – happy that we had found each other at all, and had many good conversations, each one paid for in postage stamps.

To read more about Tahir Shah's experiences in Morocco,
you will have to wait for this new book *The Caliph's House*,
to be published by Transworld in Spring 2006.

Mabrouka

SYLVIE FRANQUET

THE SEA WAS STILL and transparent as we looked out from the shade of the palm trees, some of us still half asleep. It was August and the early morning sun was already hot. Twenty people walked the narrow old jetty, and boarded the small ferryboat that would cross from the Kerkennah Islands to Sfax on the Tunisian mainland. Most of them had been visiting family and most of them attending weddings. They lugged big suitcases, carried baskets with figs, sweets and noisy chickens. Three people pulled at ropes attached to fat sheep that stubbornly refused to walk the plank and, in the end, had to be pushed on board. One of those people was me and I guess I was quite a sight – a seventeen-year-old European, very tall, sun-blonde. The sheep added to the spectacle. But everyone was friendly and helped with the sheep, probably because of the woman who had brought me to the boat. Her name was Mabrouka and I had been living with her for the last five weeks.

Mabrouka had given me the sheep. She said I was to take it back with me, and even now I'm still not sure if she did so because she liked me or just because she wanted it delivered to her family in Monastir. The sheep caused the same stir getting off the boat. By then it had eaten all the food I was carrying. The two men who were also travelling with sheep gave me the rest of their food – they were staying in Sfax – and found me some more as I had another journey, by *louage*, communal taxi, ahead of me. Here I definitely stood out from the crowd, and there was laughter and comment all around as I looked for transport. At last I found a driver who would take me and the sheep back to the family I knew in Monastir. I left the sheep in their large orchard, and soon after this strange but amusing journey I went back to university in Belgium. I never heard what happened to Mabrouka, or the sheep for that matter, but I often think of her because she was one of the strongest women I have met.

I had just finished secondary school and, as I wanted to study Arabic at university, my father arranged for me to spend the summer with a family who lived in the Tunisian beach resort of Monastir. The deal he struck was this: if I worked in the family's jeans factory, the women there would teach me some of their language. But as soon as I arrived Mohamed, the man of the house and owner of the factory, told me that I was now like his daughter, so there was simply no way I could work at the factory. Instead he wanted me to hang out with his wife Najet and their four small daughters. I was disappointed because I was very much a tomboy, boys were my only friends, and here I was about to spend a few months enclosed in the women's world.

Mohamed ran a successful business, lived in a large villa and employed two maids, although Najet did all the cooking. Our days were simple: in the morning we drank coffee before going into the garden to pick herbs, figs, peaches and all sorts of vegetables. We crushed spices in a metal mortar, made fresh harissa, a hot sauce, prepared tomatoes for drying on the roof and drank verbena, which seemed to be a cure for all female ailments. Then we prepared elaborate lunches of salads followed by a couscous or a stew.

The whole family ate lunch together, after which Mohamed went out, leaving us to sit in the shade with the female neighbours and some family members who came to visit. After exchanging greetings and asking after the health of the extended family, the conversation soon turned to sex and did not really change much after that. The women giggled and talked about what their husbands did, how they heard what others did, what they liked, what they thought they might like. If I wandered off to take some air on the balcony, they would laugh and tell me to stop flirting. Their favourite joke was to lift my skirt and threaten to remove my pubic hair with sugar and lemon syrup, as soon as possible.

It was summer, which is the season of weddings in Tunisia, sparked by the annual return of workers from France and elsewhere in Europe. Almost every other day we were invited to some part of the week-long wedding ceremonies. On the final wedding day both men and women were invited, but they sat separately to sip cold drinks and eat sweets. I preferred the women's only days, when henna was applied on the bride's hands and feet. The women would take off their white veils, loosen their hair, knot scarves around their hips and dance, totally wild, to music from a band of blind musicians. Much as I was fascinated by this exotic world of women, I longed to talk about anything but sex. Above all, I longed to talk to men.

One day, on a visit to Najet's recently married brother and sister-in-law, I met their friend Walid, a Tunisian who lived in Belgium. Walid was on holiday and staying with his family for the summer. He was a bit older than me but we had fun talking about things that were familiar to both of us. It was like a breath of normality to talk to a guy, not about sex but about Belgium, about politics and racism, and about our favourite bars in Brussels. It felt good to be away from the protected environment of women and girls, in which I had been slumbering for the last few weeks. We had to arrange our secret meetings through the sister-in-law because Walid had no phone in his house, and it certainly was not done for him to call me at Mohamed's house. We met from time to time on the beach, went for walks or a cold drink and exchanged written messages via the lady who ran the grocery store near the beach. I thought it was all very innocent and quite funny, but Mohamed did not. When he spotted me talking to Walid, he forbade me to go to the beach on my own and had Walid arrested for a few days for molesting me. This, and the fact that he had begun to walk into my bedroom after his wife had gone to sleep to 'check on me', as I was now like his daughter, convinced me I needed a break. Mohamed agreed to let me go for the weekend to the Kerkennah Islands with Najet's brother and sister-in-law, who were going to visit their old aunt.

From the sea, the islands looked idyllic, a world away from the busy beach resorts of Monastir and Sousse. We arrived by small ferry, the flat coastline shimmering in the afternoon heat, a magnificent beach lined with palm trees and fishing boats. The aunt, Mabrouka, waved at us from the shore and kissed us all when we arrived. She was very tall and had something extremely gracious and elegant about her. Her tanned wrinkled face was decorated with Berber tattoos, and her long hair was tied in two thin grey plaits on her back. We walked over to Mabrouka's house, a simple two-room building near the beach surrounded by old fig trees, where she cooked us a late lunch. At night it was so hot we lay on the roof, looking at the stars, while Mabrouka told stories I struggled to understand.

We were supposed to stay for the weekend, but I was so happy there, and so intrigued by this old woman, I asked if I could stay longer. Mabrouka seemed happy to have a new audience for her stories.

There were many stories about Mabrouka. One was that she had been a beauty and had fallen in love with a local boy when she was fifteen. Her father, who adored her, let her marry the boy, only for tragedy to strike soon after: her husband died in his twenties. Mabrouka, who was mortified, announced she would never remarry. She left the house of her in-laws and returned to the old house of her parents. When they died, she chose to live alone surrounded by fig trees in the house where the chickens and a few sheep ran loose. She also had a little blue fishing boat pulled up on the beach. Life on the islands was still very traditional and women and men were strictly segregated, their roles clearly defined. But Mabrouka chose otherwise and wanted to live like a man. Tall and skinny as she was, she wore the basic women's dress over men's trousers. She nearly knocked the men over when she greeted them by hitting their shoulder. People clearly respected her, and I was told women came to her for *baraka*, a blessing. She led her own life, seemingly happy about the decisions she had taken in life.

The islands have their own dialect, which made it hard for us to communicate, but Mabrouka took me under her wing and taught me the words I needed. In the early mornings we took her little boat out onto the flat sea, and while she fished we breakfasted on figs from her trees and on bread she had made. Sometimes I tried fishing, but mostly I watched her, admiring the ease with which she seemed to do everything and with which she handled the fish trap she had made of palm tree branches, the same as the Phoenicians used, which allowed her to catch the fish alive.

When she had caught enough fish, she told me to jump in and

swim. She never swam but watched me and smiled at my youth, while she cleaned some fish for lunch. Back home we made a fire and grilled the fish. She told me off for eating it with knife and fork, and taught me how to eat with my hands, which seemed to make everything taste so much better. The figs from her trees were the best I had tasted, slightly salty because of the saline ground. Mabrouka scolded me for being too greedy and warned that I would have stomach problems if I ate too many. I was her young apprentice: as well as Arabic, she taught me how to make bread and couscous, how to place the fish trap and, most important of all to her, how to be who you want to be. She was so strong and she made complicated things look so simple. Later in the afternoon, we slept in the shade and the stillness of the heat until a breeze came from the sea and woke us up, when Mabrouka would wash and pray.

Here too it was wedding season, but although Mabrouka would go and greet the women, paying her respects, she preferred to spend time with the men. And I followed, watching her chat and crack jokes, imagining her bragging about the size of fish she had caught that morning and remembering how far I had come from the women cackling about their exploits in bed. The night before the wedding, musicians came to play olivewood flutes, a large wooden drum and small drums made of pottery. The men gathered around them to lament the imminent loss of their freedom. These songs were often melancholic, but sometimes also very joyous at the idea of life going on, and boisterous at the celebration of manhood. The nights were almost hypnotic and seemed to go on forever, at least very late, when Mabrouka would take my hand and lead me back to her house near the sea.

On the last evening I spent with her, Mabrouka took one of her five sheep and explained that I was to take it with me to Monastir. At first I refused, but she insisted I was to take it. I hardly slept, and spent most of the night watching Mabrouka, looking at the stars and wondering how I would get the sheep back to the mainland. In the morning I ate her delicious figs for the last time – she didn't tell me off that time – and then we walked to the port. At the boat, she invoked God's blessings for me, hugged me and stood silent, strong, immobile, as the little boat took me and the sheep back towards the mainland.

Dr Jaffery

WILLIAM DALRYMPLE

I CLIMBED A NARROW STAIRCASE leading to the first floor balcony. Outside the scholars' rooms sat a line of bearded old men busily correcting specimens of Arabic calligraphy. Dr Jaffery's room was the last on the corridor.

The door opened to reveal a gaunt, clean-shaven man. He wore white Mughal pyjamas whose trouser-bottoms, wide and slightly flared, were cut in the style once favoured by eighteenth-century Delhi gallants. On his head he sported a thin white mosque-cap. Heavy black glasses perched on the bridge of his nose, but the effect was not severe. Something in Dr Jaffery's big bare feet and the awkward way he held himself gave the impression of a slightly shambolic, absent-minded individual: '*Asalam alekum*,' he said. 'Welcome.' Then, looking behind me, he added: 'Ah! The rains . . . Spring has arrived.'

Dr Jaffery's domed room was small and square and dark. Lightning from the storm had cut off the electricity and the cell was illuminated by a bronze dish filled with flickering candles. The shadows from the candlelight darted back and forth across the shallow whitewashed dome. Persian books were stacked in disordered piles; in the corner glistened a big brass samovar incised with Islamic decoration. The scene of the sufi scholar in his room was straight out of a detail from the Anvar-i Suhayli – or indeed any of the illuminated Mughal manuscript books – and I said this to Dr Jaffery. 'My nieces also tell me I live in the Mughal age,' he replied. 'But they – I think – mean it as a criticism. You would like tea?'

Dr Jaffery blew on the coals at the bottom of his samovar, then placed two cupfuls of buffalo milk in the top of the urn. Soon the milk was bubbling above the flame. While he fiddled with his samovar, Dr Jaffery told me about his work.

For the previous three years he had been busy transcribing the forgotten and unpublished portions of the *Shah Jehan Nama*, the court chronicle of Shah Jehan. He had converted the often illegible manuscript into clear Persian typescript, and this had then been translated into English by a team of Persian scholars in America. The manuscript, originally compiled by Shah Jehan's fawning court historian Inayat Khan, told the story of the apex of Mughal power, the golden age when most of India, all of Pakistan and great chunks of Afghanistan were ruled from the Red Fort in Delhi. It was an age of unparalleled prosperity: the empire was at peace and trade was flourishing. The reconquest of the Mughals' original homeland – trans-Oxianan Central Asia – seemed imminent. In the ateliers of the palace the artists Govardhan, Bichitr and Abul Hasan were illuminating the finest of the great Mughal manuscript books; in Agra, the gleaming white dome of the Taj Mahal was being raised on its plinth above the River Jumna.

The book which contained the fruits of Dr Jaffery's labours was about to be published. Now Dr Jaffery was beginning to transcribe a forgotten text about Shah Jehan's childhood. The manuscript had just been discovered in the uncatalogued recesses of the British Museum; it was exciting work, said the doctor, but difficult: the manuscript was badly damaged and as he had not the money to go to London he was having to work from a smudged xerox copy. The new transcription absorbed his waking hours, but, despite the difficulties, he said he was making slow progress.

'As the great Sa'di once put it: 'The Arab horse speeds fast, but although the camel plods slowly, it goes both by day and night.'

As we chatted about Shah Jehan, Dr Jaffery brought out a plate of rich Iranian sweets from an arched recess; he handed them to me and asked: 'Would you not like to learn classical Persian?'

'I would love to,' I answered. 'But at the moment I'm having enough difficulty trying to master Hindustani.'

'You are sure?' asked Dr Jaffery, breaking one of the sweets in two.

'Learning Persian would give you access to some great treasures. I would not charge you for lessons. I am half a dervish: money means nothing to me. All I ask is that you work hard.'

Dr Jaffery said that very few people in Delhi now wanted to study classical Persian, the language which, like French in Russia, had for centuries been the first tongue of every Delhi-wallah. 'No one has any interest in the classics,' he said. 'If they read at all, they read trash from America. They have no idea what they are missing. The jackal thinks he has feasted on the buffalo when in fact he has just eaten the eyes, entrails and testicles rejected by the lion.'

I said: 'That must upset you.'

'It makes no difference,' replied Dr Jaffery. 'This generation does not have the soul to appreciate the wisdom of Ferdowsi or Jalaludin Rumi. As Sa'di said: 'If a diamond falls in the dirt it is still a diamond, yet even if dust ascends all the way to heaven it remains without value.''

I loved the way Dr Jaffery spoke in parables; for all his eccentricities, like some ancient sage his conversation was dotted with pearls of real wisdom. Dr Jaffery's words were profound and reassuring. As he told little aphorisms from Rumi or the anecdotes of Ferdowsi's *Shah Nama* – the Mughal Emperors' favourite storybook – his gentle voice soothed away the irritations of modern Delhi. But overlaying the gentle wisdom there always lay a thin patina of bitterness.

'Today Old Delhi is nothing but a dustbin,' he said, sipping at tea. 'Those who can, have houses outside the walled city. Only the poor man who has no shelter comes to live here. Today there are no longer any educated men in the old city. I am a stranger in my own home.' He shook his head. 'All the learning, all the manners have gone. Everything is so crude now. I have told you I am half a dervish. My own ways are not polished. But compared to most people in this city . . .'

'What do you mean?'

'Here everyone has forgotten the old courtesies. For example . . . in the old days a man of my standing would never have gone to the shops; everything would be sent to his house: grain, chillies, cotton, cloth. Once every six months the shopkeeper would come and pay his regards. He would not dare ask for money; instead it would be up to the gentleman to raise the matter and to give payment when he deemed suitable. If ever he did go to the bazaar he would expect the shopkeepers to stand up when he entered . . .

'All these things have gone now. People see the educated man living in poverty and realize that learning is useless; they decide it is better to remain ignorant. To the sick man sweet water tastes bitter in the mouth.'

'But don't your pupils get good jobs? And doesn't their success encourage others?'

'No. They are all Muslim. There is no future for them in modern India. Most become *gundas* or smugglers.'

'Is learning Persian a good training for smuggling?'

'No, although some of them become very successful at this business. One of my pupils was Nazir. Now he is a big gambler, the Chief of the Prostitutes. But before he was one of my best pupils . . . '

At that moment, the cry of the muezzin outside broke the evening calm. Dr Jaffery rustled around the room, picking up books and looking behind cushions for his mosque cap before remembering that he was already wearing it. Muttering apologies he slipped on his sandals and stumbled out. 'Can you wait for five minutes?' he asked. 'I must go and say my evening prayers.'

From the balcony I watched the stream of figures in white pyjamas rushing through the pelting rain to the shelter of the mosque. Through the cloudburst I could see the old men laying out their prayer carpets under the arches, then, on a signal from the mullah, a line of bottoms rose and fell in time to the distant cries of 'Allah hu-Akbar!'

Five minutes later, when Dr Jaffery returned, he again put a cupful of milk on the samovar and we talked a little about his home life.

'The death of my eldest brother in 1978 was the most important event in my life,' he said. 'From my boyhood, I always wanted to live in a secluded place, to live like a sufi. But since my brother's death it has been my duty to care for my two nieces. I cannot now become a full dervish; or at least not until my nieces are educated and married. Until then their well-being must be my first concern.'

'And after that?'

'Afterwards I want to go on *haj*, to visit Mecca. Then I will retire to some ruined mosque, repair it, and busy myself with my studies.'

'But if you wish to retire can't you find some other member of your family to look after your nieces for you?'

'My elder brothers were killed at Partition,' said Jaffery. 'My elder sister is also a victim of those times. To this day she still hears the voices of guns. You may be sitting with her one evening, quite peacefully, when suddenly she will stand up and say: "Listen! Guns! They are coming from that side!"

'In fact it was only by a miracle that my sister and I survived at all: we took shelter with our youngest brother in the Jama Masjid area. Had we been at the house of my parents we would have shared the fate of the rest of the family . . . ' Dr Jaffery broke off.

'Go on,' I said.

'My parents lived in an area that had always been traditionally Hindu. During Partition they went into hiding, and for a fortnight their good Hindu friends brought them food and water. But one day they were betrayed; a mob came in the night and burned the house down. We learned later that the traitor was a neighbour of my father's. My father had helped him financially. This was how the man repaid him . . . ' Dr Jaffery shook his head. 'In this city,' he said, 'culture and civilization have always been very thin dresses. It does not take much for that dress to be torn off and for what lies beneath to be revealed.'

*   *   *

That week Olivia and I visited Dr Jaffery's family *haveli* in the walled city for the first time. He had been very nervous about inviting us.

'You should not make friends with an elephant keeper,' he had said, 'unless you first have room to entertain an elephant.'

'Doctor, I wish you would explain your aphorisms sometimes.'

'My friend: I am referring to you. You are a European. You come from a rich country. I am a poor scholar. It is unwise for us to become close because I cannot afford to entertain you in the style to which you are accustomed!' Dr Jaffery frowned: 'I am a simple man. I live in a simple house. You will be disgusted by my simple ways.'

'Don't be silly, doctor. Of course I won't.'

'So if I invited you to my house you would not be upset by the simple food I would serve?'

'Nothing would give me greater pleasure.'

'In that case you and your wife must come and eat some simple dervish dishes with me and my family.'

It was now early March and Ramadan had just begun. With its overwhelmingly Hindu population, New Delhi was quite unchanged by the onset of the Muslim month of fasting, but the Old City had been transformed since our last visit. There were now far fewer people about: many streets were deserted but for groups of tethered goats fattening for their slaughter on Id-ul-Zuha. Those Muslims who were out on the streets looked bad-tempered: they had not eaten or drunk since before dawn, and were in no mood for smiles or pleasantries. Even the endlessly patient bicycle rickshaw drivers muttered curses under their breath as they drove us uphill through the narrowing funnel of tightly-packed houses.

Dr Jaffery's house lay a short distance from the Turkman Gate, off the narrow Ganj Mir Khan. A steep flight of steps off the street led to a first-floor courtyard dotted with pots of bougainvillaea. Here we were met by Fardine, Dr Jaffery's nephew.

Fardine was a tall, good-looking boy, about sixteen years old; like his uncle he was dressed in white *kurta* pyjamas. Dr Jaffery was still giving lectures at the college, Fardine said. Would we like to come upstairs and help him fly his pigeons until Dr Jaffery arrived for *iftar*, the meal eaten at sunset each day during Ramadan?

He led us up four flights of dark, narrow stairs, before disappearing up a rickety ladder out on to the roof. We followed and emerged onto a flat terrace with a magnificent view over Old Delhi. To the right rose the three swelling domes of the great Jama Masjid; to the left you could see the ripple of small semi-domes atop the ancient Kalan Masjid. In between the two mosques, in the great arc of roofs and terraces which surmounted the houses of Shahjehanabad, I saw for the first time that secret Delhi which lies hidden from those who only know the city from ground level. From Dr Jaffery's rooftop you could look out, past the anonymous walls which face on to the Old Delhi lanes, and see into the shady courtyards and the gardens which form the real heart of the Old City.

In the last hour before the breaking of the Ramadan fast, the courtyards and rooftops were filling with people. Some were lying on charpoys, snoozing away the last minutes before their first meal for thirteen hours. Others sat out on carpets beneath the shady trees enjoying the cool of the evening. Nearby, little boys were playing with brightly coloured diamond-shaped kites which they flew up into the warm evening breeze. They pulled sharply at the strings, then released the kites so that they flew in a succession of angular jerks, higher and higher into the pink evening sky. While most of the fliers were quietly attempting to raise their kites as high as possible into the heavens, some of the boys were engaged in battles with their neighbours. They locked strings with the kites of their enemies and attempted, by means of the ground glass glued on their strings, to cut their opponents' kites free.

Yet, on the rooftops, the kite fliers were easily outnumbered by the pigeon fanciers – the *kabooter baz* – who stood on almost every terrace, hands extended into the air calling to their pigeons: *Aao! Aao! Aao!* (Come! Come! Come!) Above them, the sky was full of the soft rush of beating wings, clouds of pigeons dipping and diving in and out of the domes and through the minarets. The flocks whirled and wheeled, higher and higher, before nose-diving suddenly down towards their home terrace on the command of their master . . .

When the birds had eaten their fill, Fardine stood back and shouted: 'Ay-ee!' Immediately with a great flutter of wings the pigeons rose into the air and circled above the terrace. When Fardine whistled the birds shot off in the direction of the Jama Masjid; another whistle and they returned. Fardine waved his arms and the birds rose high into the air; at the cry of '*Aao! Aao! Aao!*' they obediently returned. With another flutter of wings, the birds came in to land on their coop.

'These tricks are easy to learn,' said Fardine shrugging his shoulders. 'But to become a master – a *Khalifa* – can take twenty years of training. A master can teach his pigeons to capture another man's flock and drive it home like a herd of sheep. He can make his birds fly like an arrow – in a straight line, in single file – or can direct them to any place he likes, in any formation. There are perhaps five thousand *kabooter baz* in Delhi, but there are only fifty *Khalifa*.'

As Fardine spoke, there was a sudden report, like a loud explosion. Seconds later the muezzin of a hundred Delhi mosques called the Faithful to prayer with a loud cry of 'Allaaaaah hu-Akbar!' The sun had set. The fast was over. It was time for the *iftar*.

*   *   *

Dr Jaffery was prostrated on a prayer carpet, finishing his evening *namaaz*. Fardine went to join him. Uncle and nephew knelt shoulder to shoulder, hands cupped, heads bowed in the simple position of submission.

When he had finished, Dr Jaffery rose to his feet, brushed the dust off his pyjamas and came over to Olivia and me. He welcomed us, then added: 'You looked at us strangely while we were praying. Do you never pray?'

'I used to,' I said, embarrassed. 'Now . . . I am not sure what I believe in, whether I'm an agnostic or . . . '

'You make God sound so complicated,' said Dr Jaffery, cutting in. 'God is simple. To follow him is not so difficult. Just remember the advice of Rumi: "Follow the camel of love." '

'But follow it where?' I said.

'To wherever it leads,' replied Dr Jaffery. 'God is everywhere. He is in the buildings, in the light, in the air. He is in you, closer to you than the veins of your neck.'

'But . . . '

'If you honour him and believe God is one you will be all right,' said Dr Jaffery. 'Come. The *iftar* is ready.'

He led us into the house and introduced us to his two nieces, Nosheen and Simeen. They were pretty, about sixteen and seventeen, dressed in flowery *salwar kameez*.

A sheet had been spread out on the ground, and around it had been placed a square of long hard bolsters. The *iftar* meal was laid in its centre. We sat down and Dr Jaffery handed us a plate of dates: traditionally the delicacy with which Muslims break the Ramadan fast.

There followed a succession of delicious Delhi kebabs rounded off with fruit *chaat*: a kind of spicy fruit salad. While we ate, Dr Jaffery talked of the (then) impending break-up of the Soviet Union: 'The Iranians are already broadcasting to Central Asia in Turkish,' he said. 'There will be a revival of the Timurid Empire. Just you see. Before long there will be an embassy of Samarkand in Delhi.'

After we had finished everyone lay back on the bolsters. Dr Jaffery's nieces begged him to tell us one of his Mullah Nasir-ud-Din stories and eventually he obliged.

He told how, on one of his visits to Delhi, the legendary Mullah Nasir-ud-Din arrived in the dry middle of Ramadan. The mullah was very hungry; and when he heard that the Emperor was providing a free *iftar* to anyone who came to the Red Fort he immediately tied up his donkey and went along. However he was so dirty from his ride that the Master of Ceremonies placed him in a distant corner, far from the Emperor, and at the end of the queue for food.

Seeing he would not be served for several hours, the mullah went off back to the caravanserai in which he was staying. He washed and dressed in a magnificent embroidered robe topped with a great gilt turban, then returned to the feast. This time he was announced by a roll of kettle drums and a fanfare of trumpets bellowing from the *Naqqar Khana*. The Master of Ceremonies placed him near the Great Mogul and a plate of freshly grilled lamb was put before him. But Mullah Nasir-ud-Din did not eat. Instead he began to rub the lamb all over his robe and turban.

The Mogul said: 'Eminent Mullah. You must be a foreigner from a distant and barbarous land! I have never seen such manners in my life before!' But Mullah Nasir-ud-Din was unrepentant. He replied: 'Your Highness. This gown got me fed. I think it deserves its portion too, don't you?'

After the story was finished, Nosheen and Simeen said goodnight and disappeared up to bed. But Fardine, Olivia and I sat up with Dr Jaffery sipping tea and chatting until well after midnight. At first Dr Jaffery told more Mullah Nasir-ud-Din stories, but after a while the conversation became more serious.

I asked the doctor about Dara Shukoh and Aurangzeb, and soon the

doctor was telling us about the civil war and the accounts given of it by
Bernier and Manucci.

*   *   *   **

'Come,' said Dr Jaffery, taking me gently by the shoulder. 'We must pay
our respects to the sheikh.'

We joined the queue of pilgrims, and soon passed under the cusped
arch and into the velvety warmth of the shrine.

The tomb exuded the same thick, hushed, candlelit air of extreme
sanctity that hangs over venerated shrines all over the world: the atmosphere reminded me immediately of the tomb of Saint James in Com-
postela or the Holy Sepulchre in Jerusalem. The interior was narrow
and claustrophobic. In the centre, under a painted dome, was a marble
cot covered in a thick velvet canopy like an enormous four-poster bed;
from its front beam hung suspended a pair of ostrich eggs. Between
the canopy and the raised marble tomb-cover, pilgrims had piled a
mountain of rose garlands on to a crimson drape, so that now the
material lay almost invisible beneath the windfall of petals.

The pilgrims, all men – women were excluded from the interior –
slowly circled around the balustrade, heads bowed, hands cupped in
invocation, stopping every so often to murmur prayers or recite mantras.
Outside, through the latticed grilles, you could see the dark shapes of
barren ladies clawing at the rear of the tomb. Some tied threads through
the *jali* screen: each string a reminder to the sheikh to provide the woman
with the longed-for male heir.

Dr Jaffery murmured a prayer and we left the tomb behind an old
blind guru who was being led slowly forward by a young disciple. The
guru's eyes were clouded blue almonds. As he walked, he tapped a dark
teak walking stick held in his free hand. Outside in the courtyard there
was a sudden roll of drum beats. The *qawwali* singers had struck up a
hymn: 'Salaam!' they sang, 'Salaam Khwaja Nizamudeeeeen!'

There were six *qawwals*, all dressed in high-necked Peshwari waistcoats, all sitting cross-legged in a line in front of the tomb. Two had
harmoniums; two had small *tabla* drums. Two had no instruments but
instead clapped and sang. One of the singers was a toothless old man

with a gravelly voice; he was dark and heavily-bearded and narrow-eyed like one of the Magi in Van Eyck's *Adoration of the Lamb*. He was accompanied by the quavering treble of his young grandson.

Within minutes, the crowd milling around the shrine had settled in a semicircle around the musicians. Everyone was listening intently, overtaken by the music. The *qawwals* picked up momentum. Singing faster and faster, louder and louder. As they reached the climax of each verse, the two singers raised their hands in the air and the stones in the old man's rings glinted in the light. Then the hymn began to wind down, until just the boy was singing in his soft, high voice accompanied only by the barest of bass drones from the harmonium. The singing stopped. There was a fraction of a second of complete silence. Then with a great battering of *tablas*, the singers built up to the final verse. Over and over again they repeated the name of the saint: Nizam-ud-Din! NIZAM-UD-DIN! NIZAM-UD-DIN!

At the edge of the crowd, the two *pankah*-wallahs were slowly, hypnotically waving their fans in time to the chant. All around, the devotees began to sway with a distant look in their eyes as if they were on the verge of a trance. Seeing this the *qawwals* extended their song and attempted another climax. There voices rose to new heights of passion, but the moment had been lost. There was no trance; the climax had somehow just been missed. The song ended, and a barely tangible shiver of disappointment passed through the crowd.

Later, sitting in a *dhaba* with Dr Jaffery, I remarked on how many of the devotees had been Hindus and Sikhs. Dr Jaffery shrugged his shoulders. 'Hindus and Sikhs also have their dreams which they wish the saint to make reality,' he said. 'That is one level. Also you do not have to be a Muslim to beg the saint's help in deeper matters. Many Hindus, like us, are impatient for the divine. They want to see in this life a glimpse of the face of God.'

'But the face of God that they would glimpse would be very different from the face you would see, wouldn't it?'

'Naturally,' said the doctor. 'Who is to say what is the true face of the God?' He swung his prayer beads around his index finger.

'Jalal-ud-Din Rumi used to tell a story about a far distant country, somewhere to the north of Afghanistan. In this country there was a city inhabited entirely by the blind. One day the news came that an elephant was passing outside the walls of this city.

'The citizens called a meeting and decided to send a delegation of three men outside the gates so that they could report back what an elephant was. In due course, the three men left the town and stumbled forwards until they eventually found the elephant. The three reached out, felt the animal with their hands, then they all headed back to the town as quickly as they could to report what they had felt.

'The first man said: "An elephant is a marvellous creature! It is like a vast snake, but it can stand vertically upright in the air!" The second man was indignant at hearing this: "What nonsense!" he said. "This man is misleading you. I felt the elephant and what it most resembles is a pillar. It is firm and solid and however hard you push against it you could never knock it over." The third man shook his head and said: "Both these men are liars! I felt the elephant and it resembles a broad *pankah*. It is wide and flat and leathery and when you shake it it wobbles around like the sail of a dhow." All three men stuck by their stories and for the rest of their lives they refused to speak to each other. Each professed that they and only they knew the truth.

'Now of course all three of the blind men had a measure of insight. The first man felt the trunk of the elephant, the second the leg, the third the ear. All had a part of the truth, but not one of them had even began to grasp the totality or the greatness of the beast they had encountered. If only they had listened to one another and meditated on the different facets of the elephant, they might have realized the true nature of the beast. But they were too proud and instead they preferred to keep to their own half-truths.

'So it is with us. We see Allah one way, the Hindus have a different conception, and the Christians have a third. To us, all our different versions seem incompatible and irreconcilable. But what we forget is that before God we are like blind men stumbling around in total blackness . . .'

Adapted from William Dalrymple's, *City of Djinns: A Year in Delhi*. Flamingo, London £8.99

Bohlul

SHUSHA GUPPY

> If the fool would persist in his folly he would become wise
>
> WILLIAM BLAKE

BOHLUL WAS THE JANITOR of the College of Theology – *madrasah* – in Teheran where my father taught Islamic Philosophy. The college was named Sepahsalar (Literally: Lord of the Army), which was the title of a nineteenth-century grandee who had been Persian Ambassador at the court of the Ottoman Sultan, and who had built and endowed the *madrasah* and its adjoining mosque. It was the most prestigious centre of Islamic learning in the capital, with a collegiate system similar to Cambridge, and since its inception some of the most learned and reputable Islamic scholars in the country had both studied and taught there, among them my father. When Reza Shah came to power in 1925 he embarked upon a vast and radical programme of modernisation, of which the establishment of an independent judiciary and a modern system of education, available to all citizens, were two of the most significant measures, as both had been hitherto in the hands of the powerful clergy, based in Qom and reluctant to lose their grip. The University of Teheran, the first modern university in the country, was established in the 1930s, and the highest authorities in various fields of knowledge were invited to lecture and teach there. It was modelled on the Sorbonne, where many of the dons were educated, and was open to both men and women, to the dismay of more traditionally-minded people. My father was appointed to the Chair of Philosophy, but he went on teaching at the *Madrasah Sepahsalar* as well.

The Sepahsalar Mosque was one of the landmarks of Teheran; its turquoise and white faience dome and minarets rose above the nearby Parliament buildings and the surrounding sprawl in the centre of town. You could see it on the skyline from afar, and hear the call of the *muezzin* at noon amid the roar of the traffic and the cacophony of street vendors. My school was on Parliament Square, and walking to it from home I went past the mosque and the *madrasah* every day. Now and again I would catch a glimpse of Bohlul, the janitor, unmistakable in his dervish's attire – a cloak over a flowing robe of rough wool fastened with a belt. With his long grey hair and beard, twinkling eyes and the ghost of an ironic smile, he exuded good-humour and benevolence. But who was Bohlul? And how had a humble janitor become a famous character in the city?

Bohlul had been a very rich man, with a fortune in real estate, which he had inherited from his mother, the most famous midwife of her time, at the turn of the twentieth century. She had come from a humble background but had risen to high status and acquired considerable wealth by her work. In those days professions were learnt through apprenticeship; a young woman who wanted to become a midwife would follow an older one around, assist and observe her, and gradually learn the skill. When her mistress retired or died she would take over her practice. Over the years Bohlul's mother had acquired such a reputation for competence and care that her services were sought by the wealthiest families. When she was called to the Shah's Palace and delivered a son to one of his favourite wives, she reached the apogee of her fame and fortune. She went on pilgrimage to Mecca, acquired the title of *Hajieh* (Lady Haji) and lived in grand style.

As it happens she was also a clever and prudent businesswoman; she saved and invested her money in real estate and land: fifteen houses in Teheran, which she let for good rent, and some cornfields and orchards – *baghs* – in Damavand, a green valley tucked away in the folds of the Alborz mountains to the north of the city. The valley was a patchwork of fields and meadows, orchards and woods, woven with streams and springs, surrounded by row upon row of mountains. It had a small village, which consisted of a cluster of flat-roofed dwellings, and a high-street lined with small shops – a butcher's, a baker's, a haberdasher's. The crystalline river of melted snow from the mountains that watered the whole valley flowed through it; a bridge, constructed with tree trunks and branches and mud, led to the *hammam* and the houses on the other bank, and the fields on the higher slopes. In this hidden corner of paradise every summer we took refuge from the torrid heat of the city and enjoyed two idyllic months of games and adventures with family and friends. Bohlul was a well-known figure in the area, and had owned a house in the village and a summer cottage amid his fields and orchards.

Bohlul managed his mother's properties when she grew old and retired, and he became rich in his own right. He married and produced seven children, six sons and a daughter, and set up a grand establishment – a large, elegant old house where he gave receptions and hosted a monthly *Hosseynieh* – a religious ceremony commemorating the martyrdom of Imam Hossein, the grandson of the Prophet and Third Imam of the Duodecimal Shiites. At the end of the ceremony a substantial meal was served to the participants and the poor of the district. His mother lived with him – custom prescribed that a widow live with her eldest son – and eventually died of old age.

Bohlul ran his business successfully and smoothly, and in summer he took his family to Damavand to see to the harvest. Having had no formal education himself, he wanted the best for his children, for without it they would get nowhere in the new, modern world. He sent them to the most reputable schools in town and then to university, either in Teheran or abroad – Paris, Berlin, London. They returned with qualifications that ensured them careers in the professions and the Civil Service, and in due course several of them became prominent as ministers and high-ranking officials.

Despite his large and happy family, and his material ease, Bohlul himself was not happy – the life of a property man was not for him: at heart he was a dervish – a sufi – and he hankered after a simple existence of prayer and meditation, free from material shackles. So fervently did he desire to be a true sufi, a *faqir* (poor-in-spirit), that when Reza Shah decreed that all citizens must have a surname (in the past people were known by their first names followed by that of their village, or father, or profession) he chose *Haq-Parast*, Truth-Worshipper, for what was a sufi except a seeker and worshipper of Truth?

One day he sat with his wife and told her that he was giving up the world to follow his real vocation – to be a dervish, and devote his life to the service of God, relieved of the world and its irksome preoccupations. No amount of argument or pleading prevailed.

> In this marketplace we call the World
> If there be any profit, it belongs to the contented Dervish
> Oh! Lord! Make me rich
> with Dervish-ness and contentment.

He quoted Hafiz. That is how the poet had lived, in poverty and acceptance, and Bohlul could wish for no more. He was born a sufi and would die one.

He gave his houses to the families who were living in them, lifting from them the burden of rent, which some could ill afford and which he found distasteful to demand, and his land to the farm labourers who tended it for him. Only one of his larger *baghs* did he keep in order to give to the public, *ad gloriam dei*, so that every one could enjoy the shade and the fruit of the trees, especially the children of the poor, provided they ate the fruit on the spot and did not take it away to hoard or sell. It was like a small park with no doors or walls, full of lush fruit trees, as in a fairy tale. I remember my teenage brothers and cousins once ventured into it, and came back to tell of the gorgeous fruit – apricots and greengages, apples and pears and grapes – and the teeming children enjoying themselves. Having divested himself of all his properties and possessions, Bohlul rented a small, modest house near the Sepahsalar Mosque and crammed his family into it. He then went to the mosque and offered his services as janitor. He had a tiny cell by way of an office, with an *eyvan* (an arched open space) where he would sit of an evening, murmuring his *zhikrs* (invocations), and smoking a *qalyan* (water pipe), perfectly satisfied. He discarded his civilian suit for a dervish's cloak, and took the name

Bohlul – no one knew what his real name had been – he always introduced himself as Bohlul the Truth-Worshipper.

*   *   *

The original Bohlul whose name our janitor had adopted was a legendary figure who lived in the reign of Harun Al-Rashid (*d.* 809). He was a sufi famous for his wit, his disregard for worldly conventions and his readiness to criticise the wrong-doers whoever they were, even the Caliph himself. Legend has it that he was befriended by Harun for having dared to admonish and joke with him, the mightiest man in the world. Another story relates that he was a Shiite disciple of Imam Jafar Sadeq (*d.* 765), the sixth Imam. In time his many avatars fused into a mythical figure, celebrated in Persian literature and mystic poetry as the archetypal Holy Fool, sometimes called *Bohlul-e Majnun* (Bohlul-the-fool) or *Bohlul-e Dana* (Bohlul-the-wise). Over the centuries legends and stories accumulated around his personality and life. His name became part of common vocabulary – they said a man was 'a bohlul', meaning simple-minded, but good-natured, harmless, godly.

Our Bohlul's transformation from a rich man of considerable social standing and wealth to an impecunious dervish was not without trouble. Communism had begun to infiltrate the country, from Persia's traditional enemy in the north, in the 1930s, and its first adherents were among the intelligentsia. They were soon identified, arrested and imprisoned for sedition by Reza Shah, and the doctrine itself was declared illegal. The movement was thus nipped in the bud, only to resurface virulently after World War Two. Since Communism was against property, contrary to human nature and the social order, only a Communist would give away all his land and possessions and voluntarily live in poverty. Bohlul was duly arrested and imprisoned. But after a few months it became evident that he had never heard of Communism, that he was not interested in politics, that he was just a simple, pious mystic, and he was released. That was not the end of it – he was taunted and treated as mad; street urchins threw stones at him and called him a fool, a mad man; others treated him with condescension and laughed behind his back. He bore it all with good humour and joked about it – had not the great mystics of the past been

tormented, even martyred? Who was he to complain of a little harass-
ment? Gradually people came to respect and love him, realising that he
was the genuine article, a speck of gold in a mound of tinsel. But he was
eccentric, and capable of baffling behaviour. Once my elder brother met
him in the street and stopped to greet him. Without any preliminary
response Bohlul launched into the recitation of a quatrain:

> So spoke Bohlul the Fortunate,
> Saying: 'I existed two years before God,
> For when He brought me into being,
> He had not yet acquired his divine essence and attributes.'

And having finished he walked away.

The Sepahsalar was the mosque where the memorial services
of prominent public figures took place. On such occasions Bohlul
organised and supervised the proceedings, and whatever 'tips' he received
he immediately gave away to beggars in the district. As he grew in
renown he became a favourite subject for photographers and painters.
He inspired and modelled for some of the most famous artists in the
country. I remember one large, beautiful painting by a well-known
artist, based on a line in one of Hafiz's Ghazals:

Is it a wonder that in Heaven when Venus sings the verse of Hafiz
Even the Messiah is moved to dance?

In it Bohlul was depicted as the dancing Messiah, suspended in
Heaven in graceful, ecstatic gyration, surrounded by angels. The poem,
by one of Persia's greatest sufi poets, alludes to the Pythagorean idea of
'The Music of the Spheres', to *Sama* (the psalmody and dance of the
dervishes) and to the divinely-inspired passion and eloquence of the
poet. Another artist painted several portraits of Bohlul in his full
dervish's regalia, with the long felt hat, the crook and the oval begging
bowl. One of these is mass-produced and sold as postcard and poster.
Last November in Washington I happened to visit a Persian shop, a
small emporium of goods from Iran, and there among the postcards
was Bohlul's famous portrait by Hossein Katouzian. (Alas I lost it, and

can't find it for love or money). The shop was full of Persian expatriates, and I asked them if they knew whose portrait it was. None did; they all thought he was the fruit of the artist's imagination.

There was only one indulgence in Bohlul's spare life: pilgrimage, especially to the shrine of Imam Reza – the eighth Imam, in Meshed. As he never kept any money, he could not afford the fare. So once or twice a year he would go and visit my brother, then Deputy Prime Minister, at his office. 'Would you like me to go to the Shrine of Imam Reza and pray for you?' he would say. The hint was understood and his trip arranged and paid for.

* * *

Sufism is the esoteric, mystical dimension of Islam. It is 'the Heart of Islam, and the Islam of the Heart'. In Persia to say of someone that he/she is a dervish, a sufi, is the highest praise. 'He is a true Muslim, a dervish', my mother used to say of someone whose kindness and unworldliness she admired, and whose sincerity she trusted. The opposite of the authentic sufi is the *zahed* – the mullah – whose hypocrisy and intolerance Hafiz and other sufi poets have denounced in searing eloquence. The *zahed* knows of the fear of God but not of His beauty and love; he insists on the *sharia* (Islamic law) but ignores God's injunction to mercy and forgiveness; he abstains from wine (the wine of divine intoxication) but lusts after power and wealth; he ignores the heart and pretends to know the mind, and so on:

> The Zahed could not bear the dazzle of the Beloved's Beauty,
> *So he ran away and invoked the fear of God.* (Hafiz)

The quarrel between the sufi and the mulla began early in Islam and continues to this day. Sufis were persecuted by religious authorities, imprisoned and even killed, notably Hallaj, the emblematic sufi martyr who was tried, stoned and hanged in 922 in Baghdad. It seems that since the revolution of 1979 there has been a revival of sufism in Iran, with old and new active fraternities in every town and district, to the disapproval of the authorities. Disenchanted with the *zaheds* in power, people have turned towards sufism, the real Islam. In the West, too, sufism has spread widely, through the translation of the spiritual poetry of Rumi, Hafiz and Sa'di, and the philosophy of Ibn Arabi, Sohravardi, Molla Sadra and other sufi masters. Sufism is now a flourishing field of scholarship in Western academe. Rumi is a best-selling poet in America, despite the doubtfulness of many of his translations. Even Madonna in a recent interview declared that Rumi was her favourite poet (one could say that after seven hundred years our master has finally arrived!). There are sufi fraternities in all the major cities of Europe and America. Inevitably there is the danger of dilution, of mysticism-without-pain, Chardonnay without divine intoxication. Still, Islam's universalism and spirituality, whose finest expression is found in sufism and sufi literature, is particularly appealing in our harsh and doubting age.

Bohlul died two years after the revolution, old and bewildered by the cataclysm that had engulfed the country and dispersed his family.

Nowadays it is fashionable to claim to be a sufi. From academics who have chosen sufism as their subject to politicians and businessmen, writers and artists, everybody declares to be a sufi. Yet in all my life I have only met two people who have seemed to me totally authentic: their words matched their deeds, their personalities and way of life corresponded to the ideals of sufism, which are above all the annihilation of the *nafs*, (the selfish ego), detachment from the world and its material lures, compassion and generosity and love. One of them was Bohlul.

Massoud

JUSTIN MAROZZI

I HAD LONG WANTED to meet him. Ahmed Shah Massoud was an impossibly glamorous man, the bearded *mujahadin* leader who sported his pakol cap at the most rakish angles and gave the Russians a bloody nose in Afghanistan. Now, seven years after their humiliating retreat, he was refusing to submit once again, this time to the Taliban, the iconoclastic Islamist resistance movement.

I was a cub reporter on the Financial Times, en route to a lowly yet exotic stringing position in Manila. My chances of getting an interview with him during a quick holiday in Afghanistan were considered slight. Still more unlikely was the prospect of breaking bread with him for the prestigious 'Lunch with the FT' column. I had a letter of introduction from Lord Cranborne, who did business with him in the 1980s when MI6 and the CIA were doing their best to undermine the Soviet Union's Afghan adventure. That was not a bad start, but how much good would a letter from an English aristocrat prove in the high wastes of the Hindu Kush? It would be a challenge.

Five years later, Massoud was dead, killed by a brilliant and brutally achieved act of terrorism. Two suicide bombers posing as Moroccan documentary makers secured an interview with him, then blew up their video camera. The terrorists had managed to achieve what had eluded the Soviets for a decade. The Lion of the Panjshir had been struck down on 9 September, 2001. It was a masterstroke for al-Qaeda, removing the man who would have been the West's best friend in Afghanistan. Two days later, terrorists struck again more explosively in New York. It spelt the beginning of the end for the Taliban, an

Islamist movement which had done great disservice to the Muslim world.

As for Massoud, he was simply the most charismatic man I have ever met.

*   *   *

As those Russian soldiers who fought him in Afghanistan during the 1980s would tell you, Commander Ahmed Shah Massoud was an extremely difficult man to hunt down – let alone have lunch with.

The winter of 1996 was a testing time for Afghanistan's most celebrated guerrilla leader and ousted defence minister, then leading the fight against the Taliban Islamic militia which took Kabul in September and controlled two-thirds of the country. With the first heavy snowfalls of winter upon him, Massoud was under pressure to retake the capital or reach a settlement.

After four days, a high-speed car chase and fruitless attempts to corner him in blizzards and subzero temperatures, Massoud finally consented to a press conference at his military headquarters in Jebel Seraj, a windswept town high in the Hindu Kush mountains forty miles north of Kabul. Lunch *à deux* still seemed an unlikely prospect.

Jebel Seraj was heavy with Massoud's forces, a squalid Aladdin's cave littered with the paraphernalia of war. Tanks rumbled through the muddy streets, past armoured personnel carriers, rocket launchers and shivering soldiers armed with the ubiquitous Kalashnikovs. Amid this noisy military orchestra, four-wheel-drive Toyotas with tinted windows ferried its conductor Massoud to and fro at breakneck speed.

'The Lion of the Panjshir' was the soubriquet that he earned after his exploits against the Russian invaders in the ruinously beautiful Panjshir Valley. Fearing that lunch with the FT would not be top of his agenda on retiring for the day, I asked him if he was feeling hungry. His interpreter looked long and hard at me, a stony expression suggesting very clearly that this frivolous question was not the sort of thing one asked the great man.

After some cajoling, he sheepishly translated the crude hint and, after conferring with his leader, announced in polished French that if I would like to join the commander for a private dinner I would be most welcome. The other journalists in the room, including a number of well-known foreign correspondents, were seething.

Massoud motioned me courteously into a private dining room – harshly lit and empty save for a small table, a set of chairs and a sink. It was one of the few Kalashnikov-free zones in town. Other than an uninspiring still life, the white walls were bare. There was no carpet on the concrete floor.

The trademark pakol, sported in a way which made so many female reporters swoon over the years, sat atop a handsome face lined with two decades of warfare. At forty-two, Massoud was already beyond the average life expectancy of Afghan men and admitted his best years on the battlefield were behind him. The eyes were deep, dark and in earnest as he looked back with pride to his leading role in harrying the Soviets out of Afghanistan in 1989, ten destructive years after their invasion.

A matching woollen waistcoat worn over an army sweater, khaki fatigues and black boots – he was rumoured to have a penchant for the custom-made Russian paratrooper variety – completed the ensemble of the mountain warrior. There was an unmistakable whiff of power and authority about him, but for a man who had done little else but wage war since 1973, he was remarkably gentle and softly spoken. A quiet dignity underpinned his massive presence.

'I am sorry dinner is going to be very basic,' he said in mellifluous Dari, waving a large hand over the table on which sat two steaming bowls of mutton, potato, onion and tomato stew, served with heaps of nan bread. 'If I had known you were coming, I would have had something special prepared.'

The counter-revolutionary career took off at the age of nineteen, he told me, in the wake of the coup which overthrew King Mohammed Zahir Shah, installed a pro-communist regime and declared Afghanistan a republic. He abandoned an engineering degree at Kabul University, then home to the conflicting movements of Islamic nationalism and Soviet-inspired communism.

Formal education ended there, but Massoud remained a voracious reader. After Kabul's fall to the Taliban, he relocated his home to the

Panjshir, taking with him his three thousand volumes of literature. In the little spare time war afforded him, he said he enjoyed reading the fourteenth-century spiritual Iranian poet Hafiz.

We faced each other across a cheap plastic table cover. Groping around for some culinary anecdotes for the FT column, I asked him what his favourite food was. The interpreter looked startled. Massoud was used to reporting his latest advance on the battlefield and confessed, almost shyly, that he found personal questions the most awkward to answer. The interpreter, seeing his boss was not irritated by the unorthodox line of questioning, suggested milk was Massoud's preferred night-time tipple then, as if sensing the inadequacy of the answer, declared with an air of finality. 'Commander Massoud enjoys whatever he eats.'

Subject closed. Massoud was here to talk Afghanistan and not milk-shakes.

It was something he did with ease and charm and an animation which stemmed from an intense religious faith and a profound love of Afghanistan, notwithstanding the fact that he had done much to destroy the country himself. The Russians left Kabul virtually unscathed. At the time of our interview in late 1996, after more than four years of factional fighting between Massoud and rival *mujahadin*, much of the capital lay in rubble. A decade later, it still does.

I put it to Massoud that Afghanistan was doomed always to fall victim to its deep ethnic fault-lines. The conflict at that time pitted Tajik Massoud – in coalition with the Uzbek warlord General Dostum – against the Pashtun Taliban. He shook his head vigorously and moved both elbows onto the table, citing a host of examples to prove that these divisions were not fixed. Uzbeks fought Tajiks, Pashtuns embraced Tajiks, and so on.

That ethnic mix was only one part of the problem. Afghanistan's wars had always been the creation of foreign powers, with Pakistan the master villain. 'It has been very difficult getting rid of Russia then dealing with Pakistan,' he said, stroking his beard sadly. 'Pakistan created the Taliban.'

Returning to his own background, his mood lightened and the face creased into a smile as he informed me that at twenty-five he could look back on two coups d'état and a failed provincial rebellion.

'I had a Sten gun and twenty men with me in the Panjshir. We robbed a bank and told everyone there had been a coup in Kabul. But there was nothing in the newspapers or on the radio to confirm it and people soon discovered nothing had happened.' He was now a wanted man, but the entire episode was recounted as though it were merely a boyish prank, the sort of thing Just William might have got up to on a lazy half-holiday.

My mutton was getting cold. I tackled it dutifully, expecting the worst, but was pleasantly surprised by a tender and spicy concoction. The robust potatoes were a tasty relief after the monotony of bread and kebabs and we both tucked into second helpings. After earlier long and desperately unhappy experiences in the lavatory, I avoided the glass of water which sat temptingly at my elbow. The unfortunate interpreter, who looked ravenous, was unable to grab even a mouthful, forever struggling to keep up with Massoud who was hugely, constantly engaging but never concise.

Mutton removed, we turned our attention to a plate of grapes which had seen better days. Discussing his immediate military plans, he stopped chewing and disputed the idea that he and his forces were on the back foot against the advancing Taliban. He borrowed my pen, made a hasty sketch of Afghanistan and the positions of the opposing sides, and detailed an extension of the front line into the Taliban's weakest spots. I felt it was best not to argue.

A pot of tea arrived with a bowl of toffees, walnuts and almonds. As dinner drew to a close, I asked him whether there were any plans to retire from the battlefield and perhaps write his memoirs. He laughed at first but then the gravitas of the man of war returned. 'I have never fought for happiness, nor have I fought for power. I don't want to keep on fighting one more day but while I am still alive I will do everything to defend my country.'

He made another graceful apology for our simple repast, slipped quietly out of the room and disappeared, swallowed up by the entourage of waiting generals. I never saw him again.

*   *   *

I have returned to Afghanistan several times over the years. Since his assassination in 2001, I had wanted to make the pilgrimage to pay my respects at his tomb high in the Panjshir.

In 2004, I finally made the journey into the famous valley, scene of so many of Massoud's triumphs and reversals. The wreckage of war is still only too obvious, with the rusting carcases of tanks and old field guns strewn across the countryside. Such is the state of roads in Afghanistan that a journey of little more than sixty miles from Kabul takes more than five hours.

Massoud's tomb lies in a round white building with a green dome perched on a bluff far above the foaming Panjshir River. Its position is about as wild, windswept and romantic as one could wish for, the perfect resting place for such a man.

In death, Massoud's charisma has only increased. Afghans still mourn his passing and his portraits are ubiquitous. He appears alongside posters of Ahmed Karzai to give the new president more credibility. Taxi drivers and truck drivers stick pictures of him on their windscreens. Posters of him adorn shops, restaurants, private homes and government offices. Those who met him remember him keenly. On the internet websites rhapsodise about him. 'He was Afghanistan' is the title of one. 'There was something as timeless and ageless as Afghanistan itself at the very core of him,' it goes on. 'He embodied all Afghanistan's tribulations and sufferings, all her fierce pride and independence, all her faith and hope, all her courage and endurance.' Sometimes the eulogies go too far.

Recently I looked at one website dedicated to his memory. It quoted 'Gone to the Unseen', a poem from Rumi, the thirteenth-century mystic widely regarded as the greatest sufi poet:

> At last you have departed and gone to the Unseen.
> What marvellous route did you take from this world?
> Beating your wings and feathers,
> You broke free from this cage.
>
> Rising up to the sky
> You attained the world of the soul.

You were a prized falcon trapped by an Old Woman.
Then you heard the drummer's call
And flew beyond space and time.

As a lovesick nightingale, you flew among the owls.
Then came the scent of the rose garden
And you flew off to meet the Rose.
The wine of this fleeting world
Caused your head to ache.

Finally you joined the tavern of Eternity.
Like an arrow, you sped from the bow
And went straight for the bull's eye of bliss.
This phantom world gave you false signs
But you turned from the illusion
And journeyed to the land of truth.

You are now the Sun –
What need have you for a crown?
You have vanished from this world –
What need have you to tie your robe?
I've heard that you can barely see your soul.

But why look at all? –
Yours is now the Soul of Souls!
O heart, what a wonderful bird you are.
Seeking divine heights,
Flapping your wings,
You smashed the pointed spears of your enemy.

The flowers flee from Autumn, but not you –
You are the fearless rose
That grows amidst the freezing wind.
Pouring down like the rain of heaven
You fell upon the rooftop of this world.

Then you ran in every direction
And escaped through the drain spout . . .
Now the words are over
And the pain they bring is gone.

Now you have gone to rest
In the arms of the Beloved.

I travelled to the tomb with Arif, the translator with whom I first met Massoud eight years earlier and who has since become a great friend. The temperature fell sharply. Green flags beat furiously in the bone-chilling wind. We stood silently together for a few minutes, shivering uncontrollably, signed the visitor's book and bid goodbye to the Lion of the Panjshir.

Fazlar Khan: On Top of the World

JOHN CARSWELL

I ARRIVED in Chicago in the late '80s, surprisingly translated from Lebanon, where I had spent over twenty years teaching at the American University of Beirut. This was brought to an abrupt end by the outbreak of civil war on a serious scale, and I swapped the Middle East for the Middle West. I also left the academic world for the practicalities of running a major museum in the United States. To be precise, the Oriental Institute of the University of Chicago, to which I had just been appointed as its Curator. My only qualification was a more than passing acquaintance with archaeology, for at a youthful stage in my life I had been an archaeological draughtsman on Kathleen Kenyon's excavations at Jericho, and had learned quite a lot about the discipline by osmosis. So I was not altogether unfamiliar with the pottery and artifacts of the Near East, although I was a little daunted to find I was responsible for a whole gallery of Egyptian mummies, hermetically sealed in glass cases like some macabre undertaker's nightmare (or perhaps, joy . . .)

The Oriental Institute was the brainchild of a famous Egyptologist, James Henry Breasted, who had the good fortune to meet John D. Rockefeller, who became his friend and patron and who financed the new museum in 1931. Breasted, something of a polymath, died in 1936, and the Institute fell into the hands of more narrowly focussed specialists of ancient languages, who hung out on the second floor. All sorts of interminable linguistic projects were underway, the Assyrian, Hittite and Demotic Dictionaries in the foreground. The museum and its artifacts, mostly acquired by Breasted in the days when it was possible to do so easily, by excavation or cash, was of peripheral interest to the scholars, who were only seriously interested in objects if they bore a useful cuneiform or other squiggly text. Years of neglect meant that the public areas of the museum were shabby, only attractive to under-graduates as a seriously private area in which they could tryst.

What to do? Well the first thing was to clean the place up a bit, and I embarked on a programme of stone-cleaning and brass-polishing: the building itself was a not unattractive amalgam of Art Deco and Orientalist motifs and very much a period piece. What it lacked, I quickly realised, was any extra space in the rigidly formal galleries for any form of temporary exhibition or display. What it also lacked was any space whatsoever for a Museum shop, a necessary tool if one was ever going to attract a general public apart from the amorous undergrads.

I pondered on this, and initially cleaned up the entrance hall, removed the security guard and his feet permanently on display on a desk opposite his chair, and put on a couple of minor exhibitions in the newly cleared space. These were such a novelty that they were reasonably successful outside the purlieus of the University of Chicago, and I grew bolder. I completely cleaned out one of the four main galleries, and re-displayed the artifacts in half of the gallery and kept the rest of the space empty for more ambitious exhibitions.

The first of these was intended to be both educational and lucrative. Entitled 'In a Syrian Suq', it was based on a collection of items I myself bought for no great sum in Aleppo – silk scarves, beads, spices, wooden spoons, etc – all marked up several thousand percent of what I had paid for them, and still pretty cheap by Chicago standards. To market them, I decided to build a replica of a Syrian suq in the gallery, and fill all the little shops with my purchases. I also had a series of Syrian children's cut-out toys, the paper plates which were also for sale in the suq – a kind of Islamic 'penny plain, two pence coloured' edition. I did have a problem constructing the suq, for my preparator was a very con-servative young man, to whom any angle which was not a right-angle was anathema. It was extremely difficult to persuade him that the suqs of Araby do not conform to the rigid rules of a shopping mall.

Anyhow, it finally opened for business and the general public was intrigued. That weekend – a Saturday as I recall – I was at home enjoying my lunch when the telephone rang and the young lady delegated to manage the suq said she was sick. What to do? The only answer was to return to the Oriental Institute and manage it myself. By three o'clock, business was slack (ie. none at all) and I was getting distinctly bored with my enterprise. In, at last, came a couple of potential customers.

I had some Syrian dresses for sale, and the wife was very intrigued but couldn't decide which one. I said to the husband she could nip behind my Suq and discreetly try them on. Whilst she did so, I fell into conversation with the husband who wanted to know where I was from (the Brit accent) and what I was doing, and how on earth had I hit on the idea of the suq? And as the new curator, what were my problems? I told him about my fervent desire to have a real museum shop, and he asked what the available space was. I said there was a cloakroom off the entrance hall, and we went off to look at it together.

His wife returned, and said she still couldn't make up her mind about two of the dresses. He laughed, and gallantly wrote out a cheque for both of them. I was flabbergasted, as it was well over $200 and up till then I had only taken in about five bucks, including sales tax. We parted on the best of terms, and on the way out he gave me his card and said to ring him the following week as he might be able to help me with the shop. And that was that, and I promptly forgot all about the encounter.

The following Thursday I received a phone call, and a young lady said she was Mr Khan's personal secretary and he was wondering why I hadn't been in touch? I then read his card and realised it was Fazlur Khan, senior partner of Skidmore, Owings and Merrill, based in Chicago, and one of the world's greatest structural engineers and designers. He had, apparently, meant business about the shop. We met again in his office, me somewhat contrite and he quite enjoying the knowledge that I hadn't a clue before who he was. He appointed one of his top designers to deal with the shop problem (which, alas, I didn't have the funds to build). More important, we became very good friends.

He had by this time designed the Sears Tower (then the tallest building in the world), and the Hancock building, both radically different from anything else in Chicago and utilising novel forms of construction. When we got to know him better, I asked him what it was like to be the author of the tallest building in the world, and was this the apex of his life? No, he said, that was much earlier when he was twelve, got his first bicycle, and was riding round the back streets of Calcutta. Everything is relative. He also told me (and this is a typically Chicago story) that when he was introduced in social situations as the designer of the tallest building in the world, he would inevitably be asked: 'Yea, but how do you pull it down?' A concept which he had never envisaged, but then in Chicago nothing is for ever, and always has a finite shelf life.

He did tell me that he had thought of other destructive elements connected with the building. For instance, he had calculated that if you flushed the toilet on the top floor of the Sears Tower, by the time the water reached the ground it would drill a hole in two feet of concrete. This he solved by installing intermediary tanks every twenty floors.

Because he was a Muslim, it was inevitable that he would win his firm contracts in the Arab world. The first was the *hajj* terminal at Jiddah, for pilgrims on their way to Mecca. This was an extraordinary series of floating tents. It was so successful and universally admired, that he then gained the contract for a new university at Mecca.

The plan included men's and women's sections, both of which had to be linked to the central library, but where never the twain should meet. His young assistants in Chicago couldn't understand why everything shouldn't be at right angles, and in desperation he put the final plans in a computer and programmed it for random chance. Out came an organic, hic-hoc series of structures, and this was what was built.

Another problem was the mosque. As a good Muslim, he had to admit that he had never been in a contemporary mosque anywhere in the world which was invested with the same spiritual feeling as earlier medieval mosques. He asked me one day if I knew any good mosques which they could simply copy? I said how about the Firdaus Mosque in Aleppo, and after he had seen some photographs, this is exactly what was built: a twentieth-century replica of the original.

Fazlur Khan didn't smoke or drink, played tennis regularly and was happily married to an Austrian wife and had a charming daughter. It was therefore all the more devastating to learn that he had suddenly died of a heart attack in Saudi Arabia, working on the Mecca project. He was only fifty years old.

His wife quite naturally wanted him to be buried in Chicago, and then began a tussle to get Faz back. For all Muslims, it is thought blessed to die where he did. He did eventually make it back to Chicago and was given a splendid Muslim burial in Chicago's most prestigious cemetery, properly facing in the direction of Mecca. There was a terrific party afterwards organised by his colleagues, at which everyone agreed that Skidmore, Owings and Merrill would never be the same again. It was not just that he was a structural engineer of genius, but that he was also an extraordinarily nice and intelligent person, and a great humanist.

For me, I can never look at the Chicago skyline without thinking about him, and wondering why so many years later the two most striking buildings are his, and how in spite of the enormous competition, he still comes out on top.

Poetry is More Powerful than Death

LAURENCE DEONNA

ANCIENT CITIES with their crooked lines deflecting the path of the sun, corbelled façades and bulging, lopsided walls in which everything is asymmetrical, remind us poor human beings of our own condition. Is that why we feel so comfortable in them? We also have our locked doors, our inner courtyards and our hidden staircases, and our souls are in disarray. The spirit in modern cities is obsessed with symmetry and the orderly architecture faithfully reflects a philosophy where everything is logical and as simple as a straight line! A world in which everything can be proved, demonstrated and explained, but which is as cold as a sheet of ice and as indiscreet as a pane of glass.

Sanaa, Yemen's capital, is among the oldest Arabian cities and looks from afar like a Manhattan risen from sands, but a Manhattan which reveals nothing of the lives lived behind the vertiginous stucco walls decorated with white designs. The tower-houses of Sanaa stay forever silent, guarding their secrets.

At night, the narrow streets are swallowed by darkness; the colourful stained-glass windows glint, bedded in the walls of high houses touching shoulder to shoulder. Walking here at night is akin to being an ant wandering inside Aladdin's magic lamp. Scents in the spice-market filter through closed wooden shutters. A flutter of wings brushes against me; it is the veil of a woman hurrying home with a last jug of water. Lifting the head to the sky is like the beginning of a fairytale; the silhouettes of flat roof terraces are white as lace against the starry arch. Lowering the head is imagining yourself caught in a trap, robbed, raped, never again to be seen or heard of. Yet reality is very different. With a kerosene lamp in his hand, one of the few passers-by offers to guide me through the maze of alleys.

*   *   *

The deeds of Imam Ahmed, the last ruler of Yemen, are not recorded in Sanaa but in one of the late monarch's palaces in Taiz, the former capital. In 1962 the tyrant died in this beautiful place, its walls flanked by multicoloured Yemeni style *mousharabiehs*. The new Republic has since transformed the palace into a museum. Ending a life of pomp and power, Ahmed endured a long agony after revolutionary bullets punched eight holes into his body. Here, unravelling before the visitors' gaze, are the relics of a despot who claimed to have been bestowed with God's will and possessing divine powers. The chains which paralysed the prisoners are massive! The pictures in which large sabres, caked with blood, slash, are horrendous! One panel reads: 'Dear visitor, these photos show the heads of martyrs falling like those of lambs'.

The flea-market-like displays in the museum could be entitled: 'Panoramic view of the good life of a king whose people lived in misery'. Not only imposing relics like the enormous fringed parasol that a slave once carried to shade His Sacred Majesty are displayed. All of Ahmed's belongings, down to his socks, eyeglasses and dentures, are here. There isn't a detail, not a single object, missing. Nothing has been omitted. Neither his collection of watches, clocks or jewellery, nor – it's important to note – the luxury of a hairdryer, washing machine or electric stove, for until the Revolution, only a few privileged families in Taiz and Sanaa were equipped with electricity. The 'toy department' display consists of gifts the king gave to his 'darling boys'; tops, a tricycle, a rocking horse and a life-size plush lion. 'At night Ahmed brought it out to scare people', a guard remembers.

The Imam cared little for the well being of his people, but he cared much for himself. He anointed himself with salves and creams, swallowed pills, vitamins and fortifiers by the handfuls. On display in the museum are his multicoloured perfumes lined up in huge bottles of all shapes. They were custom made for the king by Givaudan, in Geneva, Switzerland. He also kept essences to mature in cow horns for months, the old-fashioned way.

His beard reddened by *henna* and his eyes always made up with kohl, this Oriental Narcissus enjoyed admiring himself in the many mirrors decorating his palace. Other looking glasses were placed in the dead angles of narrow spiralling stairs to expose possible assassins. His intense gaze earned him the nickname 'Ahmed the Djinn' or 'Ahmed the Demon'. One legend which he spread himself had it that he was protected by spirits and that bullets would bounce off his body without injuring him. True or false, legends are born from rumours and extraordinary stories! Another tale claimed that the ruler had the front of his dress painted with fluorescent glow. Seizing the opportunity of a moonless night to appear at one of the palace windows, he faced his bewildered subjects. They were terrified, having been told that the glow stemming from their Imam was proof of his divinity.

In order to maintain an Islam without a blemish, Ahmed forbade his subjects to sing or dance in public. And woe to he who cocked an ear to music, or worse even, foreign ideas! With the exception of the ruler, foreign radio waves were to stop at the foot of Yemen's mountains. People were totally isolated and the Imam was the only link to the outside world. Non-religious books had to be smuggled into the country. 'A revolution in thoughts ends with a revolution in blood', the tyrant said. He was the sole authority. The King decided everything, for everyone, weighed the minutest detail and opened all palace mail himself. His judgement could not be appealed. He possessed vinyl records, a gramophone, and even a tape recorder which he hid under a cushion of his sofa during visits; he then encouraged visitors to talk, challenging them, encouraging them to open up and later threatened them, hand on sword: 'Listen, the *djinns* (demons) have spoken through your mouth . . . '

*   *   *

The stairs of the Taiz palace, as all stairs in the tower-houses of Yemen, are exhausting labyrinths. That is why the wide and airy flight of stairs leading to my third floor apartment situated in a beautiful nineteenth-century building, though without elevator, taxes neither the heart nor the legs of my Yemenite friends when they come to visit me in Geneva.

Visitor to our city, Ahmed Noman was over eighty years old when he climbed the stairs to my flat one winter afternoon. His grandson, Abdullah Noman, a businessman living in Geneva, had insisted on introducing him to me. Abdullah had reasons to be proud of his grandfather. He was much more than a grandfather, much more than a descendant of an illustrious family belonging to this part of Arabia, which was also the land of the Queen of Sheba. Ahmed Noman was Yemen's memory, its modern history; he incarnated the Republicans' fight over the Royalists.

This exquisite old man came dressed in turban with a matching shawl thrown over his shoulder. Reclining on the scattered pillows of my sofa, he sat facing the chimney. His subtle features were those of an icon and were underlined by the black-blue kohl around his eyes.

He squinted, the colour of his eyes faded by the brunt of a very long life; then, resting his small, mottled, almost feminine hands on his little skirt, the *footah* which he was wearing Yemeni style, he smiled at me. What a smile! Not a condescending smile, but a smile both wild and wise. And gay! The winter greyness was suddenly gone. I was once more tasting and feeling the colours of Yemen, including the colour of blood. Though the legendary Ahmed Noman was telling his life-story in a soft voice, he spared no details. For his position as prime minister of the young Yemeni republic, he had paid for dearly. He and his family had endured the cruelty of their king to the very dregs, his wild, twirling sabres beheading his brothers.

As for him, Allah only knows why the Imam of divine lineage let him keep his head, though he spared him not from hell. Ahmed Noman spent five long years withering chained in a vile prison-cell in a medieval dungeon.

Yet, this tyrant who had caused him and his family great suffering, who had decimated his family and tortured him, the old man spoke of without apparent bitterness; I could even say that he spoke of him almost peacefully. This surprised me and I told him so. His answer was most amazing: 'How could I resent him?' he said, 'Did you not know? The king was a great poet'.

Translated from the French by Iris Fillinger.

Abdul Haq

JULIET PECK

IT WAS HIS HUMOUR that was distinctive. He had a rare ability, in a time of great national hardship and suffering, to laugh at himself, at the nature of his fellow Afghans, the ambitions of America, the futility of the UN and at the frustrations of the bloody, bitter war.

Abdul Haq had a clear understanding of the West and shrewdly sized up those who came to him, whether they were offering to help or asking his assistance. He was a man who was able to cross both worlds, welcoming but distant when entertaining in his own, and confidently at ease outside. He was fully aware of his value to different politicians, Mrs Thatcher, Ronald Reagan, Charlie Wilson but he also recognised their value to him. They in turn were relieved to be able to meet with a commander of some stature, who spoke good English, who was something of a war hero, and who laughed.

We met first at the end of 1985. I was charged with collecting together Afghan war-wounded to be treated in London. It was little more than a public relations effort by the then government but I was young and keen. Introduced by a friend, Abdul asked if I would take a *mujahadin* loyal to him who had been blown up by a mine. This man had lost two hands and most of his sight. He was being treated at the Red Cross Hospital in Peshawar. The hospital refused to release him for some spurious reason, so Abdul had him smuggled out the night before the patients flew. The man was little more than a foot soldier, but he had been true and loyal and Abdul was determined that he should have his chance. In London this man was given two prosthetic arms; Abdul was content and we became friends. The Red Cross was furious.

As the end of the eighties approached and more funding came from the various sources, Abdul's establishment became larger and grander, moving into one of the hideous and uncomfortable but large houses that the Pakistanis insisted on building. The basic, dirty rooms on the outside, inhabited by his *mujahadin* gave way to large, clean inner spaces, furnished with rich red carpets and cushions, in the comfortable style of a wealthy man. There Abdul would welcome those who came, the journalists, the do-gooders, the time-wasters, the politicians, the schemers, the hangers-on and the friends. He was supported in this by the very best cook in Peshawar. It was not by chance that Abdul was a large small man. It was impossible to resist the rich food that was placed in front of one, dripping with oil and yoghurt, and delicately prepared by the man who I tried so hard to persuade to come and work for me.

One of the more bizarre events that I remember at Abdul's home was the wedding of CBS cameraman Kurt Lobeck and his American hairdresser fiancée Deborah. Kurt was a man who had followed Abdul for a number of years. He had filmed various actions by his *mujahadin* and had promoted him as a major *mujahadin* commander. In this Kurt was guilty of subjectivity, but it was mutually beneficial. Deborah in her way was a remarkable woman from small-town America. Impressed by the romanticism of the Afghans' struggle against the Soviet-supported communist regime, she had raised money for them through hairdressing and finally followed her interest to Peshawar. There she met Kurt. Finally, the pair were married and held their wedding ceremony in Abdul's compound, both dressed in borrowed Afghan finery. True to form the women were segregated from the men, always very dull. We made polite conversation on the roof terrace as the men, we presumed, had far more fun below. Deborah wore a veil. This romantic interlude was not to last. Deborah left, not long afterwards, with Barbraq, a minor commander and one of Abdul's bodyguards. She was last heard of still living with him in a mud house near Puli-Charki gaol.

Abdul gave me invaluable personal assistance. When my husband was shot in unusual circumstances, and the Pakistani police wanted to prosecute a man I did not believe was guilty, Abdul arranged for a senior member of his tribe to conduct a *jirga* on my behalf and resolution was found after the Pashtun way. Honour was satisfied on all sides.

But these personal stories should not detract from the serious nature of Abdul's commitment to his cause and his contribution to his country. Abdul was a remarkable man, not just for being a commander who spoke English and who had a good cook, but because in a country and culture which encourages and expects people to stand in groups, he was a figure who stood on his own and attempted to present an alternative.

He was young when the war began in Afghanistan. Although his family lands were in Surk Rud, Nangarhar, he had been bought up partly in the Helmand where his father worked for the Helmand Valley Project. As a student affiliated with the Islamic Youth, he opposed President Daud and was imprisoned from 1975–8 when he was freed after the Saur Revolution. All his family were involved in the resistance before the Soviet invasion, but whilst his brothers Haji Din Mohammed and Haji Qadir were based firmly in Nangarhar and allied with Yunis Khales, Abdul set up his operations in the Province of Paghman to the west of Kabul, and from here he attempted guerrilla operations. His most spectacular success in this sphere was blowing up the government's arms store, dug deep into the hillside on the edge of the city.

The Resistance was as much about politics as about fighting, and Peshawar in particular was a cauldron of plans and counter-plots. Abdul again stood apart from what could have been seen as his natural constituency. Loosely allied to Yunis Khales, whose power base was Nangarhar, Abdul resented the interference and controlling aspirations of the Pakistani ISI. To his credit he refused to have anything to do with the largely US-supported Government-in-Exile, funded from 1992–6 and widely denigrated as corrupt, inefficient and ineffectual. He was an early if tenuous collaborator with Ahmed Shah Massoud in the latter's Shura-I Nizar, an alliance of predominantly Tajik and Uzbek commanders. In the eyes of many of his fellow Pashtuns, to ally himself with Massoud was a worse crime than to cohabit with the Pashtun

Kabul government. This was an attitude visibly taken by the extremist Gulbudeen Hekmatyar, who attempted a coup in collaboration with Lieutenant General Tanai, Najibullah's Minister of Defence, in March 1990. It failed. Later Abdul was critical of Massoud, having witnessed his debacle in Kabul in the years after 1992, when the great commander controlled the city but failed to bring Pashtuns into the government. In later years Abdul urged the Americans not to rely on supporting only the Shura-I Nizar in their fight against the Taliban.

In the mid 1990s, dispirited by the failure of the Resistance in Kabul, Abdul moved to Dubai where he conducted some form of business, but he always had his finger on the pulse and was an ardent critic of the Taliban, as well as of the American's initial connivance with that regime. It was during this time he suffered a great personal tragedy when his wife and son were murdered in Peshawar, reportedly by Arabs incensed by his criticism of them in the media. He was alarmed when, after the bombing of the Twin Towers in New York, the Americans decided to root out the Taliban. A realist and intuitive negotiator, Abdul argued that a full-frontal military attack on the regime was not the way to victory. He argued that the leadership, which was extreme and increasingly isolated from society, would never be turned by bombs or negotiations. He urged that negotiations with the second-level leadership, the tribal elders and the former *mujahadin* would be more effective, turning away their support and leading the regime to collapse. But he was not listened to.

It is not certain why Abdul was travelling in Afghanistan when he was captured by the Taliban, but it appears that he was negotiating with different Pashtun leaders to secure alliances against the theocratic regime. He may have been working in competition with Hamid Karzai and by extension the American government. The sad truth is that he was taken, beaten and killed. When he most needed help, no one was there. But that is what Abdul would have expected. American policy was as much a part of his death as it was his life.

Afghanistan is a country with its own rules, rules that are founded on its particular history, religion, culture and war, even love. Abdul was a part of that country, but not that country alone. At a time when Afghanistan was playing its part on the world stage he was a player who straddled the drawing rooms in the White House and encampments in the mountains, at home in each, shrewdly finessing what he could to aid his country. Straight-talking and direct, Abdul eschewed the flattery sometimes meted out by men of lesser stature. Ridiculing the politicians, teasing his friends and laughing at himself, he brought the very best of Afghan tolerance and humour to an often intolerable situation.

Sheikh Abdu Rahim Al-Bura'i, the Sufi

BRUCE WANNELL

I ARRIVED AT ZARIBA as the moon was rising. In a large courtyard Sheikh Abdu Rahim Al-Bura'i's lanky teenage son, Jayli, presided on a mat in the sand. There was no electricity, so I enjoyed the rare luxury of natural darkness and moonlight. Jayli told me that he had twenty-two brothers and fifteen sisters, as the seventy-two-year-old sheikh had married nine wives in the fifty years he had been running the *masid*. The nine wives, even when marriage ties were dissolved (there were never more than the allowable four wives concurrently) were left with their own houses around the *masid*, and they and their children were fed and clothed out of common funds.

When Jayli's grandfather established the mosque and school at Zariba, the area had been a notorious badland of robber-nomads: this sufi centre had spear-headed a more settled and lawful life among local tribesmen. Initially, it was not easy to gain their confidence, but the first sheikh visited their families and invited all to meals of honey and roast meats, till they began to treat the *masid* as their own centre and spontaneously came to the sheikh to resolve their disputes and difficulties. A market had grown up outside the walls, allowing not only students but also locals to dabble in commerce, so that the spread of Islam was accompanied by the growth of trade. Religion brought with love had been a major factor in the evolution of society.

After the night prayer, a rumbling sound started up and continued all night – it was the oil mill, which pressed oil from cottonseed and sesame and ground-nuts for sale in Omdurman and El Obeid – the *masid* was now underpinned by agro-industry as well as by commerce.

A sudden whooping of joy from the students and a stampede towards the inner courtyard heralded the arrival of Sheikh Abdu Rahim al-Bura'i. I finished my bowl of sweetened yoghurt with Jayli and walked slowly to see the arrival – I found the old sheikh stretched on a string-bed with three students massaging his limbs.

'Such an effort,' I thought uncharitably, 'to step from the plane into his air-conditioned Pajero which stands gleaming there beside him in the moonlight!' But then I remembered all the massages I had enjoyed, a civilized pleasure I had never disdained. No doubt massage of his aching muscles was welcome to the septuagenarian, as the bumpy ride along desert tracks must be tiring, even in a Pajero.

Here was, I feared, a phenomenon comparable to other cult-gurus. The posters and photographs of the sheikh that were sold, along with his volumes of poetry, in the market outside, indicated a cult of personality that seemed far from ascetic. But this personality cult is modest compared with the monstrous self-promotion of American television evangelists. It was only after several meetings with the sheikh and close observation of the crowd of visitors that my mind and my heart began to accept a different concept of sanctity, one based not on repression and denial, but on endless and boundless generosity.

The old man certainly had a remarkable reproductive success (enviable even to monarchs and alpha-male apes), with his thirty-eight children – and all of them educated, at least in the Islamic sciences. His students and devotees were spread all over the country. I was accosted later in the streets of Khartoum by a worker recently expelled from Libya who had seen me at the *masid*, so I gave him lunch at an Iranian restaurant. In Port Sudan, months later as I was leaving the country, a petty trader who had heard my speech at the Zariba *masid* after Friday prayers gave me a long article published in the papers about the sheikh shortly after I'd left – the journalist had quizzed me about my education and my purpose in coming there. The sheikh's poetry in praise of the Prophet was known and sung not only in Sudan, but in Egypt and even in Syria – a year later, I met a *munshid* religious singer in Aleppo who regularly sang the sheikh 's religious poetry, and that of his fourteenth-century ancestor and namesake from the Jabal Bura' in Yemen.

The sheikh had also taken over one of the traditions of African kingship, that of mass marriages. At the last occasion in June, some two and a half thousand people were married in the *masid*: divorcees, the poor and unemployed, all those who could not afford the expense of marriage or were debarred from the lengthy and complex negotiations to secure a partner would come here to find a mate and be married and blessed, and even receive a little money from the sheikh to set up their new *ménage*.

I began to think differently of the oil-mill chuntering and grinding through the night: it was a good investment of pilgrims' donations to allow the *masid* not only some financial security, but also a continuous redistribution of wealth. The lorries carrying the oil daily to sell in Khartoum kept open the *masid*'s contact with the outside world, as well as offering free transport to pilgrims on the way. The profits went back into the school and guest accommodation, as well as financing a string of new mosques in most towns of the Sudan, giving focus and employment to the sheikh's progeny and devotees.

The multiplicity of the social functions of the *masid* seemed inexhaustible.

One of the visitors was a Saudi who had just flown in from Riyadh to be cured after being touched by Satan – *lams-u-Shaytan* – the Satanic stroke commonly supposed to be the cause of impotence.

Another was Zubayda, an upper-class woman from Khartoum, who had lived for seventeen years in Saudi Arabia and Abu Dhabi keeping house for her husband, bringing up her children and working in an office. On a visit to her aged father in Khartoum, she had received a phone call from her husband announcing that he had divorced her, was keeping the children and had installed his new wife in the house! Thanks to his connections with the current government, he blocked her appeals for justice and had even had himself appointed head of an Islamic Relief Charity! Her ex-husband was now in his late forties, the restless age, sick, on his own. Zubayda almost felt sorry for him. She was back at college to get a Masters diploma in nutrition so that she could eventually work and help her children. Meanwhile, she had come to ask for the Sheihk's prayers for a solution to her problems. I asked if she did not think it was time to organize an Islamic Women's Movement to protect the rights of women in Sudan, as professional women had started successfully in Pakistan. She looked at me uncomprehendingly.

Next to veiled Zubayda was a local Arab tribeswoman, dishevelled and completely naked above the waist, suckling an infant on her pendulous breasts, come to beg a charm for the health of her child. Other peasants pushed and shoved to present their petitions.

The sheikh was imperturbably kind and attentive to each one, reading the scraps of paper, answering the questions, offering a prayer, blowing on a sick child, patting a bowed head, occasionally making a joke, receiving the shower of bank notes and putting them away in his capacious pockets, always with patience and good humour; and when he'd had enough, he arose majestically and walked off in a slow procession.

Jadidi Mahmud at-Taba'i was the visitor I spent most of my time with. He was Tunisian and spoke French – it turned out that, like me, he was born at the end of August 1952, and like mine his mother was from Brussels. Beatrice van der Kerkhoove had married a cardiologist, and my mother's sister had also married a cardiologist. His father, a Tunisian *sharif*, eventually returned to his estates near Tunis and started his own, private and very profitable hospital in the capital. Jadidi had, according to his own account, the only one I had to go on, spent an extremely luxurious, dissolute adolescence and early manhood in Tunis. Aged forty, he dreamed a dream, the same dream every night for a month – Sheikh Abdu Rahim al-Bura'i would appear, summoning him to Zariba. Jadidi consulted a Sudanese neighbour, obtained his father's blessing, packed his bags and set off by lorry through Libya, Chad and Darfur. He arrived at Zariba after two months' exhausting journey. He was now living in a small room with two large porous clay water jars which cooled the dripping water. He was learning the Qur'an by heart, the basic step in any traditional Islamic education, and progressing on the spiritual path. After two years, he had been made a sheikh of the Sammaniya *tariqa*, I hoped with better justification than my own elevation to that rank a few months earlier in Ethiopia.

We sat on the sand and talked at length about our lives as the moon rose: I told him of my hopes to go on the Umra and then by sea to Egypt and to see my aged parents in England before they, or I, died; of the careless, solitary life I'd led *au jour le jour*, never thinking of tomorrow nor of the need for financial security, accumulating experiences but no material wealth, giving and sharing what I could but now in my mid-forties with neither family nor home nor established profession.

'What of it?' countered Jadidi robustly. 'If it is your fate, live it, live it to the full and enjoy it! Some of our greatest saints never had families. That didn't stop them from giving to those around them. Do likewise. Keep faith, keep trusting!'

I lay coughing on the sand till I fell asleep. Jadidi's friend, a thoughtful student who had travelled to Egypt and kept a stall in the market, woke me with a hot bitter infusion of sage leaves and ginger root to clear my chest.

In the library of the sheikh's eldest son Fatih, I came across that wonderful book of spiritual aphorisms, the Kitab ul-Hikam of Ibn Atallah al-Iskandari. One saying seemed to echo Jadidi's encouragement:

'Let it be no cause for despair, if, in spite of your insistent prayers, there is delay in granting gifts: for He has guaranteed to answer your prayers as He chooses best for you, not in what you choose for yourself, and in the time He wishes, not in the time that you may wish!'

Jadidi later told me that he'd asked the sheikh to do one of his special *fatiha* prayers to intercede for the successful outcome of my journey, including the pilgrimage to the Hijaz, the return by sea to Egypt, the reunion with my parents and brothers. I was haunted by Ibn Battutah's return to Tangier after his long absence, to find his mother already dead. Certainly in that distant stretch of central Sudan's savannah, home seemed a long way away, and the sheikh's assurances were comforting.

I spent a week at Zariba, sitting on the dry red sand in front of the sheikh's reception room during the day when he was performing his *dhikr* litanies of commemoration in a closed room. I studied in the shade of a big baobab, leaning against its trunk, and at night slept on a string bed on the back terrace; when I stood after midnight to recite the supererogatory *tahajjud* prayers under the full moon, I would see tame gazelles come out from their pen and step delicately around the sleeping guests.

The organization of the *masid* was quite an undertaking. Students, disciples and visitors were given early morning milk tea, with mid-morning *futur* of *asida* for the general public – eggs, red beans and tomato salad for guests – and mid-afternoon *ghada* of roast meat, honey, stews, *kisra* and *weka*, salad and fruit which the sheikh would heroically share with rank upon rank of guests who came to eat from the same dish with him. Late at night, *asha* of bread and sweetened yoghurt was served, a feat of organisation, mostly cooked by the sheikh's nine current and ex-wives.

There were several hundred students and disciples, mostly adolescents, willing but untidy, fifty or more visitors daily and a rush at weekends. Pilgrims arrived on Thursday evening and entered the brick and concrete compound, marching with flags and chants, drumming and dancing, till they had covered the prescribed itinerary around the tall, domed tomb of the sheikh's father where strip-lighting blazed just this one night, around various concrete excrescences, a pseudo-hillock where the older sheikh had died, some false wells occasionally filled by bucket for pilgrims. These were all significant features of the landscape of piety. Had veneration of the founder, dead barely fifty years, replaced some pre-Islamic ancestor worship?

But the *masid* was also a centre of traditional Islamic learning, strengthening and renewing the inherited but fragile cultural identity of these mostly rural Muslims. At different levels, there was the basic memorization of the Qur'an for elementary students, then the study of *hadith* traditions, of *fiqh* canon law for the more mature, and, for the more advanced, even commentaries on the Qur'an and books of sufism. In Sheikh Fatih's library, I found not only that classic of Shadhili mystic psychology, the Hikam of Ibn Atallah, but also a book of the ten variant readings of the Qur'an by Ibn al-Jazari Kitab u-Nashr fi Qira'at'Ashr, the Ihya Ulumi-d-Din of Ghazali, the supreme legal text-book Muwatta of Malik, the poetic Diwan of Umar Haddad, the great dictionary Taj ul-'Arus of Zabidi and other treasures. Reading was as much part of my Islamic journey as physical travel and meetings with Muslims.

I find the essential message of the Qur'an text convincing, the themes of preaching recur as leitmotifs in various combinations, with the personal polemic tone often supporting the traditional idea of the divine revelation fitting into the purported biography of the human recipient. The genre of prophetic utterance was perilously close to, and therefore had to be emphatically distinguished from, that of the Kahin sorcerers and the Sha'ir poets. But the Qur'an's cosmology of seven heavens, seven gates of hell, three paradises, and shooting stars to punish eavesdropping Jinn are all difficult to square with modern concepts of the universe. Our astronomers do not have seven or three of anything, their quantities are altogether vaster.

For me, and for many non-Arab Muslims, one of the most essential problems remains the relationship between innate natural religion and its culturally specific seventh-century Arabic revelation as defined by the limited geographical and historical scope of references in the Qur'an.

How Arabic should Islam be, if it is to be a universal religion?

Also, I do find the increasing identification of Ego, the Prophet, and super-ego, God, rather disturbing. There has already been enough of that in Christianity, hero-worship taken to the point of deification!

And yet, and yet, if there is not a perfect concordance of will and consciousness between God and Prophet, what does the Semitic tradition of prophecy amount to?

All this was grist to the mill of my critical mind, which worked overtime and refused to give up its addiction to examining, questioning and doubting. However much my heart wants faith, and would even be satisfied with superstition, my reason refuses to believe.

When I finally met the sheikh to talk with him, after a long wait outside his door when I almost lost my temper and banged on the door while he was performing his extended devotions, I tried to explain my predicament to him: 'My heart believes, if God wills, but my reason refuses to believe.'

He referred to verse 46 of the Chapter of Pilgrimage: 'It is not so much eyes which go blind, but rather the heart in the breast which goes blind.'

'Did you not see me in your dreams last night?'

'No.'

'You are still clouded. This intellectualism could drive you mad. Look at life and at faith from the point of view of *rahma* – mercy, not *ikhtilaf* – dissension.'

He also quoted verse 118–9 from the Chapter of Hud: 'and they do not cease to differ, except those on whom your Lord has had mercy; and to that end He created them.'

'Were men created for mercy and unity or for dissension? A Muslim must love the Prophet and therefore stick to his exemplary *sunna* habitual practice – so don't emphasize differences; just believe in the unseen *ghayb* – the all-powerful God. You cannot know all, so use allegory as well as literal commentary to approach the truth, which is all one Truth.'

'As for Arabism,' the sheikh continued, 'Arabic is the privileged language of this revelation, but never forget the saying "khatib u-nas 'ala qadri 'uquli-him" – speak to people according to the level of their understanding. You don't have to become Arab to become Muslim. So keep your vernacular language, keep your local name Bruce, providing its significance in your language is neither idolatrous nor insulting.'

The sheikh did not want me to leave until after the Friday prayers, so I took the chance for more talks with him, about dreams, idle thoughts that obstruct concentration and prayer, about asceticism. The more I saw him the more his kindness and wisdom impressed me.

'Did you hear or see me in your dreams last night?' he asked again one morning.

I was not aware of having had any dreams since coming here.

He described *zuhd* asceticism: 'renounce what is your own, God will love you for that; renounce what is other people's, they will love you for that.' The ascetic is one who envies not what is in others' hands and gives freely of what is in his own. This seemed to describe the sheikh's own practice.

To a student he repeated one of his father's favourite sayings:

'alay-kum bi-t-taqwa: wa hiya
al-khawfu min al-Jalil
wa-l-'amalu bi-t-Tanzil
wa-rida'u bi-l-qalil
wa-l-isti'dadu bi-yawmi-r-rahil'

Your duty is Piety, that is: fear God,
act according to the Revelation,
be content with little,
be prepared for the day of departure, death.

Turning to me he warned: 'Contemplating God's attributes must not go to the point of questioning His essence; the human attributes are those of *ubudiya* – being a servant of the Lord – therefore concentrate on those human attributes, humility, spiritual poverty, a sense of your own nothingness in the face of God's majesty.

'Work cleanses; service to human beings is the real expression of religion; heaven is outside time and place, outside our experience and our comprehension, and therefore described in elusive, allusive, allegorical language. The heavenly spirit breathed into each human being by God at his creation "wa nafakhtu fi-hi min Ruh-i" in the Chapter of Hijr verse 29, this is what lasts and, if God wills, this is what returns to Him, the light returning to the Light.'

I was late for the Friday sermon and prayers and was hurrying over the sand to the mosque after all the others had already entered, when the sheikh came in my direction. He took my hand as we both approached the mosque, and asked me, almost apologetically, explaining that some people were worried by the presence of a Westerner, to repeat the *shahada*, the profession of faith.

I was shocked, but repeated the formula while holding his hand. 'Ashhadu an la ilaha illa Allah, wahda-hu la sharika la-hu, wa ashhadu anna Muhammadan abdu-hu wa rasuluhu': I bear witness that there is no God other than the One God, and that Muhammad is His servant and His messenger.

The sheikh then led me into the mosque by a back stair up to the preachers gallery in full view of the assembled two or three thousand. I was confused and abashed, and did not know what to do.

The sheikh gave a powerful sermon on the text of the Chapter of the Afternoon:

> 'I swear by the afternoon,
> that man is indeed at a loss,
> unless it be those who believe
> and do good works,
> and encourage one another to hold on to
> > truth and patience.'

After the prayers, he turned to me and said: 'Now you talk to the people.'

Pushing me forward, he gave me a glowing introduction that seemed to confirm my undeserved status as honoured visiting scholar. So I talked very simply in my basic Arabic about my trip through different Muslim countries to see how my Muslim brothers were living, and to see the strength and solidarity of Islam lived in the lives of ordinary people.

I felt at first as if I were being thrown to the lions, perceived as an outsider from a hostile culture. People seemed to appreciate what I said, which was as positive and tactful as I could make it. It was obviously not the place to air text-critical quibbles. In fact the shock of repeating the *shahada* had quite driven such things from my mind. My intellectual pride and nihilistic undermining of faith suddenly seemed irrelevant, unworthy.

On Saturday, I looked for the sheikh early and found him in the furthest part of the *masid*, in the radio-room where he was giving orders by radio to his various centres at el-Obeid, Umm Ruwaba, Wad Madani, Port Sudan, Omdurman. He had just received news of the previous night's car crash, from which his son had escaped unhurt but the driver had broken his wrist. Despite his suspicion of much modern mass culture – football, cinema – there was no unwillingness to make use of modern technology.

The sheikh's youngest son, an infant, at-Tum, was climbing all over the place with a runny nose. I wiped his face clean with a tissue and the sheikh, noticing my gesture, immediately gave me a pack of tissues.

The whereabouts of the sheikh did not long remain secret and soon more visitors crowded in and were served with trays of bread and bowls of red beans with raw onion and peanut oil and fresh tomatoes, followed by basins of wild honey and ghee, then fruit and tea, a never-ending profusion.

Finally, I plucked up courage and asked for permission to leave, to travel onwards with his blessing. He looked at me and asked: 'Do you really want to go?'

'Yes.'

He embraced me, kissed me on the neck, then dug into his capacious pockets and emptied all the money accumulated there: 'Take this for your journey!'

Sheikh Abdu-Rahim al-Bura'i used to talk about his recent trip to Fez in Morocco when he was the guest of the Tijani order. The descendants of the founder, also Maliki in legal observance, quoted some fifty *hadith* in favour of praying with hands-open, hanging by the side – just as I remember the sheikh standing, leading the long lines of worshippers in prayer on the sand. This, as opposed to the arms crossed over the chest of Hanafi and Wahhabi. In some parts, these minutiae are taken in deadly earnest: one traveller who joined the prayers in northern Nigeria folded his hands across his chest and was promptly stoned to death.

Is that akin to a musician outraged at a favourite melody played too fast, with botched phrasing, or a cook enraged by a classic dish over-peppered or disfigured with tomato ketchup? Etiquette and aesthetics and fashion can command our obedience in the smallest details of taste and ritual, but not religion, not any more, not in the rationalized West.

So are the Muslims who worry passionately about the ritual efficacy of a particular gesture or length of beard or woman's veil wrong to do so? A ritual or a custom can encapsulate values and beliefs, but should remain transparent; otherwise there is the risk of idolizing outer forms, the risk of attempting – an intolerant and futile attempt – to limit the free-flowing inner Spirit.

Sheikh Abdu Rahim Al-Bura'i, the Sufi

One of the most concise definitions of sufism, that it is 'entirely about good manners', stresses precisely this attention to details of hierarchy and etiquette, not in a dry, but in a loving way. It is also a realistic way, recognizing and giving to each person or thing its proper place and value. What greater respect and courtesy than that needed in the presence of the Divine?

I keep the memory of a great and saintly man, one who had no false modesty nor false austerity, a giver, who gave back manifold everything that he was given, a fount of generosity – in that sense at least, the ideal of Muslim sanctity which reflects the unending generosity of God who perpetually sustains and renews His creation.

The echoes of this meeting have continued with me throughout my travels in Egypt and Syria, and even now in cold, damp Yorkshire.

This is a shortened extract from a book of travels in the Muslim world to be published by Constable & Robinson.

The Very Rich Hours of the Sultan of Geneina

GLENCAIRN BALFOUR PAUL

I N THE FOURTEENTH CENTURY two French brothers composed
in honour of their feudal boss the well-known illuminated manuscript
entitled *Les Très Riches Heures du Duc de Berry*. Abdulrahman Bahreddin
lived six hundred years later in a different part of the world (the western
Sudan). Few Europeans know even his name, let alone anything of the
lifestyle of the Masalit people, whose sultan or feudal boss he was when I
enjoyed his friendship in the early 1950s. I have called this tribute to him
'The Very Rich Hours of the Sultan of Geneina'. His Hours may not have
been as Rich as those of a former French Duke, but they surely showed
me a lot of colourful 'medieval' panache. The early history of the Masalit
is virtually forgotten, so I will begin with a summary of it (and will end
with a brief account of the appalling suffering inflicted on them today).

The Masalit, a substantial black tribe, had long lived on both sides of
the barely defined zone separating the much more powerful sultanates of
the Fur to the east and the Borqu of Waddai to the west. In past history
neither of the sultans concerned had paid the Masalit much attention,
except when fighting small wars with them. Nor did they trouble to
define a frontier between their respective 'states'. In those days the rest of
the outside world showed no interest at all in Darfur and Waddai. Only
one Englishman, W. G. Browne, ventured into Darfur in the 1790s,
publishing an account of his travels in 1799; but he never visited the
Masalit. The North African scholar, Muhammad Omar el-Tunisi, dug
much deeper in Darfur and Waddai and from 1799 spent seven years in
each of them. But like Browne he was a virtual prisoner in both. His
detailed account of what he was able to discover was published in

French forty years later in Cairo, but it barely mentions the Masalit apart from a throwaway observation that '*au Dar al Macalyt la beauté des femmes est ravissante, enlève la raison, et captive les coeurs*'. But he does not suggest that he had experienced such 'captivity' himself. What did captivate him were such oddities as the Fur conviction that on the top of their central mountain, Jebel Marra, the two sons of Alexander the Great were buried.

Neither during the Turco-Egyptian occupation of the Sudan (1874–88) nor during the ten years of the Mahdi's supremacy that followed until 1898 was any concern shown for defining the frontier between Darfur and Waddai. When the imperialist French occupied Waddai in 1909 they entertained ideas of adding Darfur to their Chad colony, but dropped them in the face of expected British resistance. The Anglo-Egyptian invaders of the Sudan in 1900 did nothing about Darfur until 1916, when they overthrew the Fur despot, Ali Dinar, and incorporated what had been his independent Sultanate into the Sudan as a new province. The Masalit were certainly regarded as living within its borders, but because they had long resisted Fur domination, their sultan was given a measure of autonomy as well as control of two mini-sultanates to the immediate north. The Masaliti sultan, Muhammad Bahreddin, known to his people as Endoka, was not subjected to a British District Commissioner but was given a 'Resident Adviser' – also from the Sudan Political Service but without a DC's plenipotentiary powers.

I had the good fortune to have this job from 1951 for two years, based like the Sultan in Geneina township. Endoka himself had died a few days before my arrival. Having been enthroned in 1911 by his own people he had initially resented any sign of British interference; but, come the 1920s, he had accommodated himself to the existence of a Resident Adviser. Indeed, following World War II when Geneina had been an RAF staging post, Endoka had the engaging custom on receiving a British visitor of donning an RAF helmet and goggles. This was presumably intended as a gesture of friendly respect (or so, at least, it was taken to be by the visitors).

His son and successor, Abdulrahman Bahreddin, had no such quirky habits, but was a man I much liked and admired. He was not handsome but short, stout, and pudgy-faced. I used to accompany him from time to time on tours round his 'Dar'. On one such trek we were as usual supping together under the stars, when he was stung by a large scorpion on his thigh. I had had a nearly fatal encounter with a scorpion myself at Wadi Halfa during the War and was naturally alarmed. Abo Abdulrahman simply told his accompanying retainers to bring him a leaf of the tobacco-plant, which was widely cultivated by the Masalit for chewing. None proved to grow in our vicinity, and the Sultan stretched out a hand for my tin of Balkan Sobranie pipe tobacco that was lying on our trek table, extracted a pinch, rubbed it on his thigh, and went on unconcernedly with his soup. Pain, as I was to discover later, was something no Masaliti – least of all their Sultan – would deign to admit suffering in public. But I assumed at the time that my Balkan Sobranie must have proved miraculously effective. And perhaps it had. If I am ever again stung by a scorpion I will certainly try it.

Abo Abdulrahman's younger brother, Muhammad, was a character of a different kind. Apart from being lighter skinned and less pudgy, he was the only Masaliti who had visited England, and he had come back with a black tie suit and a Harrod's dinner service – though I had no evidence that he ever made use of them. But he served conscientiously enough as the Sultan's deputy. I spent many hilarious afternoons playing amateur polo with the two brothers and my mounted policemen – the only occasions in my life when a horse and I have felt remotely conjoined as a single animal.

I recall an early experience (on foot) when I observed approaching through the tall green millet – the rains having just ceased – a cavalcade of horsemen led by Abo Abdulrahman himself, white-robed on a white stallion. He had come to attend the election of a local chieftain, the previous one having been bitten fatally by a rabid donkey. As their Sultan dismounted, the assembled electors, squatting with their buttocks on their heels, set up the traditional measured clapping, their heads turned to one side as custom required. But there was nothing flamboyant about this sultan's tours through his kingdom. His primacy did not depend on his people submitting to oppression of the old kind but on their showing a humble but genuine affection.

One of my duties was to go round the Sultan's scattered courthouses, inspect their ledgers, and satisfy him (and myself) that justice was being done. One of the offences that figured quite often in the Charge column of these court-books (written in Arabic of course) was 'Did Bordubordu'. The first time I came across such an entry I had to ask the Sultan on my return what the term meant. Though unreserved in talking to me about most things – including the local offence of transvestism by male prostitutes – he was clearly not keen to explain 'Bordubordu' in detail. However, his head judge, a saintly but supremely entertaining West African living in Geneina, was less reserved. He explained Bordubordu as the practice by which certain people could turn themselves, for nefarious purposes, into crocodiles or lions or hyenas, and he related to me a number of instances from his own experience. The most remarkable was that just across the Chad frontier a lion which had been causing trouble in a village by carrying off young women had eventually been shot dead by the local police in broad daylight; and when the populace converged on its corpse it had already turned back into the sinister sheikh of a nearby village with a bullet in his head. (I see that MacMichael, in his colossal *History of the Arabs in the Sudan*, attributes this startling practice only to the Masalit of Darfur).

We went on one trek to an area where the local headman had just been hauled over the coals by his subordinate sub-chiefs for allowing three swarms of locusts to fly into his chiefdom from the west. The nearest *dambari* (locust-wizard) had been summoned to deal with the invasion. All *dambari*s had to abstain from wine and women during their hours of business, it being assumed that such a condition of holiness would give them a measure of control over the rest of creation. This particular wizard's kit consisted of an ornamental mace, a cow's horn, and a big bag of powdered *erigs* (roots). The identity of these roots had to be kept secret from the community, or the *dambari* suspected of having revealed it was liable to wake up in the morning to find his throat cut from ear to ear by other members of the fraternity. We watched our wizard pour the secret powder into his cow-horn, bore a small hole in its narrow end, and discharge blasts of it at the invading locusts. Other ingenious procedures were used to complete the operation, including one that was said to root the locusts to the ground with trouble in their stomachs, so that they could easily be slaughtered. To me it looked as if a *dambari's* real function was simply to re-direct an invading swarm into the next parish.

Equally intriguing was the mystique attached to blacksmiths. 'Never marry your daughter', said a local proverb, 'to a donkey or a blacksmith'. The smith's trade of manufacturing metal was evidently thought to smack of sorcery. We watched these (immigrant) sorcerers producing iron out of ore, collected on donkeys from a nearby mountain, in a tall mud kiln splashed with bull's blood for a preliminary blessing. The kiln was kept stoked by young apprentices pouring more ore and more charcoal down the kiln's chimney, and the mixture was kept glowing by the blacksmiths pounding away concertina-fashion on goatskin bellows attached to clay pipes poking into the kiln through holes just above ground level. The blacksmiths were singing at the tops of their voices (when not swallowing *merissa,* home-made beer) to keep themselves awake for hours on end until the last gobbets of molten ore had seeped down into the chaff-filled hole underneath. The ore was then hammered into various shapes. These included a throwing weapon of alarming aspect, like a huge Gothic F or a recent acquisition in bronze by the Tate Gallery. But the blacksmiths' prime product was spearheads, of which there were many models. Each model had its own name: the 'No-Way-Back' with its ugly flanges pointing forwards and backwards to make it inextricable, the 'Princess's Navel' (a nomenclature less easily explained), and so on. They were all allegedly rendered lethally poisonous by dipping them in donkeys' urine, which had to be brought to the boil first.

Abo Abdulrahman, I was pleased to see, treated the operations of *dambari*s, blacksmiths, and other primaeval craftsmen with smiling indulgence.

One steaming summer day I watched him, stood beside one of the shrinking pools of valuable water, pointing out to a European water engineer where barrages might be constructed to hold water longer in that particular catchment. He looked like an inverted African Canute, challenging the waters to *recede.* Out of what was left of the pool waded a bevy of jet-black Aphrodites with waterlilies in their plaited hair, and the foremost of them kneeled at the Sultan's feet to proffer him a single cream-white waterlily. The tuberous roots of these lilies, incidentally, were judged a delicacy, eaten like potatoes – though the one I tried tasted like nothing so much as a musty mothball.

Perhaps the Very Richest Hour in the Sultan's programme was a ceremonial gathering of the tribes in their drum-beating squadrons, eight thousand horsemen and camel-men having assembled to ride past him and such foreign notables as came to witness the ceremony. Accompanying some of the squadrons were flautists pointing their instruments of antelope-horn to the sky, their heads thrown proudly back. There were even prouder individuals sporting medieval regalia, coats of chain mail, plumed helmets, and brass shin-pads. English pageantry has had nothing to match it since Crécy. When darkness fell, hundreds of fires were lit in the arena. Close to the tent we occupied was a local orchestra of eight musicians with flutes, wooden drums, and gourd rattles, led by a prancing pipe-player in a conical hat, its perimeter dripping with leather bootlaces decorated with cowrie shells.

In the far north corner of Dar Masalit lay the smallest mini-sultanate in the world, that of Tini, ruled by a Zaghawi sheikh. This was the only place in the Sudan where the ancient ostrich-feather fan-ballet of central Africa was to be seen (though I witnessed it twice in Waddai). At Tini it was performed by eight of the local Sultan's sisters' sons, in black waistcoats over white tunics. They were drawn up before their lordly uncle amid his women in their curious headgear – brass bows tied to the scalp with a leather cross-strap, the horns pointing forward and strung from tip to tip with strings of coloured beads. The dancers were in fours, the two lines polka-ing towards each other while their fans – black feathers on a three-foot red wand – were canted upwards in the right hand, twiddling as the elbow straightened. They seemed, as perhaps they were, an echo of a temple frieze at Memphis, Negro captives dancing for a victorious Pharaoh.

I spent a lot of my spare time finding my way to sites of antiquarian interest. The last one, just before my transfer to Kutum, was Kidongi Baldanga and was not easy to reach. I had to borrow a horse off a kindly Masaliti from the nearest motorable track, and the reins of the horse consisted to my delight of a motor-bicycle chain. Kidongi Baldanga proved a good example of the practice of local chieftains in the past (as I had discovered in a number of other places) of building their dry-stone or brick 'palaces' on the tops of hills, having first got their people or their slaves to flatten the chosen hilltop at enormous labour to provide at an imposing height a level plinth. But the interest of Kidongi Baldanga for the purposes of this article is that a local peasant told me that Abo Abdulrahman had recently come there to have a look. Could he have caught the infection from his Resident Adviser?

The Sultan owned and cherished a large herd of giraffes in the forested scrubland between Geneina and the Chad frontier. None of his subjects, however hungry, would have dreamt of interfering with the herd; and I loved to watch these great beasts floating gracefully through the trees, their long necks enabling them to munch foliage far above the range of lesser herbivores.

Altogether the Resident Adviser's job was hugely stimulating and I owed much of my enjoyment of it to Sultan Abdulrahman. He died in 1965 and was briefly succeeded by his son Sa'ad, before a more 'democratic' form of local government was imposed by the authorities in Khartoum. I understand that the Bahreddin family retains the old standing amongst the people, but power and authority now reside with an official appointed by the central government.

Since 2002 the Masalit – as Western media have, without much effect, made manifest – have suffered atrociously and are still suffering (as I write) from the appalling brutality of Arabs known as the Janjaweed with evident backing from the Sudan government. There are, I am aware, two sides to this ghastly clash of cultures, a small minority of the Masalit and other black tribes in Darfur having reportedly rebelled against Arab domination. But whatever these rebels may have done, nothing can possibly justify the barbarities of the Janjaweed. Tens of thousands of defenceless Masalit have been mercilessly slaughtered, and tens of thousands more have had to seek refuge across the border in Chad. The Masalit, I should add, are no less Muslim than their Arab persecutors.

El-Janna is the Muslim Paradise, and el-Janeina (or Geneina) is simply its diminutive verbal form. If Abo Abdulrahman is now looking down from up there at his old Sultanate he must sometimes wish that Dar Masalit had indeed been swallowed up by the French in 1909 and become part of Chad, instead of being left to suffer today from its incorporation into the Sudan.

Paradise Point

EMILY YOUNG

IN THE SUMMER OF 1969, I found myself, an eighteen-year-old English girl, camping on the coast of the Sindh desert in the South of Pakistan, looking out over the blue Arabian Sea. We had travelled from the North, my companion and I, in an old blue Ford van, decorated with Hindi invocations, Om Shanti, and such. The van had a small rusty chimney sticking out above the battered rear door, attached on the inside to our little stove, which had kept us warm through Himalayan snow storms, but was now not in use. The temperature this far south was in the low hundreds. Humidity was in the high nineties. It felt as though you were walking through a hot shower, but the water never quite materialised. Our blue van contained all we needed for survival on the road.

I was travelling with a young Californian man, who was avoiding the American draft, being an Assiniboine Sioux; the Vietnam war was not something he wanted to get involved in, being, apart from anything else, rather beyond his areas of enthusiasm, which were psychedelic drugs and travelling. In order, as he put it, 'to wash his mind free of American bullshit', he was travelling as far as he could from the USA, and its culture. We were drawn to mountains. I was interested in finding out where I would eventually stop, having left England with no plan other than to leave. I had met him in Italy, at the start of my travelling time. He had a share, with the rest of his tribe, in an oil well that had been found on ancestral Sioux land in Montana, and received a hundred dollars a month from that. We lived simply.

We had been in Afghanistan for some months, where we began to attune ourselves to desert life, mountain life; we had spent the summer living in the foothills of the Himalayas, in Swat. I remember the night sky there, dark blue velvet, strewn with diamonds; you could reach out and clutch handfuls of starlight. Swat, beneath the orchid and snow-decked shoulders of the mountain K2, was a land of abandoned Buddhist stupas and milky-white rivers, running through deep valleys terraced with emerald-green rice paddies. We had lived in a village nestled above the Swat River, and grown used to the sound of the rushing snow waters below, and the hospitality of our neighbours, Pathans, mountain people, descendants of Alexander the Great, with sea-blue eyes. But when the snows came, we went south, like birds. We were light-footed. Due south, till we hit the coastline. And when we arrived it was hot, and humid.

When we reached the sea, we turned right, westwards, and drove along the coast road till we found a tea-house, where, along with drinking sweet tea, we asked about a place to park the blue van for a while. In Pakistan there is always an English speaker. We were told to follow the coast road and we would find the ruins of an old, abandoned, never-finished holiday resort. We drove along the rough road, untarmacked, across stony stream beds, gullies, through bare scrubby yellow desert, a warm mist rolling around us. Deserts are, by definition, deserted. We saw no one, no beast, no fowl, no creature at all. This was a most wonderful nowhere: the Sindh desert meets the Arabian sea; there was the sea, the sky and the sun, and that was it. We found the promised camping spot: it comprised four or five concrete shells, perched on the crumbling cliff edge of the desert, where the desert washed away to become sandy beach. It was utterly abandoned; the sun had bleached the cement and the concrete, the breeze from the sea scudded gently across the floors, where sand had drifted in and out. Dried grasses whispered in corners. We chose a shell, with a roof, to keep us dry should the rain fall. It suited us well.

Sand, sea, sky, sun, all conjoined by the softness of the air, and the fierceness of the light, everything touched by moisture. There was a constant flow of moving air, from the ocean, hot, humid, but somehow cooling, pleasant on the skin, making it a place of stunningly acceptable simplicity and sensuality; there was very little to do there but wander, slowly, damply, about, breathing the warm air of the sea; the air smelled of winds, and sand. We would wander out to watch the sunset each evening, wondering at the stars as the sky cleared, at the Southern Cross and the Milky Way as they came out to greet us, and in the morning we would wander out to watch the sun rise again. We would read and watch the sun burn up the sea. We swam in milky water the temperature of tepid tea, the colour of Northern eyes. Sea-blue. Sky-blue. Beneath the sea-blue. The land, the desert, was misted into invisibility; we didn't want to go there or even look in that direction. We lived with our backs to the land, always looking south, the light-filled south, across an infinite sea to an infinite sky.

Sometimes we saw dolphins leaping, leaf-shaped metallic slips of dark light breaking through the surface of the sea, gleaming and cavorting, from another world. Or the tiny bobbing head of a turtle, taking so long to get somewhere.

Often in the evenings we smoked chillums of hashish, and danced in the warm wet moonlight, laughing, like the good hippies we were.

Remembering it now, it seems a dream time, heavy with light, where I floated, the sand beneath my feet shifting, the air like water, water air, where our bodies too were insubstantial, reflections of sunlight, strong light, dancing on water, through water. Coursing photons. A roar of golden light in the distant south, an insistent rhythm and rhyme of sea waves moving towards us, washing through us and passing on, holding us in a quality of stillness, locked in locked out. Translucent sea, milky, blue and gold. White bones, wide land, washed clean by years of golden empty light. Hearts beating. Eyes too wide open. Speechless. Close to death in some way. And bliss.

The name of the place was Paradise Point.

There was no one there, and nothing happened.

Every now and then we would drive along the coast road to the tea-house, to buy food, and drink tea, and be chatted to by employees from the local nuclear power plant. One could see this dome of a building from the road on a clear day, out on a point, shining and shimmering, a mirage. They wore clean white shirts and western trousers, they spoke English, smoked cigarettes. They called me 'Baby'; they thought that was 'cool'; they had watched Hollywood movies. They made me nervous. Their Western ways intruded into my bare blue heaven.

We had been there for a while, when one morning, as the dawn broke, we woke to hear steps in the sand and gravel outside the walls of our shelter, our house, and later, when we went outside we found, lying at the door, a gleaming grey sea creature, white-bellied, resting quietly on shiny green leaves. On looking closely, I decided yes, it was a small very freshly killed shark. A baby shark. But where had it come from and who had left it and who had leaves like these in this wilderness of desert and sea? There was no one around. Not a soul.

We ate the shark later, grilled over driftwood on the beach, drinking warm beer. It was delicious.

A couple of days later, there was a basket of turtle eggs. Again no one to see. I scrambled them, and they were so dry as to be almost uneatable, and I wished they had stayed where they had been laid, in the sand. But we appreciated the gift of them.

The third gift: some silver fish; again, wrapped in leaves. Still no person to thank.

But the next time we went to the tea-house for food and Hollywood badinage, there was a group of men whom we hadn't seen before; fishermen, tall, athletic, dark, five, six of them, sitting in the shade, on the benches under the palm thatching. Lounging perhaps I should say, as they were so relaxed and at home with themselves. Their machine guns lay casually over their thighs. The men from the nuclear power plant did not like them, it was plain to see. The fishermen wore aviator sunglasses and shiny gold watches, and very little else. They chatted softly among themselves, smiling a lot and laughing, chuckling, flashing white teeth. They were at home in this place. They looked East African, very, very, very black, with lots of shiny curly hair, but their beautiful faces were Asian. They looked like they were the true inhabitants, the kings of this place. Their dark eyes were brighter than the sea glinting behind them. One of them, the youngest, approached us and asked in lilting English if we had enjoyed the fish. We told him of our surprise and gratitude, and asked him to visit us whenever he was passing.

He came a couple of days later. We sat in the shade, and drank tea, and he asked us questions, full of enthusiasm and goodwill. He was twenty, and his name was Abdul. Over the next weeks we became good friends. He almost always carried his gun, but we never saw him use it. His watch was a Rolex, he told us, a 'good watch'. His sunglasses were RayBans because, again, they were 'good'. His gun too. He was genial, playful, full of pleasure in life, smiles and small jokes. He was also courteous, careful, very generous. He was fascinated by us, by our stories of where we had lived, what we had done, why we were there. He loved to listen to our collection of cassettes, our Californian rock music.

His English was good, and he proved a good neighbour. He lived nearby, or sometimes did, as he and his companions travelled up and down the coast, in their fishing boats, staying where the waves, the fish and the whim took them. Their boats were kept 'along the shore', invisible to us. He would appear in our bay, rowing his dark blue and decorated boat, with its high prow, calling out to us about a swimming trip, a drive inland, some fun activity. We were always pleased to see him.

One day Abdul appeared with a Land Rover, to take us on a visit. We drove off across the scrubby land, inland, with Abdul pointing out deer, and eagles, snakes slithering away, lizards; animals did of course live in this place, it was just that we didn't know how to see them. Leopards, and bustards lived there, still, and tigers used to.

We were going to visit his family, who lived in one of the curiously invisible local mud castles. It was fortified, with barricades of thorn branches around the outside, to keep wild animals out and domestic ones in. But built of mud as it was, it looked vulnerable and I could easily believe that one heavy monsoon rain would wash it all away. But it was obviously old, and could do whatever it had to do to survive in that land. The building was three, maybe four floors high, otherworldly in its strangeness, its unfamiliarity. It was exactly the same colour as the surrounding landscape, dun, yellowish, dull. Inside it was dark, with wooden floors and beams, a place of shadows. It was inhabited by dark children and women who flitted past doorways, laughing, hiding from us, dressed in bright embroidered clothes. The lengths of brilliant cloth which the women so gracefully threw back over their shoulders were of a richness completely at odds with the sere landscape outside. On the ground floor, goats and dogs wandered about, and chickens. There was a peacock, maybe two. Above, woven woollen rugs and cushions in reds yellows and purples were laid out on the floor, reminding me of life in Afghanistan. We sat and sipped tea, and communicated in the language of curiosity and friendliness that involves a lot of facial expressions, and waving of hands, Abdul answering questions for us. Babies were presented to us to admire, smiling, sleeping, eating and laughing along with their siblings and cousins in what looked like an idyll of tribal family life. Children played and ran and shouted, and the women chattered and sang and prepared food, or stitched fabrics, or swept mud floors, or washed clothes in spare water. We spent the day there, and on into the evening. We were fed, everyone sitting together on the carpets. No segregation for the women from male strangers here. The old men smiled and nodded, the young men were absent, who knows where. No electricity, no running water, (water, that most essential and precious thing; smooth, dark, clear, sweet water), communal living, an ancient way, seemingly untouched still by the industrial world at these close quarters, in a mud castle in a bare desert; the women, as I remember them now, are like burnished butterflies of grace and strength.

Who knows what else went on there, what tragedies of constraints, illnesses, passions, deaths. They must have existed, but I saw none.

We were, though, bemused by how these people could survive there when so little was provided by nature, that we could see. There was a well, a small vegetable patch, and there was hunting, and there was fishing. We had initially assumed the fish market was what kept our new friends going but the shiny watches, the guns, the Land Rovers: it was obvious there was money coming from somewhere. It become clear that Abdul's way of life was not in fact simple. We learned that some night trips were indeed fishing trips, but that others were of a different sort, the boats going out to sea without lights, out to the freighters that could be seen passing on the horizon on less hazy nights. The port of Karachi lay some miles further down the coast to the East and was never short of cigarettes, or electrical goods, or alcohol, or watches. Or guns. Or gold. Perhaps there was an old tradition of smuggling, piracy. It would be easy to believe.

Abdul took us on outings in the Land Rover to see local wonders: a nest of snakes, a ruined fort of sagging mud, the remains of a temple with carvings and a stone foundation, a sea cave where the water was cold; he showed us where to watch long-legged birds, invisible from feet away, sand-coloured and delicate. He showed us strange mosses that drank from the mist, and lichens of orange, yellow, green, purple and black, growing on rocks. Sometimes in the evening we could hear the honking of water birds a long way away. We did not know the names of things, but we were happy to see and admire, and move on to the next quiet marvel.

At night we would watch the surf illuminate itself with the phosphorescence of tiny sea creatures glowing there. We watched as turtles the size of tea-chests made their slow and lumbering way up the beach, late at night, oblivious to us, leaving tank tracks in the sand, and then worked long and hard to dig a safe place to lay their eggs, so many ping pong balls, and then struggled slowly back to the ocean by the time the sun was rising, as they and their ancestors had done for millions of years, on sandy beaches just like this, the moon shining gently down. The eggs were so vulnerable to us who sat and watched, but we would not touch them now. We worried for these ancient creatures, green turtles, leaving their tracks, so obvious that they had been there, so obvious what they had done, and we wanted the tide to come up faster, and hide the tracks, the evidence, quicker, quicker.

Abdul took us one day to a bay, along the coast a bit, where a large cliff jutted out into the sea from the desert. We climbed to a ledge halfway up the rock, some twenty feet perhaps, and gazed down into the emerald green water below. There was a sheer drop.

'Look' said Abdul.

And there, beneath us, was a turtle, a green turtle, bobbing quietly along, its head sticking out of the water, its body angled down into the water.

Suddenly Abdul dived into the water, and reappeared moments later, holding on to the creature's shell, at the front, just behind the head. Then, with Abdul strung out along its back, the turtle headed out to sea, further and further away: we jumped into the water too, to watch them race through the glassy depths. Dimly, through the dense expanse of luminous green-blue water, we could see the two of them turning and diving, and it looked like playing, Abdul's legs flying out behind. The creature dived, and Abdul held on till the turtle went too deep, and then he burst exultantly up into the air and sunlight shouting, laughing.

Other times we would take the fishing boat out, and when we saw a little black head bobbing along, a match head in the blue, we would get as close as possible without it noticing us. At the last moment, we would slip into the water, and try to seize hold. After some tries and failures, I too was able to catch the shell and hold hard onto the bony edge, and, eyes wide with fear and delight, and straining to hold on, trying not to breathe water, I would go down and away until, my ears hurting and my lungs bursting, I had to let go, and I would hurtle back up, like a cork, my head full of the dreamy green-blue of the world below the sea surface, the sound of roaring silence, and the astonishment at the feel of the power of this ancient thing, this green turtle. He, she, was so alien under my belly, allowing me, for a brief moment, to be like them, at home in the ocean, a sea creature, alive in the waters. The turtle: my unwilling, unwitting guide into my own atavistic reptilian past. I know I had no right to steal a ride like that, but my joy in that theft was fierce, breathtaking, and my heart pounded, and he must have felt it too.

Again, my memory is of an infinity of warm translucent blueness, an emerald half-light, all-encompassing, the dream-like weight of it shot through, like glass, with gold: a soaring, a flight through something almost solid: the memory swells into a longing to return there.

We stayed there for some months more, until we were drawn by the mountains again, and headed North. We kept in touch, and I heard that Abdul had married an American girl, a traveller, and started a family. The world moved on: I've lost touch for many years now. My travelling companion is dead, killed in a car crash. Perhaps I'll go and visit Abdul one day, perhaps I could find him. The place will have changed, and him too; maybe it's a good thing to leave him there in my blue memory, carrying the dream of what was a wild place, and he, a wild boy, still part of that light-drenched desert, laughing, eyes flashing, diving with green turtles in a warm and emerald sea.

The Peace Maker

PETER CLARK

IN 1990, WILFRED THESIGER returned to Abu Dhabi to attend the opening of an exhibition of his photographs, arranged by the British Council. He had known the town and the region over forty years earlier during his great journeys across the Empty Quarter of southeast Arabia. Thesiger had known and loved pre-oil Arabia and its people.

We had brought over from Oman Bin Kabina and Bin Ghubaisha, two of Thesiger's companions during his historic explorations. Thesiger dedicated *Arabian Sands*, describing those years, to them. Then they had been teenagers. Now they were bearded patriarchs in their sixties.

One morning Thesiger said, 'The man I'd really like to see is Musallim bin Al Kamam. I haven't seen him for over forty years. His picture is on the spine of the dust-jacket of the first edition of *Arabian Sands*.'

In *Arabian Sands* Musallim is described – in the late 1940s – as being middle aged, but he must have only seemed so, for he was then in his late twenties, ten years younger than Thesiger. He was born into the Rashid tribe of Dhofar, the son of a minor sheikh. He and his father acquired reputations as peacemakers among tribes. His father had given assistance to Bertram Thomas in his desert travels in the 1920s. A generation later Musallim provided similar services for Thesiger. He knew all about the tribes and their conflicts, was resourceful and wise; and very well known. A story tells how in Inner Oman in 1947 Thesiger was pointed out as a Christian, and an old man asked, 'Is he the Christian who travelled last year with bin Al Kamam and the Rashidi to the Hadhramaut?'

Musallim helped Thesiger with contacts but never travelled across the Empty Quarter with him. However his quiet authority and dignity left an enduring impact on Thesiger and all who met him and spoke with him. He was a good listener, patient and curious, and could make friends with anyone. As such he had all the qualities of a negotiator and in the following decades he negotiated truces with tribes all over southern Arabia, and travelled from Yemen to Baghdad.

An hour after Thesiger expressed the wish to see Musallim I was in my office and the British Embassy phoned me: 'We have a Musallim bin Al Kamam here who wishes to see Umbarak bin London.' (This was the name by which Thesiger was known in those parts.) I immediately went to the Embassy, and met a man clutching a camel stick. He was perhaps seventy, neatly built, lithe of body and bright of eye. He had heard about the exhibition, travelled over from Oman, and wanted to see Wilfred. For the next week Musallim was with Wilfred every day.

For the rest of my time in the Emirates Musallim often dropped into my office. I would have to abandon British Council financial returns and spend the next hour or so in fascinated conversation about Southern Arabia and its changes in his lifetime. I learned a lot from him.

His Arabic was difficult to follow. My Arabic – he said – was like that of a Syrian school teacher. I do not know if he went to school but I remember him writing his name for me, slowly and with effort: Musallim's skills were in speaking, listening and acting on evidence thus acquired. Reading and writing were inessential to his way of life. He had not lost an iota of his integrity in adapting to the transformations of the late twentieth century, looking on them with detached curiosity and acceptance: it was all part of the unfathomable purpose of God. He often dropped into our house, bringing some dates from Dhofar, meeting my family including my widowed mother-in-law, whom he told me he would like to marry. This offer was made without irony. For him, the world was full of extraordinary things and becoming my step-father-in-law was no stranger than, for example, the modern island city of Abu Dhabi, which he had known when it had only one tree and no building taller than the residence of the then Ruler.

On one occasion I accompanied him to call on Edward Henderson at that residence, in the early 1990s the Centre for Documentation.

Musallim had known Edward Henderson in Dubai in the 1940s. The guards at the gate challenged Musallim as we went past, but not me. I was in a Western suit. He was in Bedu clothes, neat and clean, but clearly not a recognisable part of bourgeois *modern* Abu Dhabi. I felt furious. This man had been a legend in southern Arabia over forty years earlier. Even the President of the United Arab Emirates, Sheikh Zayed, would have treated him with respect. But Musallim was not angry. He smiled tolerantly at what I thought was ignorant and insulting behaviour.

Musallim never gave notice of any visit. On the outskirts of Abu Dhabi there was a community of Rashid tribesmen. I would always, after a visit, take him where he wanted to go, and we generally ended up there. He would sit in the passenger seat of the car, clutching his camel stick and squatting with his feet up, as if he was sitting on the ground.

He invited me to Dhofar and I did see him and his family at Thumrait, fifty miles from Salala. They lived in a breeze block government house, with a couple of camels in the enclosure. His son was working with an oil company and was later to study at Loughborough University of Technology. Musallim and his son suggested we take a few days off and travel with the camels into the Empty Quarter. A fascinating idea, but, for my pattern of life, alas quite impossible. But it was proposed as if it was the simplest idea in the world. It seemed to make Thesiger's pioneering explorations somehow an extended picnic.

I saw Musallim for the last time at Muscat airport. He was not well and was going to India for treatment at Omani government expense. He died soon afterwards. But on that last sad encounter there was a smile, a cheerful and curious acceptance of the manifold wonders of the world. Flying across the Indian Ocean. Peace-making among warring tribes. Camel riding in the Empty Quarter. Calling on strange Ingiliz friends in Abu Dhabi. A son studying modern management at a place called Loughborough. Musallim's tranquil and tolerant friendliness made him one of the most remarkable people I have met. Life has been the richer for having known him.

The Absent Mirror

SABIHA AL KHEMIR

'I, HILAL, FROM BANGLADESH,' said the gardener, 'and you?'
'From Tunisia,' I said.

'Muslim, al-hamdu-lilah,' he said. 'You new in Qatar?'

'I arrived a few weeks ago. I live in London.'

'How long you stay in Doha?'

'I don't know,' I said, 'perhaps till the museum is built. I am on a consultancy mission for a new museum of Islamic art which will open here, in Doha in 2006.'

Hilal was no longer listening. He was holding the bushes back and talking about cutting, and more cutting. To him, the garden was far too overgrown, too wild and, as he muttered to himself, he seemed particularly bothered by the state of the palm tree which had, probably, not been trimmed for years.

'You're free to do what you want,' I said, 'all I ask for is a beautifully blossoming bougainvillaea.'

As he kneeled before the sad bougainvillaea, Hilal seemed immersed in deep thought. When he finally spoke, I thought he would declare his plan of action, but he simply said: 'Hilal love garden, garden will love Hilal.'

I drew the curtain leaving Hilal to his dialogue with the garden and came to the empty page. This was the weekend, my day off from museum work and the time to write my contribution for *Meetings with Remarkable Muslims*.

'Write about your father,' Barnaby had suggested, and I said nothing. Deep down, I was stunned. I didn't have the presence of mind to ask:

'Do you know about my father?' Now, I am thinking: Why should he know about my father. How would he know that my father's life was intertwined with the history of my country. He probably meant I should write about him as a father in a Muslim, Tunisian family ... I dare not phone Barnaby to ask what he had meant but now, I have to decide: do I want to write about my father?' Barnaby's suggestion was unsettling – it was like suggesting to someone who had never seen a mirror to write about its reflection.

My father passed away when I was a few years old and during those few years, he was hardly on his feet. His poor health was the result of time in prison and years of resistance against French colonization. After Tunisia's independence in 1956, he was a tired man. He never recovered. Though long gone, my father's permanent absence has always weighed like a silent presence. And the consciousness of being this remarkable man's daughter has been a constant companion and a significant reference. But do I want to write about my father? The empty page gazes at me. Something in me resists breaking the sacred silence. I don't really want to write about my father.

In an attempt to avoid the gaze of the empty page, I pace around, searching in my mind for the remarkable Muslims. I gather my washing and load the machine. Memories tumble, crowding ... different places, different times, from the seventh to the twenty-first century, different kinds of encounters, some bringing insight in split seconds, others, an inspiration throughout my life. Flashbacks take me to Cairo, to Houston, to Budapest, to Korba, to New York.

Mary Belle sat on a public bench having lunch. 'If I met her on a moonless night,' I thought, 'I wouldn't have been able to see her – she is so black!'

' ... and what's *your* name?' asked Mary Belle.

'Sabiha,' I said

'I work over there!' she said, gesturing beyond the trees. 'I help an old lady and she gives me a place to stay.'

'Do you think I should get married?' I asked.

'It depends.'

'It depends?'

'Do you love him?'

'I am thinking about it.'

'If you're thinking,' said Mary Belle with arched eyebrows and an unequivocal tone, 'it's a very bad sign, the heart doesn't think. You see Sabina, the mind gets us into knots. Thought is the enemy.'

I looked at Mary Belle. Her layers told of a keen appetite.

'What does she know?' I thought, 'Black American Christian, probably evangelist . . . she calls me 'Sabina'! What does she understand of an Arab, Muslim woman – I am invisible to her!' I stopped listening to Mary Belle's ramblings between the full mouths.

The autumn colours of Central Park were fire to my thoughts; the bench where she and I sat was at a decisive crossroad in my life journey. She finished eating, folded the paper bag neatly, held it between her palms and declared: 'al-hamdu-lilah!'

Mary Belle was a Muslim? Having heard her thank God in those Arabic words startled me, bringing the insight that it was her who was invisible to me and that a Muslim could also be a large, black, American woman, eating a hamburger in Central Park!

This was 1991. I had just come from the Metropolitan Museum in New York where I had submitted my report on a trip across North Africa and parts of Europe. I had been working as a consultant looking at art from al-Andalus, Islamic Spain, for an exhibition to be held the following year in the Alhambra palace in Granada, and later in the Metropolitan Museum in New York.

The journey took place during the first Gulf War. Everywhere I went, televisions were broadcasting the events of the war. In a hotel in the city of Marrakesh, in the south of Morocco, the television screen seemed to fill the room. Queues of Kurdish refugees stretching for miles . . . families were spending nights on their feet, half-awake, waiting for their nightmare to come to an end, wondering whether they would be able to cross the border into Turkey and leave Saddam's cruelty behind, whether they would have a chance for a new life.

One image was particularly penetrating: a big close-up of the face of a newly-born, nestling to his mother's bosom, his head covered by a flowery scarf, vibrant and happy, in flagrant contrast with the appalling reality. Even now, the image is still so vivid before my eyes, it interrupts my writing.

I get up and walk to the kitchen, looking for words perhaps. The turning and tossing of the washing machine takes over, suddenly so loud, almost violent. I find myself facing the drum, watching the bundle of clothes intently. For a moment, I was the bundle of washing itself, thrashed about, turned, splashed, squeezed . . . I can't distinguish any particular items in the washing; the bed-sheet seems to take over everything . . . black knickers appear suddenly. I laugh, not at the knickers, but at the words of a woman I had met in Spain during that same journey. Talking to me about the English, the Spanish woman had said: 'Their habits disgust me. Apparently, they put underwear and kitchen towels in the same wash load!' 'Do they?!' was my hypocritical reply. At the time, I didn't have the courage to say that dirt was dirt and ask why we have to subjugate everything to discrimination.

Departing from London before Spain, I had gone to Tunisia, Egypt, Algeria and Morocco. It was in Morocco that I had a particularly memorable experience. I visited the Royal Library in Rabat and some other collections, housing a number of special manuscripts. In the Ben Youssef Library in Marrakesh, the manuscripts were kept in modest conditions. Walls were covered with overloaded shelves. In a tiny room at the back, an old man, in the traditional *djellaba*, sat like a forbidding guard. 'Someone will come and assist you,' he said, gesturing to the chair. I waited quietly. He was writing intently, tracing letters on a piece of paper, and seemed absent from the reality of the room. It was quite dark, only the paper and the man's face, as he bent over, were in a pool of light from the desk lamp. The beads of his rosary, to the side, were also luminous.

'You're sent from New York?' he asked.

'Yes, by the Metropolitan Museum.'

As he traced the letters, his movements seemed to dictate the flow of the conversation.

'What is the Metropolitan Museum?' he asked some time later, 'What's in it? Has it got our manuscripts?'

'Yes,' I said hesitantly.

'And our carpets? Our ceramics? Our woodcarvings? Our metal-work? Our past? The key to our future?'

I shrank and froze. I felt attacked. There had been many tense moments in this trip already. I was, after all, sent by the Americans during the Gulf War. Someone in Egypt had asked jokingly whether I was a spy. And now, I was representing America in Marrakesh!

'Is our past well looked after, at least?' he asked in an ambiguous tone.

'Yes, very well looked after,' I replied without looking at him.

He sighed before he remarked: 'They know about our history more than we know about it ourselves. We learn about their history, their civilization in admiration. Do they learn about ours in the same way?' His spoken words paused while he traced the diacritical marks to a letter, then he added: 'They keep it, study it, catalogue it . . . and in a way, own it. I admire their seriousness. They don't waste time!'

The silence was back. And I was wishing whoever was going to assist me would turn up soon.

'He won't be long,' said the old man as though he had heard my thoughts. In my embarrassment, the silence seemed heavier and the light of the rosary beads, a threat. The old man dipped his pen in the inkwell and continued to trace his letters. For a moment, it seemed as though he had been writing for eternity and that the manuscripts covering the walls were his work, not the work of calligraphers going back centuries.

'Are all these manuscripts from the Medieval period?' I asked in attempt to lighten the silence.

'What do you call the Medieval period?' he retorted, 'Medieval for the Muslim world is different from Medieval in the Christian world. The Muslim era did not start till the seventh century of the Christian era. Their seventh century is the first century for us.' He smiled and added: 'No wonder Christians and Muslims have difficulties under-standing each other – we're not even living in the same time! They misunderstand us and we misunderstand them. Prejudice is returned with prejudice. We all reap what we sow!'

I was contemplating my failure to lighten the silence, when, suddenly, I could hear someone's steps approaching. I felt a great relief.

'This is Ahmed,' said the old man, introducing the assistant who was to help me.

'Hello,' I said wholeheartedly, offering my hand. My enthusiasm gushed, welcoming his arrival and the start of a different experience in the Ben Youssef Library. A different experience, it certainly was.

'Hello,' said my hand.

'Hello,' it reiterated. 'Hello,' it insisted, reaching out. 'Hello,' it whispered, now lost in mid air. But a whisper or a scream, the voice of my hand was not to be heard. The assistant did not budge. He simply said with a stern and a dry tone: 'I don't do that!' It did not sound like: 'no, I don't shake hands with a woman.' It was more like 'no, I don't do drugs,' or 'no, I don't touch dirt.' In that short moment, my hand froze and died. The hand of a corpse it was, and I wished the earth would split and swallow me. There I stood, with my hand still extended. It would not act on my instruction to retrace its step. But, did I, in fact, have the presence of mind or the will to direct it? No, the freezing had gone to my mind too. And why did it feel so dramatically painful? A hand given but not taken. A cold moment of rejection making the woman in me feel exposed, naked, stripped of her dignity and pride.

That night in Marrakesh, it rained all night, I lay down listening to it, regular and rhythmic. I stayed awake till dawn, as though watching a moment of consciousness. There were times when I thought I had exaggerated the effect of the assistant's rejection. Yet, now, the moment comes back vivid, potently symbolic.

Suddenly, the sound of the washing machine filling with water becomes unbearable – I have the strange feeling that there could be an overflow which would submerge the house. In the eternity of that intense moment, when my given hand was not taken it died, and it seemed that its death would spread to the whole body. But in reality, the moment was cut short by the old man.

'Don't you know,' he said to the assistant, 'don't you know that it is said in the Qur'an '*wa itha huyyitum bi tahiyyatin, fa-hayyu bi-ahsani minha aw rudduha* (When a greeting is offered you, meet it with a greeting still more courteous, or (at least) of equal courtesy)?'

It was awkward. The verse from Surat An-Nisa (Women) sounded like a retribution. The young assistant said nothing. He retreated aside, not because he had realised that he had done something wrong, but simply out of respect for the old man. The look in his eyes transformed the camera zoom lens in my hand to a machine gun. In that moment of estrangement, I had the feeling that all of us wanted to leave the room. I certainly did not want to spend time with the assistant; but I was on a mission and I had to accomplish it. I had already been waiting for quite a while that morning and it was time to start if I were to make use of my two days in the Ben Youssef Library. It was unexpected but there I was, in an Arab Muslim country, feeling in the place of the other, the outsider, and I did not know how to get through. Something in me wanted, perhaps, to launch an attack, but there was no need, the old man had come to my defence. The assistant reached for a manuscript on the shelf with the intention of starting the work. But, to my surprise and his, the old man intervened again: 'I will deal with this myself,' he said, 'you're relieved of your duties for the day!' The assistant's ears turned red. He mumbled 'goodbye' in an apologetic tone and left.

The old man gathered his tools quietly and rearranged them in a box, during which time I regained my composure. He chose a manuscript and opened it gently. On the peach coloured paper, the confident sweeps of the letters in dark brown came below the line, round and graceful.

'This is thirteenth-century paper; it came from Shatiba in Spain but the manuscript was written in Morocco, here in Marrakesh.'

The old man's eyes shone with pride. But I could not respond to his enthusiasm. I was still feeling strange as a result of the assistant's attitude.

'How could I not read the signs?' I blamed myself.

'What signs?' said the old man, 'Are you supposed to guess his fanatical attitude just from looking at him?'

He got up and started gathering manuscripts relevant to my research. He held each manuscript as though he were in prayer. And not only the Qur'ans, all manuscripts without exception, including scientific manuscripts and poetry, as though the prayer was in the beauty of the line traced on the page. The old man opened the window so that I had enough light to take photographs. He was patient as I took time with extensive notes for my report. Every now and then, he made a comment as though talking to himself. The link between his comments was not particularly apparent.

'I feel that so many out there hate us simply for being Muslim. I don't think they even know what that is. And some of our own kind are busy distorting Islam into an ugly state.'

He reached to a folder and opened it to show me a single page with three beautifully calligraphed lines.

'You'll see many single pages here and there!

'Manuscripts scattered across the world, their pages separated, their spines broken, their voices lost.' He spoke about manuscripts as though he was speaking about close friends.

'These manuscripts you're looking at in different countries,' he added, 'many of them were once held in the same library, but are now dispersed around the world. And all the manuscripts that you will find are a tiny fragment of what there used to be. Once upon a time, the library of Cordoba housed two hundred and fifty thousand handwritten volumes. We are guilty. Both Muslim and non-Muslim dealers have been separating pages to sell them one page at a time for maximum profit. And hundreds of years ago, the Reconquista burnt our books.' What came to my mind after the old man's last comment was an Andalusian manuscript 'Hadith Bayad wa Riyad' or 'The Story of Bayad and Riyad', kept in the Vatican Library in Rome, a love story illustrated with elegant miniatures, with scenes set outdoors in the lavish gardens of al-Andalus – both architecture and other details link it undeniably to Muslim Spain or Morocco and its accomplished style suggests that a miniature school must have flourished in al-Andalus. Yet only one manuscript of this kind has survived; the others probably perished in the bonfires of the Reconquista.

We had been working for hours when I paused to ponder over the last page of a particularly beautiful manuscript. I was wondering whether the colophon included the signature of the calligrapher, as calligraphers hardly ever signed their name.

'Can you read it?' asked the old man astonished.

'Yes, I can.'

'Katabathu al-'yadd al-fania li-'abdihi . . . ' ('written by the perishable hand of the servant of God . . . '). The old man's face lit up.

'Bless you my daughter,' he said. His smile revealed a joy at my deciphering the thirteenth-century script. Somehow, he had not expected a 'modern'-looking woman who had lived in Europe for a long time to have the interest or the ability to read the old Arabic script. His eyes suddenly filled with kindness.

'I'm sorry about the young man,' he said, referring to the assistant.

I was disappointed when I did not find information about where exactly the manuscript was copied and by whom. In fact, I did not find the name of a calligrapher in any manuscript. The signature of the calligrapher was missing even in the most wonderful work. But the old man laughed at my disappointment.

'The calligrapher saw himself as a vehicle through whom a bigger passion was channelled. A whole vision and a cultural mentality are reflected in these manuscripts and these other objects that you call "Islamic art"! That's why the artist is often absent.'

He laughed again, this time with an edge of sarcasm.

'If you look at these objects simply as pretty objects, then, I tell you my dear, you can find prettier objects in the shops. When I say I admire these Westerners who research our past, catalogue it, gather information about, I mean it! What have we done about our past, our history in the Muslim world? And what are YOU doing with it? Becoming yet another scholar of Islamic art? How can you start to see or understand what's reflected in this so-called "Islamic art" if you're not interested at all in the source of that reflection? You'll never understand anything about these objects if you don't link them to the culture that produced them. Unless you're not interested in that culture!'

The silence around his speech heightened and he stopped. A moment later, he asked, 'Where are you going next?'

'Spain.' I said.

'You're crossing from one country to another,' he said. 'This was once upon a time simply the Muslim world. Morocco and Spain were culturally one. That's why it is difficult to differentiate between manuscripts produced in Morocco and those produced in Spain. No boundaries.'

He smiled unexpectedly. 'In any case, boundaries don't exist,' he added, 'we make them; they are our fences and we think they can keep us safe!'

'The link in your journey is the Andalusian era, looking at material which was at one time part of one reality. Your journey is a journey in time!'

The following day, the old man worked with me again, while the assistant watched our complicity with bewilderment. When, later on, the old man insisted I join him for a brown couscous in his sister's house nearby, the assistant was particularly taken aback.

The old man, his sister and I sat at a round table in an inner garden with running water. We ate in silence. Only the chirping of birds could be heard. We were surrounded by orange trees. It was as though the gardens in 'The story of Bayad and Riyad' had come to life.

'My sister cooked this couscous,' he said proudly as he watched me eat with a happy appetite. I had not eaten brown couscous since I was a child, when my grandmother used to cook it. So, the meal, cooked by the old man's sister, was responding to a bigger hunger than that of the stomach!

The silence of his smile seemed to recognise a nostalgia for my own culture. A warm look rested in his deep brown eyes. The afternoon sun was shining softly. And a sweetness emanated from the earth that had been quenched by the plentiful rain of the night before. We sipped our mint tea in serenity. The falling leaves seemed to cascade from the sky, like a blessing. The world out there seemed far away, but not for long. News from the radio inside the house, an update on Iraq's invasion of Kuwait, reached us in the garden.

'This is a time when one no longer knows who the enemy is,' said the old man. 'We have always thought that the enemy is the other but, in fact, the enemy is within the self.'

'The Iraqis invaded Kuwait and looted the Museum of Islamic Art,' he added, 'The al-Sabah collection with its extraordinary holdings is now in the hands of the Iraqis who will hide it in order to sell it for a fortune or destroy it for the sake of it. History meaning nothing. The past, essential for Humanity's story of continuum, gone. And we are helpless, not even worthy of our role as witness.'

There was a moment of inexplicable shame among us. The sun was leaving the horizon, the earth under our feet became mud.

'Your exhibition will mark a significant date,' he said in a neutral tone. 'It will celebrate the five hundredth anniversary of the discovery of America.'

'Without the Arabs in Spain,' he added, 'there would have been no Christopher Columbus and without Christopher Columbus, there would have been no America!'

I did not understand what he meant.

'What are you celebrating with this 1992 exhibition anyway? The Muslim dynasty was defeated in Granada in 1492; the departure of Abu Abdil, the last Muslim ruler, brought nearly eight hundred years of Muslim rule in Spain to an end. With Ferdinand and Isabella, the Reconquista was ruthless towards Muslims.

'Perhaps I would have liked to be a Muslim in the thirteenth or fourteenth century,' he said. 'Being a Muslim today is not the greatest of feelings. How to explain what it feels like being born, living and dying within a culture that is being oppressed? And the feeling, the certainty, perhaps, that this culture will not stand on its feet during my lifetime?

'If life is a game,' he added, 'it's much more fun to be winning the game than losing it! The problem, to be a winner, someone has to lose!'

He laughed and both his sister and I did not know whether to join in the laughter or not. It was not clear any more whether he was serious or joking.

'More tea?' suggested his sister before disappearing indoors.

'Promise me,' he said intently, as though profiting from his sister's departure and as though this was a special pact between him and me, 'promise me, that on the night of the opening of the exhibition, you will remember Abu Abdil leaving Spain, the night of his defeat.'

After our last glass of tea came the time to part, and when the old man extended his hand to say goodbye, it felt as though his hand was saying hello, returning the greeting that was offered to the young assistant and was never returned.

That second night in Marrakesh, it rained again. I had a remarkable dream. My hand extended in mid air, filled with water, emptied and filled, filled and emptied, until from the fertility of the palm sprang beautiful flowers of all colours which I presented to the old man. When the old man shook my hand, a drape covered my body, wrapping me inexplicably into a comforting *sitr* (a word which I find untranslatable, but it encompasses 'sanctuary' and 'blessing') which has never left me since. The dream was so real.

The opening of the exhibition took place in March 1992. The Generalife gardens of the Alhambra Palace were sumptuously lit with candlelight for the occasion and I did think of Abu Abdil, of the night he left Spain; I had the feeling that he was there among the guests, perhaps in a dark corner where he would not be visible. It was not difficult to feel his sorrow of loss and failure – I was already feeling it in relation to my personal life: it had already become clear by then that Mary Belle was right and it was a mistake to marry the man! And how idiotic it was to think, during my encounter with her, that in a dark night I wouldn't be able to see her. On a dark night, I wouldn't be able to see anyone, black or white!

Very recently, after so many years, I found myself in Marrakesh again and went to visit the Ben Youssef Library, only to find it shut. It was as though it never existed. I was told that the manuscripts had been moved to the capital to be housed in better conditions, which I was pleased to hear. But when I mentioned the old man, no one recognised who I was talking about.

'What was his name?' everyone asked.

'The guardian of manuscripts,' was all I could say.

Who was this absent man whose name I did not know? Was he a figment of my imagination? Why did he touch me so much? Perhaps the reason we are deeply touched by someone cannot always be explained. He was religious, yet there was in his personality a timelessness that encapsulated the old and the new, the traditional and the modern, the Eastern and Western. And it was perhaps no coincidence to find him in Morocco. Isn't the Maghreb, North Africa, the Western part of the Muslim world, a space of link and transmission? His questioning unsettled my perception of the art of the Islamic world and my approach to it as someone from a Muslim culture who has been schooled in the West and who is looking at something within from the outside. He raised many questions and I am still thinking about them today.

Twelve years later, I find myself in the Gulf, consultant for a new Museum of Islamic Art. The Americans are in Iraq. The holdings of the Iraqi museum have been looted, Babylon destroyed. The television screen is filled with atrocious images of dying civilians, casualties of precise bombing for democracy, broadcast by al-Jazeera close by. I feel that I am on the same journey, a journey in time, as the old man described it. The two days I spent working with the old man remain unforgettable. When I reflected on my own perception I realised that when I was made to feel an outsider, I saw him in a negative light and that I was not really able to understand him. He only gained my trust once he took a position with the assistant. Through the years, I have needed his hand to extend towards me, that hand which became for me the symbol of my culture's acceptance of a woman who crosses boundaries, embracing tradition and modernity, often standing on the bridge between cultures. On that sometimes lonely bridge, there have been a few remarkable meetings over the years, meetings with Muslims and non-Muslims.

As for the old man, perhaps he has forgotten about a Tunisian sent by the Americans to look at manuscripts, but then again perhaps he has not. My relationship with old manuscripts was shaped partly by his perception of them. As I leafed through manuscripts and manuscripts, watching the harmony of the page, the tracing of the lines, the fading of ink . . . I was introduced to a sublime space and I fell in love. I became aware of the name of the calligrapher absent. I was touched by the calligrapher who had not signed his work, the work to which he gave his entire life; the experience has left an indelible impact on me, enough to emerge years later in a work of fiction entitled 'The Blue Manuscript'. Somehow, the calligrapher of a manuscript I saw in Dar al-Kutub in Cairo was the same as the calligrapher of a manuscript I saw in Madrasa Ben Youssef in Marrakesh, one written in the thirteenth century, the other in the sixteenth. As he gave the best of himself, with his self-effacing, the calligrapher was all calligraphers. The man who gave of himself, while remaining absent, was, in fact all men. The absent calligrapher, the absent guardian, and my absent father became all one and the same.

Now, when I pick up these thoughts to edit them, by some kind of coincidence, the washing machine is drumming away in the background – it is the weekend again! And for a moment, it seems that the washing machine's cyclical turning never came to an end. But this is of course a different wash and another cycle.

A few weeks have already passed and the bougainvillaea has already bloomed, its flowers a beautiful ruby colour. The garden has returned Hilal's love.

Mehmet

MARY CLOW

MEHMET WAS SLIGHT AND NEAT, dark of course. His eyes never met mine in all the weeks we worked together, and when I took papers into his office he always stood up, but stared down. Like himself, his room was neat and dark. It must have been originally some kind of domestic space – a pantry, perhaps? The film company had taken over an empty villa – an Anatolian Alpine chalet, two storeys, a red-tiled, pitched roof with gables, verandahs, and extensive servants' quarters designed for laundry or cooking, now bereft of equipment, hard to define. Someone said it had been the former Vietnamese Embassy, before the Vietnam War, and could not be torn down due to ownership disputes. This made sense as it was surrounded by open ground – a wasteland, odd in the centre of Ankara, within sight of the main hotel where the production unit lived. Some early mornings as I picked my way across the rough grass, the camels of nomads, overnighting, would pull themselves up, groaning and spitting, as I scuttled for safety into the office. It beat dodging taxis in W1.

The production had expanded into every nook and cranny of the villa, in the manner of film companies who commandeer property with the ruthlessness of soldiers at war. Our wardrobe department in the semi-basement below 'broke down' costumes in great tubs of water and chemicals. Masters of arcane arts, they knew how to age a textile by a century in an afternoon. They worked under enormous stress, often all night, patching, stitching and refurbishing uniforms wrecked on that day's battlefield, good enough to fight again, as army surgeons might do in real war. The office staff worked above, tucked into bow windows, or at trestle tables spread between double-doored reception rooms where Vietnamese bureaucrats had once gossiped and sipped tea. The Turkish caretaker, who must have made that tea, still worked in the villa as guard and cleaner: he came with the building. It took me a long time to understand that his extended, multi-generational family – wife, grannies, children – lived there also, invisibly integrating with us, like mice in a nursery tale. If I left my desk I would come back to Turkish coffee, a tiny cup amidst the scattered papers. If I was off for the day, the desk would be dotted with offerings, black, sweet, congealed.

In what had been the formal entrance lobby of the villa, our hideous Gestetner copier roared and thrashed out script changes and call sheets for the next day's shoot. A perpetually exhausted Third Assistant Director wrestled frantically with its inky guts and sulky tendency to seize up after one of the frequent Ankara power cuts. When I first joined Tony Richardson's Woodfall Films three years before in London, that had been my job, and now every day I gave silent thanks that I worked as Personal Assistant to the Producer.

The film was set in the Crimean War, a peculiar historical aberration in which England and France (ancient enemies) joined Turkey to attack Russia. The *causus belli* was a punch-up between Orthodox monks at the Holy Places in Jerusalem – that is, between Russians (subjects of the Tsar), and Greeks (subjects of the Sultan) – a dispute which little affected nations who now would go to war and lose brave sons in deluded conflict. The parallel with the Vietnam War, which raged at this time, was apposite: the difficulty was to make that point clear.

The Charge of the Light Brigade could not be made in the Crimea, certainly not near Sebastopol, Russia's major warm-water naval base. For the actual charge, the script historically asked for six hundred horses trained to ride in formation, for a cavalry attack. Furthermore, filming great costume battles needed space controllable for sequences that might take all day to set up with only one chance to shoot. And we required men, thousands of them, disciplined, cheap. The Turks had the last great horde of trained mounted cavalry in the entire world and, besides, were prepared to rent four thousand troops from their regular army: it was an offer we could not refuse.

Up and down three flights of Mayfair stairs where tubercular housemaids had once coughed out their lungs in a nineteenth-century firetrap – our offices – Woodfall went into pre-production. Blow-ups of Roger Fenton's Crimean photographs hung over my desk and I signed up for language lessons at the Turkish consulate.

'Honey,' said my boss, the Producer, 'take care of Colonel Günes.' Günes means sunshine, my elementary Turkish lessons taught me that. The Colonel of Turkey's elite cavalry hit London for the weekend like a coiled spring. I collected a wad of cash from the office accountant, who as always griped as if it came from his own pocket. I found Jan, Tony Richardson's Polish driver, who regarded the notes as his own from now on. Office myth had it that Jan had been won in a poker game. Built like a goblin, he had two teeth – no more – and the same number of hairs on his head. He drove the company Mercedes like a Valkyrie, and was equally comprehensible. 'Jan – take him wherever he wants to go – don't lose him, he doesn't speak English. Pay for whatever he asks, on Monday put him on the plane, and give me an accounting.' Jan excelled at this kind of duty.

On Monday I was handed a grubby paper, much worked over and pocketed. The accountant yelped with an anger that was personal (he hated Jan). 'I can't put this through the books!' I ran my eye down the list – drinks, dinner, show-tickets, drinks – to the last item, the largest by far: GIRLS. Back to the typewriter, we rephrased the accounting to read: entertaining expenses. The accountant growled, but put it through the books.

Then Jan produced another list, items the Colonel wanted taken out to him in Ankara. I went off to Simpson's Men's Shop on Piccadilly, and rather pink-faced ordered fifty pairs of Y-fronts with athletic supports. The Colonel was smartening up his cavalry.

Lord Cardigan, commander of the Light Brigade, was said to pay his own tailor to make his famous 'cherry-pickers' britches, so that they stretched tight over his regiment's bums in the saddles. At that time I knew an old lady who had known an old lady – the second Lady Cardigan – who in Edwardian widowhood lay on a sofa, smoking cigars, wearing the last pair of his Lordship's cherry-picker trousers.

We flew to Ankara to make the film and my luggage full of men's underwear was waved through Customs, and delivered to Colonel Günes. For two months the shoot continued, through July and August, on the burning plain around Ankara where we had installed the dressings of the freezing Crimea with faked forts and cannon – which the contemporary villagers often stole in the night. It was gruelling work – strong men frequently collapsed from sunstroke or dysentery – but being on the set was an escape for me from the chalet and the stuttering Gestetner, the unreliable electricity, a desk covered with old, cold coffee, and the grim thwacking from below of instant ageing.

One evening at the office I took some papers to Mehmet. The Production Manager, Tariq, was with him, and for once I saw Mehmet's eyes blazing, his cheeks flaming and a wild exultant look on his face. I backed away to my own desk, wondering what could have been said to arouse such a gentle man: it was disturbing to see him distressed. Tariq was quite a different sort who kept whiskey in his filing cabinet and tried to get me to drink with him if no one else was around. I never accepted and avoided him whenever possible. He stopped in my doorway now, his expression coarse and suggestive.

'Don' let that boy look fool you,' he said, unpleasantly, 'wife just 'ave 'nother bebby. Now THREE son!' and he gestured obscenely as he passed.

I was in my mid twenties and I guessed Mehmet was about the same age. Although we had no common language or even eye contact between us, I felt an affinity with him, and sympathy for his tiny children whom he must rarely see, working the insane hours of film production as we all did. Thinking this, I returned to his office with the receipts.

After long days in the 'Crimea' where men dropped like flies, I was not amazed to find him down beside his desk, on the tiled floor. Mehmet was kneeling, crouched over, murmuring quietly. His dark hair was immaculate as always and the soles of his socked feet pointed towards me. At that moment I heard a call from a distant mosque. The Turkish bookkeeper – husband, young father, Muslim – Mehmet was saying his sunset prayers. All the tension, intensity, exhaustion of film making was stilled for a minute as I stood, afraid to disturb the skinny figure who whispered into the darkness his certainty that there is one God and Muhammad is His Prophet.

The Embroiderer of Azemmour

SHEILA PAINE

FATNA HAD NEVER actually seen a dragon, nor indeed a griffin. They were creatures not indigenous to the Moroccan coast, so that she had no idea what the patterns she worked represented. She sat with other little girls in flowery frocks, perched on low stools in front of their embroidery teacher, piercing the linen cloth with her needle, twisting the red silk into rows of long-armed cross-stitch that filled the background and left the animals as blank spaces. She was dimly aware that these exotic white shapes came from somewhere outside her own confined world, but it was only much later that she felt the mesh of rigid stitchery that defined them hedged her own life too. Her embroidery was known as Assist work, but for Fatna it belonged to her home town of Azemmour and was her heritage and fate.

To reach the house of her teacher, the *ma'allema*, Fatna put on a headscarf, ran down the steep staircase of her home and out into the small square just inside the Bab Kasbah. This arched gateway led from the new French part of town into the old port, through stone walls topped by castellations and pierced by two mean windows that spoke of defence, irrelevant to the shad fishing that became Azemmour's main trade. When the walls were built by the Portuguese in the early sixteenth century they were to fortify a small conquered town trading in cereals and horses. And also in fabrics, which is perhaps how Fatna's Renaissance patterns reached Azemmour.

Still in that small square were weavers' workshops hung with scarves that few could buy, each a tight room brimming with looms, men and the din of shuttles. Fatna's path to her teacher's house took her through the square across rough earth spiked with stones, down past the small white mosque, its rickety facade topped by plaster merlons, to the back of the town where a trickling fountain set against the old ramparts served as a wash-house. The flaking walls, the unsold scarves, the idle men and boys, bespoke the isolation of a port where ships no longer called. Not that ships had ever jostled masts in the tiny walled harbour, as in other ports of European conquest – the Portuguese stayed only thirty years. But in that time they built a fort, an armoury, a powder magazine, bastions defended to seaward by glowering cannons, and ramparts that encircled the town on its spit lying between the estuary of the Oum er Rbia river and the Atlantic. As a child Fatna had loved running along those ramparts. They were unsure walls enclosing gardens of henna, simple squares of whitewashed houses, pomegranate and olive trees, sunning cats and lines of laundry. At intervals they disappeared completely where they had collapsed into a slithering cascade of ill-set stones and rootless weeds, leaving gaps too wide for Fatna to jump across.

Under the colonization of the French she had been allowed to go to school, where she had been taught only French and embroidery. The origins of both were unknown to her and brought a stirring of territories beyond her own boundaries, which were tighter even than the walls, the sea and the river. She never left Azemmour, never stepped onto the bridge and looked back at the white spine of its reflection in the river, or understood that beyond the bridge were roads and, further still, a railway line that could have taken her to Casablanca, to Marrakesh.

Her French lessons, compelling her to describe a *visite au marché*, shared nothing with the little old man who sat outside the Bab Kasbah with a few oranges and bananas as his sole livelihood. *Une journée au musée*, had she benefited from a more comprehensive education, would simply have entailed a description of the town she lived in. But Fatna's horizons were entwined with red thread and scraped with a needle.

For her embroidery lessons, the French had been obliged to use local women as teachers and therefore continued the local tradition. In the case of Azemmour, this had been the work of the Jewish women of the town, and was part of the extraordinarily rigid structure of Moroccan needlework. Brought to only six towns by Andalucian refugees from the southward advance of Christianity, the embroideries of Tetouan were mirror cloths, hung opposite the marital bed for forty days to keep away evil spirits; in Chefchaouen intricate covers for dowry chests; in Rabat curtains that concealed the women's living quarters from the outside world, embellished with flower petals in floss silk, while within hailing distance of Rabat across the Bou Regreb river, women of the pirate stronghold of Sale worked architectural motifs in chunky stitchery. In Meknes they covered scarves with scattered flowers; in Fez cushion covers were thickly embroidered with strict borders. Tangier, Casablanca, even Marrakesh – which is a Berber town and therefore the home of weavers not embroiderers – have no such tradition. Then there was Azemmour, out on a limb with its style shared with Assisi, Sicily, Avila in Spain, and Parga – an ancient Venetian port on the coast of Greece. Fatna's father had thought it important for her to learn, indeed to have extra lessons with the *ma'allema* though his small grocery shop hardly met the modest expense, as it would assure a marriage.

As soon as Fatna was fourteen, her school lessons and carefree running long since at an end, a husband was presented to her, known to her father from the mosque, but not to her. Her embroideries as a dowry lowered the marriage price he should pay. Had she not had those serviettes, towels, tablecloths to account for her childhood, she would have been chided with 'who does nothing at home?' All she could bring to the nuptial bed was a smidgeon of French and, above all, sophistication in DMC threads: reds 814, 815, 816 for the solid background, then for outlining black 310 and green 890, 895, never any other colours, nothing more.

By the time I met Fatna, her husband had died, being of course very much older than her, her waist had thickened and she had a succession of daughters. Her home was still in the square inside the town walls near the Bab Kasbah, a few balconied rooms from where she overlooked the apathy of the unemployed and the deprivation of a town that had missed out. The French had long departed. Tourism, as the main source of revenue in Morocco, had not touched Azemmour, by the 1980s washed up into poverty, but Fatna was still embroidering. With new zeal she had moved into teaching her skills to the local young women and her own daughters, all increasingly dressed in shirts and trousers of jazzy design, supposedly Western. It seemed a hopeless task.

Some years later I returned to Azemmour to look for her again. Through the Bab Kasbah into the narrow streets of the town. A sharp left turn where the next stall still had homemade bread, but now also hairgrips, soap and gaudy plastic toys from China. Down past the workshop of weavers on the left, still there, past the little mosque and on to the fountain, unfrequented now that most homes had water. The end, really, of the road. But then a young woman, Kenza, was brought to me. Her mother, Fatna had died of cancer in her early fifties. She took me to her home.

In almost all Moroccan towns, the French, under the instruction of General Lyautey, refrained from destroying the labyrinth of cool tangled passages designed to confuse invaders, and from swamping them under colonial boulevards of Haussmann inspiration, but built their *villes nouvelles* alongside the existing towns, leaving these intact. Azemmour had merited only a main square outside the Bab Kasbah, named by the French the Place du Souk, and a miserably wide avenue, the Avenue Mohammed V, that merely led outside the town again. Just off this avenue, down a narrow alleyway only a few yards long, between the Cafe Marco and a greengrocers, is Kenza's home – two rooms abutting the street, a doorway leading directly into them, and something of an unseen pattern of further rooms, full of people.

Sisters, cousins, aunts and Kenza herself continue Fatna's embroidery, knowing it is time to jettison Renaissance creatures on tablemats and to think about the road out of town to the tourist shops. But how to persuade foreigners buying yellow baboushes, rugs and tagines to choose embroideries instead, has defeated Kenza and she still hasn't crossed the bridge to Marrakesh.

Dressed in an embroidered jellaba that holds in its stitching the Mediterranean world, Kenza is a replica of her mother. She will try again with the only thing she knows. As nobody wants tablemats, she is making velvet gowns with collars, cuffs and belts embroidered in classic Azemmour style, but not with dragons and griffins. With rabbits. And in bright blue: DMC 796.

Ali Bulent

ANGELA CULME-SEYMOUR

M Y SON-IN-LAW Colin Crewe had just opened a jewellery shop in Brompton Arcade, with Annabel Jones. It was called Jones and it is still going, in Beauchamp Place. At that time, in the autumn of 1968, they were looking for somebody to work there, someone presentable and who knew about jewels, and could speak a few languages. Annabel said that she thought her father, Timothy Jones, might know of somebody, and soon he produced a Turkish gentleman whom he had known in Paris. He knew about jewels since his childhood when he had loved to play with them at his grandmother's knees and later, when he was married to Faiza, one of the beautiful sisters of King Farouk, and they had often chosen and bought her jewels together, hundreds and hundreds of them. Now he was in London with neither job nor money, since Nasser had grabbed all his wealth and property in Egypt. He and Faiza were divorced. 'He's a charming old boy,' Colin said, after they had seen and engaged him. 'You must meet him.' His name was Mehmet Ali Bulent Rauf.

I met him on Friday, November 29 during a weekend at Berghane in Cambridgeshire. I hadn't really wanted to go. It was very cold and I would have to return on the Sunday because it was Katie's christening. But when I arrived Sally had put the heating up, as she always did when I came, though Colin would turn it down again later, and the house was warm and I felt happy to see Sally. Colin and the 'charming old boy' were not yet there, and Sally and I went into the big country kitchen and started to prepare chicken, and drink wine.

Then we heard a car outside and Sally said, 'There they are, Gran,' and a minute later this big man, wearing a rather dreary beige sort of overcoat made of Burberry stuff, and leaning on two sticks, came down the steps into the kitchen. Colin introduced us. He kissed my hand, and I had a look at him. He was tall, about six foot one or two, and with a bombé chest, quite thick around the waist and with long legs, which he often told me later on had been much admired at some ball in Paris when he was dressed up as King Louis Quatorze. Colin took him away to the drawing-room with a drink, and left alone in the kitchen Sally said, 'You must go and talk to him Gran, really you must.' 'But what about you? I'd much rather stay here with you,' I said, but in the end I went, and there he was sitting by a roaring wood fire drinking whiskey and smoking. He had discarded the dreary coat and was wearing a dark blue suit; I looked at his face more carefully. He had a high forehead with curly grey hair combed back and a bit to one side, a moustache, deep greeny brown eyes with quite dark, heavy shadows underneath, and a sort of twice-doubled chin which ended in his neck, though not at all a runaway chin. He talked almost perfect English and had great charm, and if I have made his appearance sound unattractive it did not seem so, or to matter. He was unlike any other man I had ever met.

He had been a friend of Eddie Gathorne-Hardy, Anne's brother, who was in Egypt when he was living there, and one of the first things Ali told me was how Eddie had said to him, 'Well, I've given up sex, my dear, it makes life so much less complicated.' 'Very good advice,' Ali said. 'No more sex, no more entanglements or getting attached – all that is over for me,' he continued. 'Oh well, yes, I suppose it's best,' I said. It was almost as if he wanted to make that quite clear, and afterwards he told me that the weekend before, he had stayed with Lees and Mary Mayall, whom I had known in Paris. When they heard he was to meet me they said to him, 'You be careful, you'll fall for her.' But he had been determined not to.

Ali was born in Constantinople (as it then was) in 1911, still in the days of the once-great Turkish Empire. His father was an army officer who had been educated in France at the École Militaire, St Cyr. On his mother's side he was related to the Khedive Ismail who had ruled Egypt from 1863 to 1879, whose own grandfather was the then famous Khedive Mehmet Ali Pasha. Faiza's grandfather and Ali's grandmother were brother and sister. This lady, one of Ismail's daughters, was said to be one of the richest women in Egypt, owning ninety thousand *fedehs* of land, for each of which she had a piece of solid gold each year. When she was in Turkey she lived in Emirgan on the northern shore of the Bosphorus, and as a boy Ali was often rowed across to visit her and play with her fabulous collection of jewels. He told me many stories about her.

We all went to bed early that night. Ali had had an operation on his hip only four months before; but quite soon he was using only one stick, and he kept it for the rest of his life. The next morning it started to snow and I was afraid it would be too deep for me to get to the station and down to the christening the next day, so I rang up a weather centre and they said it would not last. 'I shan't have to go today, after all,' I announced. 'I can stay until Sunday.' 'Oh, thank God,' Ali said. 'Now I know you're not going away I can relax,' and he smiled and looked happy. I was pleased, though I soon found that he often paid fulsome compliments, sometimes just to cheer people up.

That evening, the Saturday, David Grosse came to stay and after dinner he and Sally and Ali and I played scrabble until two in the morning. Afterwards Ali used to tell people that it was over a game of scrabble that I had won him.

A month or two later Colin rang me up one day when I was in the Stanhope Gardens flat. 'I have something to ask you, I don't think you'll mind. The thing is . . .' The thing was that Ali needed a room, there was still a spare one in our flat – I wouldn't mind, would I? Of course I wouldn't; and the next day Ali moved into the room next to me, in fact in bed at night our heads must have been less than a foot apart, with just the wall between us on which quite soon we were tapping goodnights to each other. He knew a lot of people in London and often went out to dinners and dancing, in spite of his broken hip, and he loved to kiss beautiful girls. It was not surprising that Ali was sought after and a success with so many people. He had an unusual and distinguished appearance, great charisma and he could talk well and knowledgeably about almost any subject you could think of; he was funny without being that sort of professional 'amusing man'; he had a formidable memory and could tell stories of his childhood days in the family house above the Bosphorus, and visiting his grandmother (the one with all the jewels), the richest woman in Egypt, and his life with Faiza.

One evening I went with Ali to a party given by a rich Greek called Niko Goulandris. We started off with a very potent vodka, and that evening we danced, hugged, kissed, and got drunk, and from then on we seemed to be together – regarded as a couple – nearly all the time. We never became lovers, then nor later, not physically I mean. I remember that Ali did look extraordinary that night at Goulandris's party. We were meant to be dressed as gypsies. Ali's hair was parted in the middle and left to hang down in wild grey curls, and he was wearing an open-necked shirt of purple, a scarlet necktie, and a sort of orange cummerbund that I had made out of the remains of some curtains. The length he first gave me to sew was at least two feet too short to go round his middle. 'You mean to say I am bigger than this?' he said, holding up the cloth. 'Your waist measurement is nearly sixty inches,' I told him. 'Dear me,' he said, 'I suppose I must eat less.' But of course he didn't. He loved good food and was a superb cook.

One day I said to him, 'You don't believe in God and that sort of thing, do you?' and to my surprise he answered, 'I'm a very religious man.' He said, 'Where do you think you come from?' 'From my mother and father, I suppose.' 'What about your soul?' 'Oh, I shouldn't think I've got a soul,' I said. 'Of course you have,' Ali said, 'a very big one.' He never sat down and explained or taught me all that he believed; some of it seeped through to me during the years we were together. Occasionally he did explain something I had heard him say to others, or I had read or come across when translating one or another of the books concerned with his beliefs. I think all I did learn was intuitively rather than intellectually since I am the least intellectual person I know. Ali's way was the way of the sufi, with his own thoughts, feelings, ideas, understanding, his own mysticism on top as it were, and I shall not write about that side of him specifically.

Meanwhile the time for me to go to Greece – April 23 – was drawing nearer. I had arranged months before to travel by ship from London to Athens, but now that we were almost there I only half wanted to leave. I hated to be away from Ali for so long. But we said we would meet in Istanbul on my birthday, August 3, and we would stay there together for all of his month's holiday.

He gave me lunch before going to Waterloo to catch the boat-train but he was silent and depressed and only ate a little smoked salmon. As the train pulled out we waved and tried to smile at each other and I think we both wished I wasn't going. When I found my cabin on the ship there was a huge hamper of fruit and a great heap of flowers from him. After I had left he went to Yorkshire for the weekend, but on the way he had his suitcase stolen, in which was his much loved Qur'an, a suede waistcoat from Hermes in Paris (a relic from his rich days), and a new pair of pyjamas from M&S which I had given him.

From the ship I wrote all the time, posting my letters at Marseilles, Genoa, and Naples, where there was one from him, rather impersonal, which I realised afterwards may have had something to do with the Turkish language; in Ali's young day it was considered *mal élevé* to use the word 'Ben' (I) too much. So in that first letter he wrote, 'Your departure would have been too painful if it was not for the fact that your presence remains so clearly in the memory . . . ' not even 'my' memory.

He was a bad correspondent. At Athens I stayed for several weeks in Peter Mayne's flat in Pangrati, where I slept on the terrace and could wake up in the mornings and look straight across at the Parthenon, and I remember doing a drawing with the Parthenon in the background and some plumbago growing in a pot on the terrace. I used to wait up there for the postman to bring me Ali's letters; they seldom came.

By the middle of July I thought I should go towards Turkey, and I went to an island called Thassos, calling in every day at the *poste restante* to see if there was a letter from Ali confirming that he would be in Istanbul on August 3. But every day the sulky man signed with his head that there was nothing. (Two months later, back in England, several letters from Ali arrived in a dirty package, sent on from Thassos PTT. I should have been more demanding with that dreary creature.) I left Thassos and went to Alexandroupolis and sent Ali telegrams, but no answer came.

Well, I thought, at least he would know where I was staying. I had told him before I left England. If he was in Istanbul he would find me. So one Monday evening I boarded the train and we rattled away through the night towards Turkey. About midnight we arrived at the frontier. Now there were new sounds, new words in a language I didn't know; up and down the platform boys were calling 'Çay! Çay! Çay!' and 'Karpuz! Kapuz!' and there were trays of something that looked like milk but turned out to be *ayran*, made from yoghurt and water, and there were *simit* – little circles of hard bread with sesame seeds sprinkled on top; even water was being sold. A policeman got into my carriage and bought me some tea. He was sweating and fanning himself with some newspaper, and presently he undid the top buttons of his uniform, leant back and fell asleep. Sometime in the early hours the train trundled forward again and I too slept, and when I woke up the policeman had gone, and we were very slowly approaching what I thought must be the outskirts of Istanbul.

It was half past five in the morning. There were the tops of some minarets, then a lot of dull, dirty buildings, another minaret – and then we pulled slowly into Sirkeci Station.

I found a very old, brown taxi and gave him the address of the hotel. Then, for the first time in my life, I crossed the Galata Bridge, looked back and saw the six proud minarets of the great Sultan Ahmet mosque, the Haghia Sofia, Süleyman the Magnificent, and closer, the Yeni Cami whose steps were covered by strutting pigeons. All these names I did not know, of course; Ali was to teach me them and many more, and often test me on them. I saw the Golden Horn and the steamers leaving the Bosphorus for the Sea of Marmara and the Princes' Islands, and the ferries hooting impatiently at stray fishing-boats as they made their way up and down the sea from the Asian shores to the European side, back and forth. But before I had time to take it all in we were rushing up steep streets, screeching round corners, until eventually we stopped under a hanging sign saying 'Büyük Londra Oteli'.

I paid the taxi all the money he asked for, knowing it was too much, and went into the hall where a sleepy clerk rose to his feet behind the reception desk. No, they were not full up, and no, there were not any messages for me. I went upstairs, and found a small room which looked over the gardens of the British Consulate, cool green lawns under tall trees with pigeons cooing. I lay down on the narrow bed and at once fell asleep. When I awoke three hours later, I went downstairs – still no messages – and had a small glass of tea, and then found my way out into the busy street. Peasant women were still wearing 'şalvas' – baggy, brightly coloured trousers – in those days. Later they took to ugly dun-coloured coats down to their ankles, and greenish or brown headscarves. In 1968 the scarves were all, like the trousers, patterned in brilliant colours.

I tried to decipher the writing of advertisements on the walls from Lesson One in *Teach Yourself Turkish*. People looked at me without smiling. The smiles would come later Peter had told me, and then I would find the Turks the most hospitable people on earth. At the end of the street on the corner of the Balik Pazar I went into a button shop, really nothing but hundreds and hundreds of buttons. The owner was Greek, and he told me I should be careful going about the streets of Turkey, a woman all alone, it was dangerous, the Turks weren't friendly like the Greeks. He himself would escort me, later on, that evening, he said. Yes? Well, no thank you, I thought. 'My husband will be here by then,' I told him, and then I went back to the hotel before I got lost.

By now there was a different person at the reception, and he handed me a bit of paper with a telephone number on it, telling me that a gentleman had called the day before. 'He expected you yesterday, not today,' he said reproachfully. 'Well, anyway, could we call this number now?' He looked sad and said that unfortunately it had rained so much in the night that now the lines were down. We would have to try later on. How much later? Well, who was to know? God willing, that very morning.

I went back to my room and sat on the windowsill, looking down at the gardens. The hours passed slowly. Perhaps Ali would just come, if he knew the telephone lines were down. But by lunchtime they were working and there, miraculously, was his voice. He would fetch me at three o'clock, so I went into the hotel restaurant and ate a leathery omelette and a good salad, followed by a tiny cup of Turkish coffee. Then I went and sat near the window in a small, seemingly unused, dusty salon. I watched the people in the street, the taxis tearing along, the overcrowded buses, the vendors of cucumbers, watermelons, tomatoes, and figs, and pushcarts loaded with selections of haberdashery, safety-pins, thread, scissors, ribbons, elastic, looking-glasses, and suddenly there was a voice behind me 'Ah! at last!' and Ali stood in the doorway in his dark blue suit looking very large, and beside him, his cousin, in whose house we were to stay, a tiny woman with short white hair, full lips, and eyes as dark and gleaming as two black olives.

Outside the hotel another big and very old taxi was waiting, so I fetched my case and we got in, Ali in front and the cousin and I in the back. We were going to see the cousin's sister-in-law, Nesrin. She turned out to be a small very thin lady with a certain French elegance; later on, alone together, Ali and I called her 'Cat Face' partly because she adored cats and also because she looked rather like one – almond-shaped green, cat-like eyes, wide cheekbones. She had beautiful slender hands. She was married to the cousin's brother.

Then we drove along the shores of the Golden Horn, noisy, dusty streets where we constantly had to jam on the brakes and sound the horn. There were horses and carts, and men bent almost double with sort of saddles on their backs, enabling them to carry enormous loads, and making it impossible to turn their heads to see oncoming traffic. Boys, bicycles, half-starved dogs and cats weaved in and out of our way; watermelons, piled high on carts, sometimes fell off and rolled under our wheels. Now and then Ali would point up a narrow side street and say, 'Look – up there – that little mosque at the top – built for Sultan X – in the eighteenth century,' or, 'Look quick – up there,' and halfway up the wall of some half-ruined house would be a tiny sort of miniature stone chalet sticking out on its own – a bird house. Or there would be a carving or a very old 'cumba' almost touching the houses opposite. Ali was an extraordinary guide, he seemed to know every corner, every stone of Istanbul.

Finally we reached the tomb and surrounding mosque of Eyup Sultan, standard bearer to the Prophet Muhammad. The tomb stood behind a green iron grill and was surrounded by headscarved women and men standing with their heads bowed and their hands in front of them, palms facing upwards as if in supplication. Ali prayed like that for a minute or two, then passed his hands over his face and turned away.

We drove back to Eminönü, to the quayside where men were frying fish in swaying little boats; the cousin disappeared, and Ali and I were at last alone together on the ferry to Beylerbeyi.

As we crossed the mouth of the Bosphorus, where its waters ran into the Sea of Marmara, Ali pointed out to me a line of trees near the top of a hill rising in the distance, behind the town of Üsküdar, which we were now approaching. 'You see where those trees stop?' he said, 'up there, up there – a small white square? That is my brother's house.' 'Your brother!' I had forgotten Ali had a brother. 'Is he like you?' 'Not at all,' Ali said and laughed, 'but you will soon see. They will all be there to meet you.' The ferry stopped first at Üsküdar, then Küzgüncük and then Ali said, 'See? That square pink house by the water – that's where we're going to be.' I saw for the first time the house which I was to get to know so well, and the room which would be mine, only a metre or two from the sea, behind tall grey shutters. We passed it silently, the engines already cut as we approached the quay.

We disembarked and walked along a narrow street, past the dentist, the tiny shop where they grilled kebabs, a big store that sold rolls of material and was run by a man we called 'The Ox', and then through a wooden door in a high stone wall, and into a big, dark, cool garden. There were earth paths overgrown with weeds, running between low box hedges, steps which seemed always to be wet and slippery, and some tall trees near the water's edge. One of them had half blown down in the previous night's storm.

We went indoors; nobody seemed to be about. Ali showed me my room, one big bed up against the window, and the waters of the Bosphorus slapping against the stones just outside. 'It's very small,' Ali said. 'Will you be alright?' 'God, it's the best room I've had all summer,' I told him. 'The best room I've had in my life, I should think.' The bathroom was next door. Just then the bath was full of clothes but the taps worked, cold water came rushing out of them, which was just as well because you needed buckets of it to throw down the lavatory. When I had washed and unpacked my things I went through a room that seemed to be a dining-room and out onto a terrace close to the water, and warmed by the setting sun, and there was Ali with Mahmoud, his brother.

Immediately he saw me he rose and bowed deeply over my hand and spoke in beautiful English. No, he was not like Ali at all. For a start he was extremely thin. He wore rather baggy grey flannel trousers, a white shirt, and a green silk scarf tucked in at the neck, Noël Coward style. His clothes looked like old, once-good English. He had smooth white hair brushed back, and a large moustache, whiter than Ali's, and brown deep-set eyes in a thin face. He offered me tea – 'Or a drink?' he suggested. 'Yes, I'm sure you'd like a drink, no?' Ali frowned and said something in Turkish, and Mahmoud laughed scoffingly, made a movement of impatience and muttered something like 'ridiculous' or 'what nonsense'. 'We're going to have drinks upstairs in the grand salon in a minute,' Ali explained. 'Münevver – cousin – doesn't like to have drinking going on in the downstairs rooms.' 'Good heavens, why not?' I asked tactlessly. 'She's a Mevlevi Dervish,' said Ali in a voice that indicated that was enough.

But Mahmoud snorted again, 'Mevlevi Dervish! *Tu sais, mon cher, depuis qu'elle est allée à Mecca, elle est devenue Haci, elle se croit sainte, eh?*' and he roared with laughter. '*Elle se croit sainte, eh?* – Thinks she's a saint!' Ali looked cross, and again said something in Turkish that sounded disapproving. Then he sat down and lit a cigarette. I went to the edge of the terrace and looked at the green, fast-running water. There were large jellyfish floating down, and a lot of rubbish, watermelon skin, swollen tomatoes, old newspapers, dead fish, a dead cat, all drifting towards the Sea of Marmara.

A young woman appeared carrying a boy of about one year old. She had a round smiling face, pink cheeks and bright brown eyes. She turned out to be the cousin's companion, help, cook. Her husband Hassan had been Müevver's chauffeur-gardener for many years, when he decided to get married: would Hacani find him a bride? So the cousin found Fatma, a girl from Georgia, brought up by foster parents in a mountain village. She was only sixteen when she married Hassan, who had a kind, strong face and as well as gardening and doing odd jobs, drove a *dolmus* between Çengelköy and Üsküdar. Fatma loved gaiety, make-up, dancing, going to the cinema and being modern, like going about without a scarf over her head. Hassan disapproved of all these things, but she worked on him gradually and in the end got all she wanted.

A ferry announced its departure from the nearby quay with a loud, insistent hoot, and a swirl of water round its bows as it started off downstream for Istanbul. 'Sixty-six! It's Sixty-six!' cried Ali as it passed quite close in front of us. 'Sixty-six? Of course it isn't,' said Mahmoud, who always disagreed with everything Ali said. 'It can't be!' 'Of course it is,' Ali insisted. 'Look!' 'It must be rebuilt then, it must be.' 'How, rebuilt?' said Ali. 'It's the original one! It's English,' he explained to me. 'It arrived soon after the First World War, brand new. We all used to rush about and say I'm Sixty-six! I'm Sixty-six! It seemed very modern and fast then. Well, there it still is!' 'Still going strong,' Mahmoud now agreed. 'Born 1820, still going! Johnnie Walker!' and he roared with laughter again.

The cousin came back and retired to her room and Ali and Mahmoud and I went upstairs to the 'grand salon' which ran from the back of the house, overlooking the dripping green garden, to the front, directly over the sea. Long grey shutters were permanently half-closed, so all the lamps were lighted. There was a grand piano with photographs in silver frames on it, many of Ali's ex-wife Faiza, looking beautiful and elegant, a grandfather clock, several antique and uncomfortable chairs and ottomans, upholstered in cream and crimson brocade, and on the walls pictures of sultans on horseback, and many writings in the old Ottoman script, in gold or black.

Nesrin was there making tiny *börek* (little triangles of very thin pastry called 'yufka' filled with white cheese or sometimes mincemeat and dill, and fried) to go with the drinks, and there were black olives, slices of cucumber, honey melon, and little squares of some sort of hard cheese. In 1968 there was a choice of white cheese, which was soft, or hard cheese, and that was it. We drank *rakı* and talked English or French and I was ashamed when the others sometimes broke into Turkish and I knew no more than my Lesson One. Afterwards we had dinner downstairs with Cousin and drank only water. This cousin was called Münevver which means the 'enlightened one', or the 'intellectual one', names which suited her. She was also funny, changeable, sometimes malicious, and deeply involved in her Mevlana Way. In the afternoon visitors used to come in twos, threes, fives, tens and at the door of the salon remove their shoes, and then bend over Münevver's hand and touch her wrist with their foreheads, as is deemed proper for a younger person to an older, respected one. They often sat round in silence for hours, waiting for her to speak. She had been to Mecca the year before Ali and I arrived.

That first night in Beylerbeyi I lay propped up in my bed for as long as I could keep awake, watching the lights of the fishing-boats, sometimes just in front of the house, the great dark shapes of the tankers heading towards the Black Sea, to Russia and Bulgaria, and the busy ferries. The last one glided up to our quay just before midnight, while others sailed swiftly downstream, like the Sixty-six.

In the morning I got up and went into the dining-room where I found Ali already sitting in his dressing-gown, smoking and drinking black coffee. He got up and went into a tiny kitchen in the back somewhere and made coffee for me and brought white cheese, black olives, rose-petal jam and sort of toast made over a naked flame. Then Münevver called him and he went into her room and they talked for several hours. I sat in the garden, on the terrace by the sea, and struggled on with *Teach Yourself Turkish*.

Later that morning we went into Istanbul on the ferry and had lunch in a draughty passage, part of a restaurant, that led out into the noisy street where rain was pouring down.

Afterwards we took a taxi up to Haghia Sofia and Sultan Ahmet, the Blue Mosque. Every day, when Ali was not talking to Münevver, we went on one of Ali's Guided Tours. He knew and remembered so much detail, so much history, where everything was; it was he who told the taxi-drivers which steep narrow streets to take in order to find some half-hidden church or fountain or tomb. Gradually I learnt to appreciate the mosques and museums and churches he took me to and disregard the noise and crowds and dirt of the streets, and I loved the round scarlet wooden trays that fish were displayed on, the fruit market piled with watermelons and peaches and grapes and figs where Ali knew the good things and passed by others; I loved the Bosphorus and the birds that flew so swiftly, always in groups of seven, just above the surface of the water; and I used to love to look at the skyline of Istanbul silhouetted against the setting sun, while we were going back to the pink house on the 7.40 ferry, drinking little glasses of hot tea.

It was during this time in Istanbul, that one of Münevver's much loved but rare visitors turned up, a wandering dervish; I can no longer remember his name. He used to walk from village to village talking to people, and in Istanbul he used to frequent the cafés and restaurants where students gathered, and tell them to renounce violence, drugs and gambling. He was a fairish man with very blue, kind eyes and a thin face. With Ali and Münevver he talked and talked, and when Ali told him that he was living in England now, he cried excitedly, 'But you must go back there! Go at once! We have been watching England for the last thirty years.' 'I am going, anyway,' said Ali, but he was excited too and he turned to me and translated.

Unlike Münevver, the dervish sometimes drank quite a lot of *rakı*, and one morning, very early, I heard him walking about the sitting/dining-room, where he had slept, banging into things, moving chairs, knocking over books and papers. It was his shoes, Ali told me later. He had removed them the night before and in the morning could find them nowhere. Perhaps he had left them outside but none of us could go into the garden, because of the fierce dog, even when the house was shaking from an earthquake one night and we longed to. We dared not while he was unchained, which was every night until Fatma tied him up again at eight in the morning.

The dervish used to call me 'our daughter' and once when Ali and I were playing backgammon, he came and stood behind me and put his hand on my head and said, 'I think it's time our daughter won a game.' I had, in fact, been on the very point of losing (generally I did) until that moment, when suddenly I got all the dice I needed.

From Angela Culme-Seymour, *Bolter's Grand-daughter*,
Bird Island Press, Oxford, 2001

Three Stories

PEREGRINE HODSON

T HE DUST BLEW through the windows of the bus as it rattled
through a landscape without shadows or people. It was my first
time in Iran, I was eighteen years old, and I was on my way to Isfahan. So
far, my impressions of the country were mildly disappointing. Tehran
was too modern for me, and Isfahan beckoned – an ancient city so
beautiful, the Persian saying went, that it was *nesfe-jehan* or half the
world.

Isfahan! It sounded like somewhere in the Arabian Nights, shimmering with gold roofs, with a spice bazaar to dizzy the senses. But the
bus was uncomfortable, the heat and the dust were oppressive, and the
sun-bleached terrain was monotonous, like a vast abandoned quarry,
with no sign of life, not a house or a tree. Occasionally a car or a truck
flashed past, momently interrupting the tedium, and then there was
nothing again, just rocks and dust and sand.

Out of the window I half-glimpsed a figure walking by the side of
the road: a moment of mild surprise – someone walking, miles from
anywhere – and then the figure vanished in the dust behind us. The next
moment I lurched forwards as the bus shuddered to a halt, and an old
man in dusty white clothes – the figure I'd glimpsed earlier by the side of
the road – climbed onto the bus. He was wearing a loosely tied cotton
turban, and had a staff in his hand. The driver said nothing and the old
man made no attempt to pay, but simply bowed to the driver and
walked down the bus towards me.

Then he's sitting beside me, looking into my eyes, and to my surprise
his eyes are blue – not pale blue like the sky, but dark blue – the colour of

lapis, a colour I've never seen before in someone's eyes, and as I look into his eyes, I see . . . what do I see? Intelligence certainly, and curiosity, humour and humanity.

Now, years later, when I remember those eyes, I am a little afraid. So much has happened since then: the Iranian Revolution – the *Inqelabi Islami* – the Islamic Revolution and the Pak-sazi – the 'Making Clean' – the Russian invasion of Afghanistan and the war with Iraq; the first Gulf War, 9/11, and the war against the Taliban; Guantanamo, the 'Axis of Evil' and Abu Ghraib. Fallujah. Let's not talk about Palestine or Chechnya, Salman Rushdie or Yassir Arafat, Hitler or Usama bin Laden. The words, the names and the events echo like heavy heartbeats – dom beh dom, breath by breath, second by second – and all this time, the man's eyes have been with me, invisibly encoded somewhere in a network of synapses, in the warm dark of my brain, gazing intently.

Now, when I try to interpret the meaning of the look in his eyes, I'm uncertain. Why, after all these years, do I seem to remember his eyes more clearly than the eyes of my own brother? He has looked through my eyes for so long, I'm unsure whether he is inside me, or beyond me, with me, or against me.

I knew almost nothing about where I was, or where I was going, but I'd already begun my journey in the footsteps of Jalaluddin – or at least I'd read some translations of his poems. I'd even bought a copy of *Teach Yourself Persian*, but I was a lazy student – *danesh-ju kheili tanbal budam* . . . and I could hardly manage more than a few words to the old man with the silver beard sitting beside me. I was not a good *taleb*, and yet, without knowing what I was looking for, perhaps I found a teacher. *Pir. Qutb.* The words conceal as much as they reveal. Or a teacher found me.

It's so long ago, and so many sad and terrible things have happened since, it's difficult to imagine how it would be if we could meet again and yet, somehow, if it should ever happen, I believe the look in his eyes would be the same as I remember.

I have not been faithful, but I have not lost faith.

*　　*　　*

I'm stupid with hashish, twenty years old, and everywhere I go in Morocco there's *kif*. Smoke it, eat it in cookies, drink it in tea – it's everywhere. If you want to know the street, you have to walk the street, and sometimes it's fun, but it's better to keep a clear head. Maybe bad stuff's going to happen soon, but it's okay – it's mercifully hidden some time in the future – and in the golden-clouded arrogance of youth I'm unaware of it.

There's a festival in town – and the streets of Moulay Idris are full of Berbers and pilgrims who have come to worship at one of the five holy cities of Islam. I feel as if I've fallen into another earlier world that could so easily be described by the cliché 'biblical' – but that would be another country, and this is North Africa, towards the end of the twentieth century.

I'm travelling on a scholarship to study Arabic, but my heart's not in it. I walk among the crowds of men in brown and grey jellabas who are followed a few respectful steps behind by anonymously veiled women, between sweating porters pushing carts of vegetables and fruit, shouting and cursing their way through the narrow lanes, past stallholders who gaze watchfully over mounds of raisins and pistachios, and beggars calling the faithful to pity the poor. Maybe it's all the dope I've been smoking, but I feel like a tourist watching one of those shows put on by the locals, even though the pilgrims are real, and the Berber tribesmen with their horses and wives and tents are real, and the camels and beggars are real.

There seems to be a distance – or a difference – between me and the people whose language I have come to learn. I would like to dissolve my Western identity in the warm ebb and flow of the people milling around me, but something makes me wary – a lack of trust, maybe, or a lack of faith – and I hold back.

I remember E. M. Forster's subtly ambiguous advice to those brave spirits who dream of making their home in another culture: 'Only connect'. But I can't forget the story of Dives and Lazarus, the rich man crying out for a drop of water from the flames of Hell to Lazarus, the poor man comfortably nestled on Abraham's bosom. Never a completely happy image. I think of the great gulf fixed between Dives and Lazarus: the distance between myself and the people around me seems correspondingly immense, and I'm not so sure I want to make the connection anyway, even if I could go the distance.

It's mid-afternoon, and I'm sweating and getting irritable with myself when suddenly I catch the scent of mint in the air. I find a chair at a tea-stall and sit down with a glass of mint tea to watch the passers-by. Then, as if by some elegantly pre-arranged signal, a modest *tableau vivant* unfolds in front of me. A water-seller, dressed in red, carrying a great glistening skin full of water, festooned with brightly polished brass cups, stands in the middle of the square, and in front of him there's an old man, who's angry. The old man's beside himself; shouting and shaking his fist in the water seller's face, and then the water seller takes the old man's hand and kisses it – and kisses it – and, as I watch, the anger goes out of the old man until he's gentle and humble, and finally he accepts some water from the water-seller and bows his head in gratitude and drinks some water from a shining cup.

This is the moment I realise what's happened: I've just witnessed a miracle, not a wide-screen technicolour miracle, but a miracle, and even as I register what's happened, I find myself walking towards the water-seller. He sees me coming and smiles, raises his hand, and says something to me in French.

'*C'est toi?*'

First fear, then uncertainty. Why is he talking to me in French? What do I say? Play safe. Maybe.

'*Peut-être,*' I say, and immediately I regret my cowardice. The water-seller smiles.

'*Oui, c'est toi,*' he says.

My mind swims with the possibilities of what's just been said. Mistaken identity? No mistake. He knows what's happening. Maybe it's happened before. Maybe it'll happen again, Insha'allah.

As I reach out my hand towards him, I hear myself repeat the question – the simple question – also in French.

'*C'est toi?*'

The water-seller takes my hand.

'*Oui, c'est moi,*' he says.

I hear the certainty in his voice, and as he holds my hand I notice the odd formation of his fingers – not an ordinary handshake, nor a secret handshake, but an odd, sensory pun, like a confession of humanity, and then we're standing together, in the dust and the noise of Moulay Idris, and everything is made by faith, un-made and re-made, again and again, until the water-seller lets go of my hand and we stand facing one another.

Even now, I look for the meaning of that meeting and other initiations, conscious and unconscious, revelations, and hidden demonstrations, and I ask myself whether this, finally, is all we're seeking. Water in the dust. Kindness in a stranger.

Then it's time to part.

'*Au revoir.*'

Insha'allah.

*   *   *

The first time I met Abu Hamza was in Kabul, early 2002, a month or so after the fall of the Taliban. He'd just been released from a Northern Alliance gaol where he'd been held with other Taliban fighters, and now he was on his way home, back to England. He was lucky. Several men in prison with him had been taken to Baghram, and one or two ended up in Guantanamo, but Abu Hamza was on his way home to Burnley, Lancashire.

He was still emaciated from three years of imprisonment, with long hair and beard, Taliban-style, still wearing the clothes he'd worn in prison. His gaunt features, black beard and hollow eyes were startlingly like the face of a desert ascetic gazing from an icon or a medieval fresco – until one remembered that Abu Hamza's faith was Islam, not Christianity.

The next time I saw Abu Hamza was in Burnley. He still had a beard but it was neatly trimmed, his face had more flesh, and he'd put on a lot of weight. He was glad to be home, but he had difficulty sleeping. Sometimes at night the images of his time in prison came back: the dripping darkness of the metal container where he was kept for days, the beatings and the shootings, and the Taliban prisoners with him, one by one dying of malaria. Sure it was good to be back and have some home cooking, but sometimes . . . sometimes it was hard. Abu Hamza's voice trailed away as he looked towards the dark clouds over the hills around the town. Afghanistan. *Jihad*. The memory of those who were *shahid* (martyrs).

A week or so before the trial, Abu Hamza came to stay with me in Gloucestershire. He liked the hills and valleys dotted with sheep, the stone-built walls and the winding lanes of the village. The war in Iraq had just begun, and every day the gigantic roar of the B-52 bombers reverberated over the valley, as they thundered over from America. Abu Hamza shook his head. 'It's a bad business, Perry man. You know what happened to the Russians in Afghanistan. The same's going to happen to the Americans in Iraq.'

One afternoon I took Abu Hamza to the village church. The Victorians restored the fabric long ago, dutifully scouring away the pious paint and grime of centuries, but they left an old Saxon font, and the worn stone effigy of a crusader. Abu Hamza laid his hand on the polished stone head of the dog at the crusader's feet, touched the stone sword at the knight's side, then turned to me and grinned.

'We whupped them, Perry man, didn't we? The Muslims whupped the crusaders.'

Gradually his smile faded and his face became thoughtful.

'All that way to Jerusalem – in those days! He went a long way for his religion, didn't he?' and then, as if he was addressing the memory of the ancient knight, Abu Hamza lowered his voice and whispered, 'You went a long way for your religion too, didn't you?' and for a second or two – a heartbeat maybe, or a breath – there was a balance between past and present, stone and sunlight, the *jihadi* and the crusader.

İrfan Orga: Flight, Flame, Farewell

ATEŞ ORGA

İRFAN ORGA – Ottoman child, Republican son, second-generation pioneer of the skies – found his destiny, Margaret (two weeks married), in London in 1943: according to their rings on 22 July, the day Palermo fell to the Americans. That first moment, she turning right at the corner from Inverness Place to Terrace, Bayswater-land, profile hesitating, gazing coolly, would come to be remembered like an arrow through the heart. Irregularly beautiful, early twenties. Follower of Saladin, defender of Parnell. Admirer of Pushkin, Rilke, Elizabeth Bowen and Graham Greene. Norman-Irish. Born during an air-raid, I joined them one Monday evening fifteen-and-a-half months later. In 1945 father was ordered to a new Air Force posting – arriving Gaziantep in the south-east of Turkey, close to the Syrian border, 8 August. Mother and I followed, to encounter life and language with a Greek family in İstanbul. We were not to stay. Declining the hand officialdom offered him, preferring asylum to arrest, father made it back to London in the run-up to Christmas 1947, landing Northolt, 23 December – prospectless if not possessionless. The charges against him, filed by the Turkish Ministry of National Defence, (21 December 1946) claimed as 'established fact' that 'Captain İrfan Urga [*sic*] lived with a foreign woman [and, under Article XII of the Military and Civilian Retirement Law, is] considered as having resigned his commission [. . .] he has been dismissed'. Omitting to recognise he had been sent to the Turkish Embassy in London in command of Turkish fighter-pilots training with the Royal Air Force, a Complaint Petition calling for a recoup of monies 'spent on the defendant during his period of study [*sic*] in England' plus corresponding penalty, was issued. At the (unattended) hearing in the Third

Law Court of First Instance, Ankara, Monday 12 September 1949, a guilty verdict was returned, the judge, Abdulkadir Ozoguz, levying a fine of 49,761 lira 44 kuruş including costs, plus interest. £135,000 in modern equivalency.

İrfan – 'beloved darling [. . .] without whom this life would be meaningless and empty' – and Margaret (two days divorced) – loved 'more than anything else in the world' – were married in Paddington Register Office, 9 January 1948. Six weeks later the Aliens Department of the Home Office advised that he could remain and work in Britain. For a while he did the round of Embassy receptions, and accompanied a Turkish trade delegation to Newport and Cardiff in May 1949. Annually I would go with him across the park on April visits to the grand Consulate building in Rutland Gardens, where he would queue uneasily to have his Certificate of Nationality stamped (1948–59). In August 1950 *Portrait of a Turkish Family* was published, tracing his İstanbul story from the last sultans, through the Allied Occupation, to the Atatürk years. Banned in Celal Bayar's Turkey, and only finally translated into Turkish in 1994, it caught the attention of the English-speaking world. Caroline Moorhead celebrates it today as 'a poignant memory of lost love . . . sad and magnificent . . . one of the great memoirs of the twentieth century,' (*The Independent*'s 'Book of a Lifetime', 11 February 2005).

Father's tales, the passacaglia of his mortality, became the silk-and-emblem of our family, the legend of who we were. Our name 'Orga', adopted under the 1934 Turkish Surnames Law, he told us, was derived from that of a river, the Urga between Nizhniy Novgorod and Kazan on the trail east to the Urals. The fantasy of a young *bey* in Eskişehir sticking a pin in a map to find an identity fired my imagination. But the thought (years subsequently) of the old water-gods returning to haunt him for losing their vowel (Captain 'Urga') sent shivers.

Contrasting the straightforward parent who brought me up, father was complicated, the paradoxes of his personality, the unanswered questions of his story, were many. That, for example, he was on the one hand assertive, on the other nervous of confrontation. That he preferred a reclusive lifestyle and shunned publicity yet courted public recognition through being a writer. He cherished the Republic of his early manhood, yet hated, with fisted passion, the price its laws were to ask of him. He upheld his Islamic values and customs, yet was a Kemalist without Friday ritual, celebrating the feasts of the Catholic year. Christmas was always special (even in hardship), when food *alla turca*, drink, gifts and happiness could never be enough. The more the wine the mellower and softer he became, a social after-dinner cigarette smoke-circling into hours of reminiscence.

I was never tempted to cross swords or take him to the edge. I knew the sting of his hand, and that once his temper was roused, his eyes turning cold, his jaw hardening, it was as dangerous as being in a cage with a lion unready to relinquish his kingdom. Not that he was unloving or uncaring, far from it, only that, to survive the position he found himself in, he needed to have a battle strategy – regimental order. People noticed. During the second half of 1951 we'd taken rooms just south of Dublin – at widow Mooney's, 82 St George's Avenue, Blackrock, close to the Strand. March, thirty-seven years later. A rain-and-sunshine after-noon. There the house stands, atmospheric in its late Georgian lines. New faces live there now, and the once wild garden has been tamed. Searching for anyone who remembers, I get into conversation with a man who points me towards a run-down area on the outskirts of the town. I find Lillian, last of the Mooney daughters, the simple-minded girl who'd scalded my father into hospital when I'd accidentally set the place ablaze. Not knowing who I might be, she brews a cup of tea and talks, defensively at first, then more freely. She remembers a couple, with a child. Turkish. Nice lady, very protective towards the boy. But a stern man with broken English, seemingly a tough disciplinarian, too tough. A man of good taste. The boy? Yes, quite a rascal, spent his days in their garden up the pear tree at the end talking to Miss Fitzharris and her Rhode Island Reds next door. Never played with other children. In bed by seven. The couple used to have their evening meal with a bottle of wine – or was it Martini? There was always a pot of marrow bones on the boil – because marrow and soup, the man said, did you good. Lots of packing cases and strapped trunks, fine books, Oriental carpets . . . A short name the child had. 'A – tesh?' . . . ? Faded eyes stare. The October fire, the fire the whole avenue knew about, she'd blanked from her memory. But not the strangers from across the sea.

My father was a man who watched – and taught how to watch. Some time in the mid-fifties, a grey-skied, rainy spring morning, we were in Kensington Gardens, taking the North Flower Walk from the Long Water towards Lancaster Gate. A pale girl sat on a bench, dressed thinly for the weather in a cheap cotton dress, make-up worn, tense with the tiredness of the night. From Paddington Green maybe, or Inverness Terrace, perhaps even the tenement house we called home, three in a cramped back room for one. A prostitute, I heard muttered, don't catch her eye. Warning maybe, yet father never denigrated their calling. They had a place in his heart. Maybe in his İstanbul youth, off the gas-lit lanes of Tünel down the former Grand Rue de Pera – 'public parade for the stylish and high society, anonymous lair for the styleless' – his relationships had embraced friendship, love.

He possessed a strong sense of historical moment. Not just VE Day, which he and mother shared with the throngs in Trafalgar Square. But the passing of men, the insurrections of Europe, the rituals of ceremonial. In February 1952, a bitter wind blowing off the Thames, we went to the lying-in-state of George VI, our feet wrapped in newspaper. In 1965 we watched the state funeral of Churchill on television, naval ratings pulling the coffin at sixty-two paces to the minute. The 1956 Hungarian Uprising took us to the Hungarian Embassy to see the communist star torn from the national flag. The royal salutes of the King's Troop in Hyde Park, Henry VIII's hunting ground, became a pilgrimage. The sight, sound and smell of seventy-five black horses galloping and wheeling out of distant woodland, harnesses jingling, pulling their six battle-green thirteen-pounders from Gallipoli and the Somme, nearside riders in gold-frogged, hussar-cut No 1 Dress, the earth-pounding thunder of each 'Fire!' ricocheting off the walls of Park Lane, drowning out the voices of Speaker's Corner: this, we used to imagine, was what it must have been like to witness a charge at Waterloo or in the Crimea. Battle of Britain flypasts, Spitfires and Hurricanes leading heavy Wellingtons and Lancasters, were another highlight each

September during the early '50s – the banshee wail of the All Clear, the high drone of Merlin engines taking him back sentimentally to the days when he'd first met mother and flown with the RAF.

The world stage drew my father. He followed Suez closely, he was appalled by Hungary, by Czechoslovakia twelve years on, he analysed Cuba, he grieved for Kennedy. Concerned, he watched developments in Russia, the old enemy. He welcomed the principle if not the actions of the 1960 Turkish coup. He had firm ideas about the Cyprus issue: for a Rumelian west of the Bosphorus, Cypriots were colonials, Turks by adoption rather than mainland inheritance, a viewpoint he could not help. In outlook he was an old Ottoman first, a liberated Turk second, a modern European only selectively. What his thoughts were on the 1915 Armenian massacre he never voiced. As a child he would have been too closeted to know of such atrocity, as a man too brainwashed by the military to question. When it came to Greeks he was divided. How, following the First World War, they'd raped and carried off women, bayoneting unborn children from the womb, how they'd been routed by Mustafa Kemal's men and driven into the sea off Smyrna in September 1922, invariably released emotions. Yet in Bayswater he felt comfortable in their company. In Costas's tiny red-and-white stripe-poled barber shop at 175 Queensway, the Turkish Baths end, where everything was debated and purveyed from current affairs to cologne and condoms, he'd have his hair cut short and sleeked back while olive-skinned, liquid-eyed girls of seductive accent and delicate cleavage demurely manicured the hands of coffee-drinking patriarchs. Never did I hear a negative word. More than once these people had been his saviour, a pushed-in-the-hand pound note going a long way.

Exile in the 1960s was spent in rural East Sussex – Kipling country. Tiny as it was, Spike Island – the white house on a hill foretold by a fortune-teller – father loved. Its stillness, the deep night 'powdered with stars', the galaxies of the Milky Way, the blackness of the night un-polluted by city lights. A place where humans and noise didn't exist. The garden spirits ruled everywhere. We were enveloped by Nature in all the awakenings and cadences of its seasons – the damp-green smell of the earth, the scent of flowers, the waves of June yarrow, the rustle of animals, the majesty of oak and beech, the sway of birch, the wind. But not everything was idyllic. My mother, aristocratic example of the landed Irish gentry – 'more than a class but just less than a race' as Annabel Goff described the breed in *Walled Gardens* (1990) – increasingly led her own life in London publishing, daily taking the breakfast-car train to the City. Leaving a trail of unpublished stories and novels, she'd always wanted to be an author in her own right, not the uncredited poet-editor behind father's words and ideas. Bitterly, she would accuse him of having crushed her talent. Disparagingly, he would waive her attempts to talk about religion or the supernatural, stiffening in mute discomfort, reluctant to get involved lest perhaps it might unleash his own psychic sensitivities.

Life in our weather-boarded, corrugated-roofed 'castle' was not without incident. The first evening a paraffin stove blew up in a sheet of flame before being carried out to expire under a damson tree. Then a stranger came by with a gun – supposedly, he said, to pot a rabbit or two but his threatening manner seemed to issue an unspoken challenge. A sleepy lane of grass and hedgerows ran through our land, Footpath 49C on the Wadhurst map, petering out in ruts and ditches behind the Rock Robin inn. Once, local lore went, it had been the post-road from Tunbridge Wells to Hastings, haunted by a coachman whose coach had lost its wheels, his horses their footing, down among the stones and naked roots beyond the big beech. 'Rock Robin, rock . . . ' One day a cadaverous elder, taking objection to father's attempts to cut back the brambles and hawthorn, angrily set about him, his parting 'git back t'where ya com' from' inflicting a suppurating wound. To hear once more the *muezzin*, to sway with the waves that had carried him as a child. To see 'the dim, haze-hidden face of the city' he'd captured in *The Young Traveller in Turkey* (1957), to drink in the long, twin-towered profile of Kuleli (the Ottoman military college by the Bosphorus, the *alma mater* of his youth), throwing 'its white reflection to the blue waters'. To catch again the whiff and smoke of grilling fish on a Black Sea wind. Nothing but a dream. Newsreel footage of Istanbul's domes and minarets, streets and skyline, he found painful to watch. Likewise leafing through photographs of friends and the places he'd travelled, or his green Ottoman-scripted wartime notebook, treasured away in the depths of a mildewed, rotting leather briefcase once luxurious. Another afternoon a huntsman cantered up, churning the wet grass into mud. Knowing the distinction, father reminded him this was a footpath, not a bridleway. Reaching down with his crop, rearing his stallion, the man belly-laughed. 'Bloody foreigners' shouldn't meddle in things that weren't their business.

One frosty November morning in 1970 a card came in the post for a hospital appointment *baba* didn't need. Walking his garden, he touched the trees he'd planted, pausing here to prune, there to commune with the queenly cherry before the kitchen window. When the day arrived, the appointment was with death. Forgotten by a world he'd once fancied to command, speared by the arrows off mother's tongue, he slipped away from us with a beatific smile, his brow at rest, his pallor no longer flushed by the heat of fever. That heart-attacked, gout-ridden, medicated summer had been one of pain, of blue eyes darkened with anxiety and sickness. But not that night. Unconscious, he just wanted to go. Those moonless hours, the phone call from the Kent and Sussex, Ward 14, the walk home through the woods, branches dripping, my mother never having had time to say goodbye, his faithful old labrador, Lâle, black as coal, howling in her loneliness, the aura of light trembling behind the trees, I have remembered all my life. Sunday the twenty-ninth.

I know little of the music my father listened to as a young man. Yet I fancy Deniz Kızı Eftalya who made her early reputation in the waterside cafés of Galata during the Occupation years may not have been unfamiliar – along with 78s of *Light Cavalry*, *Old Comrades*, parade-ground *marcia*, brothel tango, a grace or two of Chopin. Eftalya, Siren of the Ottoman Bosphorus, legend has it, was famous for going out in a caique with her Greek father, singing away the summer evenings. No one ever saw her – but her songs, echoing across the waters off Büyükdere on the way to Sariyer, childhood retreat and tragedy of the *Portrait*, were there for all to hear. Deniz Kızı, they would say, the Mermaid.

I know even less of what he read. Yet I think it must have been eloquent.

Come she said to me
Stay she said to me
Smile she said to me
Die she said to me

    I came
    I stayed
    I smiled
    I died

Nâzim Hikmet, lines on the
back of a photograph *d'amour* ...

Flight, flame, farewell. Old Kuleli soldiers talk still of the airman and the Irish girl, the 'eagle' who forsook all for 'a foreign woman'.

Ghosts

Leo Africanus

SARAH ANDERSON

SMELL IS THE MOST EVOCATIVE of the senses and it is the smell of the tanneries in Fez that hit me and made memories flood back, memories of the first time I had been there and had had that serendipitous moment stumbling on the life of Leo Africanus or El Hasan ben Muhammad el-Wazzan-ez-Zayyati.

It was an Iranian photographer who introduced him to me. We were staying in the same hotel, not one of the almost two hundred innes . . . Every of these innes are three stories high, and contain an hundred and twenty or moe chambers apeece. Likewise each one hath a fountaine together with sinks and water-pipes, which make auoidance of all the filth', but in some modern building. Since the photographer seemed to be on his own; I suggested that we meet for a drink; and during the course of that evening and many others, as we searched out little-known parts of Fez, he showed me the Fez of El-Fasi, the man of Fez, which probably hadn't changed that much in five hundred years. For me, being shown Fez through the eyes of a photographer who understood the culture was illuminating. The Bou Inania Madrasa built at legendary cost, or the early fourteenth century Attarin Madrasa, both early Islamic schools of learning where students lodged, are bound to have been visited by El-Fasi, as were the narrow shopping streets with their crammed shops and donkeys and mules jostling for space: 'Then followes the herbe-market, wherein the pome-citrons, and diuers kindes of greene boughs and herbes doe represent the sweete and flourishing spring, and in this market are about twentie taverns; for they which drinke wine, will shrowd themselves under the shadie and pleasant boughes'.

There are many myths about El-Fasi but it is generally supposed that he was born in Granada sometime between 1489–96 and left for Morocco as a young boy with his parents, settling in Fez probably as a result of the post-1492 Spanish policy that made it uncomfortable for Muslims to stay in Spain. What was it about him that intrigued me so much? Firstly, I found his descriptions of Fez mesmerizing: 'In Fez there are divers most excellent poets, which make verses in their owne mother toong. Most of their poems and songs intreat of love. Every yeere they pen certaine verses in the commendation of Mahumet, especially upon his birthday'.

Secondly, after studying in Fez, a seat of great learning, he had travelled widely. I had been round the world by my mid-twenties and although I had had my eyes opened to different places, peoples and cultures, I had never stayed anywhere long enough to get to know it in depth; El-Fasi ostensibly travelled for the Sultan on commercial and diplomatic missions, but in reality it was probably chiefly to satisfy his own curiosity. His descriptions of elephants: 'This wittie beast keepeth in the woods, and is found in great numbers in the forests' and of giraffes ' . . . so savage and wild . . . It is headed like a camel, eared like an oxe, and footed like a [missing word]' are acutely observed. In 1518 he was captured by Christian corsairs near Tunisia but due to his intelligence and general worldliness he escaped being instantly sold into slavery and was instead taken to Rome to be given to the Medici Pope Leo X, renowned for his patronage of the arts. El-Fasi spoke Spanish and enthralled the Pope with his love of literature and his adventures and travels to remote African kingdoms, Constantinople, Egypt and possibly Mecca. Opinion varies as to whether or not he actually became a Christian but the likelihood is that he was baptized and the Pope gave him his own name – Giovanni Leone – from which time he became known as Leo Africanus. I think it would be wrong to look at his adoption of Christianity as mere opportunism, indeed it is tempting to speculate that he saw much in common between Islam and Christianity. Perhaps being a Christian did make it easier for him to travel freely around Italy, which he did until the death of his patron Pope Leo in 1521, but I like to think that because there is much in common between enlightened Islam and enlightened Christianity, Leo

Africanus reconciled the differences and embraced the religion of his host country because of its essential sameness.

'We have the same God' is a sentiment I have often heard expressed in the Arab countries where I have travelled. The sound of the muezzin in Muslim countries is certainly more regular than anything now produced by the Christian Church – but bells heralded both the thrice daily recitation of the Angelus and the Mass more regularly then than now, a sad loss for everyone.

In Bologna Leo Africanus lodged with a Jewish physician and humanist, which shows his liberal attitude towards those of other religions. Jacob Mantino, who had also come from Spain, helped Leo compile an Arabic-Hebrew-Latin medical dictionary (the Arabic part still exists in the Escorial Library in Spain). Wandering round the streets of Bologna peering through sixteenth-century windows, I like to imagine Leo and Jacob working together on the medical dictionary, tempted by the kind of food and drink described by the sixteenth-century Flemish traveller Andreas Schott in *Journeys*: 'Bologna the Fat is a proverbial saying. Here can be seen fine, broad fields which produce not just wheat, vegetables and other crop, but also wines of every kind, including the very finest to be found in Italy. Fruits of every variety abound, nor is there any lack of places for fowling and hunting. In Bologna they make two cuts of exquisite meat and the sausages and charcuterie are without rival in the whole of the country.'

I met Leo Africanus again in America – Sebastiano del Piombo's Portrait of a Humanist in the National Gallery of Art in Washington D.C. painted *c.*1520 is reputedly of him. It is not surprising that the Christian corsairs who captured Leo recognised that he was a cultured scholar and deserving of special treatment. I would be rather intimidated at the prospect of meeting him; the three-quarter length painting is of a rather gaunt-faced, sad and pensive man wearing a dark robe and holding some kind of manuscript while standing beside a table covered with books, a globe and a quill pen. But if I was able to overcome my initial apprehension I think it would be wonderful to sit and talk to this many-faceted man who was possibly the role model for Shakespeare's Othello, who influenced Corneille and who appeared in séances to

W. B. Yeats as a spirit called 'Leo'. What would I ask him? His travels, his scholarship, his faith – it would be hard to know where to begin. Amin Maalouf's Goncourt-winning novel *Leo the African* does much to capture the cosmopolitan Leo and certainly brought him to much wider prominence when it was published in 1986.

Leo Africanus' most weighty work was *The Description of Africa*, divided into nine books and based on his own travels and observations; it has been shockingly neglected until now – the last English translation was done in 1600 – but a modern English translation is being done in Canada. He also translated the Epistles of St Paul and compiled a biographical encyclopedia of twenty-five Islamic and five Jewish scholars. He is exactly the kind of person needed today to help bridge the cultural divide and the seemingly increasingly large gaps between the three religions of the Book, which in their essence have so much in common. Leo wrote that if he was vouchsafed a longer life he wanted to write about 'all the regions of Asia which I have travelled, to wit, Arabia Deserta, Arabia Felix, Arabia Petrea, the Asian part of Egypt, Armenia, and some part of Tartaria, all of which countries I saw and passed through in the time of my youth'. What a pity he died before being able to do this.

There are many different theories as to where and how Leo spent his last years. A few chroniclers say that he stayed in Rome, but I like to think, along with the majority, that he returned to North Africa and died in Tunis having reconverted to Islam. Whatever religion Leo practiced he seemed to be able to incorporate facets of the other without diminishing either. Dialogue with people of other faiths has to be the way forward; and this rather lugubrious-looking man would have made an excellent bridge between Christianity and Islam. A truly remarkable Muslim.

The Leo Africanus quotes are from: *The History and Description of Africa and of the Notable Things Therein Contained.* Translated into English 1600 by John Pory. Hakluyt Society. 3 vols 1896.

Encountering Ali

JASON ELLIOT

'YA ALI!'
This muttered invocation, unheard in the nations of Sunni Islam, made me turn my head. It had come from the lips of a young man ranging kebabs over a bed of white-hot coals, above which a blinking neon sign read 'Ali Baba Restaurant'.

Despite the cold, the door to the place was open and beckoned with a friendly smile from the cook, I went inside for an evening meal. The owner, after I had eaten, invited me to join him at his table, where he was puffing on a small water-pipe. His name was Khalil. He was a stocky, handsome man, with cropped black hair and watchful, dark eyes the shape of almonds. He must have been thirty but his manner conveyed the calm and authority of an older man. We liked each other and settled into conversation. Then, after the last of the customers had left and the cook been despatched with a wad of notes from the day's takings, we were joined by Khalil's younger brother and one of the waiters.

There was the usual flurry of exploratory questions. They'd had an English visitor, one of them said, a year or two ago – perhaps I knew him? No, he wasn't English, a voice corrected him, he'd been French. But what was I doing here alone? What did I think of Iran? What would I be writing about? How much would I make from the book? Did I have a wife, and did she work? What was the pound worth? Where had I been, and where was the best place so far? Frequent refills of tea accompanied this gentle interrogation. By now I had had ample practice with the answers and, sensing my interlocutors were as good-natured as they

were hospitable, and in such a way as to show I wasn't too serious, I said:
'I wasn't sure, mind you, about coming to Tabriz.'

There were some indignant cries of 'why ever not?'

'I've heard,' I said, ' – in Tehran – that the people of Tabriz have a
bad reputation.' The three heads tightened closer to hear the charge.

'What do they say about us?'

'That the people of Tabriz are unkind and fanatical.'

'That's *exactly* what makes us angry!' Khalil's brother, a younger
and more passionate man, raised a retaliatory finger in front of me.
'What do they know?' Then, simmering down, added almost ruefully:
'We're not like the Persians anyway. We're Azeris.'

'That's right,' said someone, 'we're Turks, like all the great families of
Iran.'

At this point the door opened and a melancholy-looking, white-
haired man in a tired suit joined us at the table, and greeted us in
Azeri. Then, realising there was a Persian-speaking guest, he switched
languages.

'Have you heard the one about the Christian and the Muslim?' he
pulled up the sleeves of his jackets and, looking down to brush aside a
few crumbs, set his elbows on the table and looked at us in turn, as if to
say, 'then I'll begin.'

'You'll like this,' said the brother, refilling my glass of tea with a
complicitous wink. 'He's a doctor. And his speciality is jokes!' But the
crux of the long and complicated tale that followed, and ended in eye-
watering guffaws all round, evaded me. It had all hung on a word I didn't
know, which was dutifully explained with a gesture from one of them
resembling a bottle being opened. Jokes about circumcision, it occurred
to me eventually, must have been circulating since the Crusades.

'Are you from London?' asked the doctor. There was a comic glint
beneath his sad features. 'I've been there a few times,' he said wistfully.
Then he lit a cigarette, gazed upwards through a curl of ascending
smoke, and sighed. 'Paris once. Frankfurt, too. They used to be beautiful
places before you let so many Arabs go and live there.'

Khalil, who had kept silent for most of the time, now put aside the
mouthpiece of his pipe, exhaled a long and expanding plume, and

recalled the time he had met an Arab from Kuwait one evening in a nearby street. He was looking for a place to eat, so he brought him to the restaurant. As they arrived, the Arab had looked up, seen the sign '*Ali Baba*', shuddered, and fled into the darkness,

'The forty thieves!' he chuckled. '*Ali Baba and the forty thieves!* He thought we were going to rob him!'

'The Arabs don't understand us,' added the brother. 'They think we're all *Hezbollahis* or something.' (He meant the much-feared and hardline *Ansar-I Hezbollah*, not the popular Palestinian resistance movement of the same name.)

'For one thing, they're Sunnis.'

At this, there were a few solemn nods of assent.

'If you were Muslim,' one of them turned to me suddenly, 'which would you be: Sunni or Shi'a?'

'Shi'a of course!' interjected the brother.

I said I understood that there were different kinds of Shia: apart from the main body of Twelver Shi'ism there were the Ismailis and the Zaidis and the Nizaris, the Ahmadiyya, the Druze too in the Lebanon, and some others I wasn't too sure about.

'Yes,' said the waiter, 'but they're not really Muslims.'

'They've made up their own religion!' With good-natured passion, Khalil's brother started up again. 'Look,' he went on, 'there's only one kind of Shi'a, and that's our kind. We believe –

' – there are others,' said Khalil gently. 'The Ismaelis – '

'I'll get to them. We believe,' he tapped his finger on the table, 'that Ali was the rightful successor of the Prophet – peace be upon him – and the first Imam. But the Sunnis put their caliphs – you know about the caliphs, Abu Bakr – and the others? Good. They put the caliphs in his place – the place of Ali, who was chosen by the Prophet himself at Ghadir Kumm. We don't agree with that.'

'They said Ali was too young,' said the doctor gloomily.

'But Ali was himself the fourth caliph,' I said.

'Yes, but he was also the first Imam. It's – complicated. The Sunni have their caliphs, and we have our Imams.'

'The Twelve Imams.'

'Yes, twelve. Ali's son Hassan, was the second Imam, and *his* son was the third Imam, Hussein, who was murdered – *murdered!* – along with his whole family, by the caliph Yazid, the Ummayyad, at Kerbala – you know about Kerbala?'

I nodded.

'Good. After them . . . after them – '

'After them came Imam Zein al-Abedin,' said the doctor.

'And after Imam Zein al-Abedin came . . . came the fifth Imam. . .'

There was a pause; Khalil's brother was running out of steam. A few names were hurriedly proposed, put aside, and re-arranged like a puzzle. It was slow going; but we got there in the end, and I wrote down the succession in my notebook at the table.

Muhammad Baqir was the fifth Imam. His brother, Zaid, became the founder of the so-called Five-Imam Shi'a, or Zaidis. The sixth was Imam Ja'far Sadiq, perhaps the most famous of the Imams – whose son, Ismail, was chosen as successor by the Ismailis – the 'Seveners', so-called – who founded the Fatimid caliphate in Cairo in the tenth century.

The seventh, the son of Imam Ja'far, was Imam Musa Kazim; the eighth Imam Reza, who himself nearly became caliph, and whose famous shrine is today in Mashad; the ninth, Imam Muhammad al Taqi; the tenth, Imam Ali al-Naqi; the eleventh, Imam Hasan al-Askari, who married the daughter of a Byzantine emperor; and the twelfth and final Imam, Muhammad – known also as the *Mahdi*, the Rightly Guided, *Sahib az-Zaman*, Lord of the Age, *Sahib al-Amr*, Lord of the Divine Command, *al-Qat'm*, He who will arise, *al-Muntazar*, the Awaited, and the *Baqiyyat Allah*, Remnant of God – and whose earthly disappearance in 940 marks the beginning of that enigmatic period known as the occultation, during which the Imam is alive, but invisible.

By this time, the original question – Sunni or Shi'a? – had been forgotten. But the events of thirteen centuries ago had not. We had touched on one of the pivotal moments in the history of Islam, the repercussions of which, pulsing across time like the radiation of an extinguished galaxy, still inform the pattern of events in the Shi'ite world, and especially Iran. Outwardly at least, the great schism that divides Islam into Sunni and Shi'ite camps arose over the question of a successor to the Prophet Muhammad, who died in 632, leaving no male heir. A consensus of the Prophet's closest companions elected Abu Bakr, his father-in-law and intimate friend, to lead the community of Moslems. The Majority who supported this appointment of a successor, *khalifa*, became known as the People of Tradition, *sunnah*; a small group of others believed that the role should remain in the Prophet's family, and supported Ali, his son-in-law and cousin. These later became known as the partisans, or *shi'ah*.

But the split in opinion was more than political. The very role of successor was perceived differently, with the Shi'a laying stress on the initiatic dimension of succession; only Ali, in Shi'a tradition, had been chosen by Islam's founder for the task of interpreting the mysteries of the Qur'an, conveying the esoteric inheritance of the revelation and serving as a channel of Divine Grace flowing from the family of the Prophet. The choice of Muhammad's successor was not without controversy – contention, even – but three times Ali was passed over in favour of the earliest caliphs, Abu Bakr, Omar and Uthman, the latter from an aristocratic Meccan clan, the Ummayyad, which had earlier strongly opposed the Prophet.

Uthman's assassination in 656 brought Ali at last to the caliphate, and for five years his followers' hopes were realised. But like his predecessor, Ali too fell victim to an assassin's blade, and a cousin of Uthman, Mu'awiya (and the first of the Ummayyad caliphs, so-called) rose to power. Power there was: in the early decades of Islam the Arabs and their allies made extraordinarily rapid territorial conquests; their armies, by the time of the Prophet's grandson Hussein, had already penetrated into north Africa in the west, advanced through Persia as far as Khorassan, and laid siege to Constantinople.

They ruled over an ever-vaster empire. As the new government grew wealthier and stronger, there was frequent opposition to its methods (and even its religious integrity); the question of succession was still controversial, and the worldliness of the caliphate brought accusations that it had become no more than a privileged autocracy – a hereditary kingdom, in other words – that had largely forsaken the theocratic spirit of Islam's earliest days. Resistance came to head in 680, when Ali's second son, Hussein, agreed to put himself at the head of a revolt against Yazid, the second Umayyad caliph. He first planned a pilgrimage to Mecca, stopping en route in Kula to discuss plans with his supporters. But word of his movements had reached the wily Yazid, and the advance of his caravan – followers, guards and family, numbering seventy-one in all – was checked at Kerbala in Iraq. Then it was attacked.

The tragedy is commemorated to this day among Shi'ites everywhere, who recreate the burning afternoon on which Yazid's troops, ignoring their pleas for mercy, slaughtered even the women and children of Hussein's caravan, and finally the Imam himself.

Yet it is wrong to call Shi'ism a sect. Not only is its influence too vast, but on fundamental matters of doctrine it is not different from Sunnism, and in this sense belongs to the orthodox community of the faith. The dispute between Islam's two main bodies is nowhere near on a par with the schism between the Eastern and Western Church, and nothing in the division approaches the magnitude of such bitterly disputed theological conundrums as the nature of Christ or the Virgin, the *filioque*, Purgatory or infallibility; it more resembles the divide between Anglicans and Methodists or, even more approximately, Russian and Greek Orthodox churches.

In fact, the separation can be said to have borne unexpected and far-reaching intellectual fruits. After the occultation of the final Imam, followers of Twelver Shi'ism – lacking an earthly heir – were largely diverted from politics towards religious and scholarly goals. Most of Islam's early educational institutions came to life under Shi'ite tutelage, and in both art and science it was Shi'ite scholars who were to be found at the intellectual vanguard of the era. During the tenth and eleventh centuries, when the disciplines from non-Islamic sources became available in Arabic for the first time, they were given a much warmer reception in Shi'ite circles than in their Sunni equivalents, where interest lay more in the orthodox pursuits of religious law, *hadith*, jurisprudence, literature and theology.

Perhaps a predisposition for the esoteric, as well as sustained periods of persecution and seclusion in the lives of its leading thinkers, had given Shi'ism a stronger intellectual stomach and a greater power of assimilation of ideas initially beyond the Islamic pale. It ingested entire philosophies – Hermetic, Pythagorean and Aristotelian, as well as more arcane Alexandrian and Chaldean traditions, metabolising them, as it were, in accordance with its own psychological and spiritual needs. The process is one of the least known in Islamic history; but the results manifest in such extraordinary documents as the encyclopaedic corpus of the *Ikhwan al-Safa'* or Brethren of Purity, whose treatises are saturated with neo-Pythagorean and Hermetic lore. In a particularly fertile marriage with sufism, this philosophical-religious heritage blossoms anew in the visionary metaphysics of the twelfth-century mystic Sohrawardi, and is again reborn in the Safavid era with the Illuminationist teachings of Mulla Sadra and Mir Damad.

In the transmission (and subsequent legitimisation) of this sapiental legacy, the role of Ali is again crucial. It is through the conduit of the first Imam that the Hermetic dimension enters into later Shi'a thought and, like the life-giving channels that nourish the different quarters of the beloved Persian garden, flows into the adjoining oases of theology, metaphysics, and sufism. It is through Ali, too, that the majority of sufi orders – including those of the Sunni world – trace their lineage to the Prophet.

'*Ya Ali!*' How often I heard the name! It is uttered at the outset of countless undertakings, as a benediction on parting from company and, often with a deep sigh, as a self-fortifying invocation. The sanctity of the first Imam permeates the fabric of all Shi'ism; he is both warrior and master of chivalry, champion of the poor, compassionate towards his enemies and exemplar of both worldly and spiritual virtue – attributes which both glorify and redouble the iniquity of his demise. And it is this tragic hue, along with the semi-divine status of the Imams and the theological paradox of the occultation, which loosens Shi'ism from the more pragmatic spiritual atmosphere of Sunni Islam and, I think, imparts to it a quality more akin to the bathos and mystery of the Christian Passion; the tragedy of Ali's murder and that of Hussein and his family; the generations of persecution by cruel and worldly rulers; the suggestion of a secret tradition imparted to a spiritual (and, implicitly, rightly-guided) elite, as well as the promise of an Awaited One – all contribute to the personal intensity with which Ali is venerated throughout the Shi'ite world. His Christ-like portrait – the very iconography of which suggests a syncretic inheritance – is everywhere in Iran. His face is dark and handsome and unlined, his beard is full and flows gracefully around unsmiling lips. A blazing nimbus radiates from behind his saintly head, which is wrapped in swirling folds of deep green, the colour of Islam and its saints; sometimes in larger portraits his body is enveloped by a supernal glow. But doom-filled shadows haunt his serene features and, more often than not, tears brim in the seraphical eyes, which are turned heavenward with an almost reproachful gaze, and the whole tragic story seems to be compressed darkly behind them. The effect is almost gaudy, but the message is unmistakable: that of a man bearing, as only a saintly warrior can, the full burden of a wronging of cosmic proportions.

Jason Elliot's book about Iran, *Sons of Adam*, will be published by Picador in 2006.

Meeting Muhammad

TED GORTON

I'LL NEVER FORGET my first meeting with Muhammad. He was tall, portly, with a reddish-blond beard. A bit of a dandy despite not being particularly handsome, or perhaps to compensate: he liked to wear a pistachio-green jacket over his sky-blue robe from the tailors in Almeria. He was a Spaniard, but thought of himself as simply a Muslim and an Arab. His name always puzzled me: not of Arab origin, it may have come down to him along with the colour of his beard from some Visigothic ancestor, and could be related to the Spanish surname Guzman. His full name was Abu Bakr Muhammad bin Abd al-Malik bin Isa bin Quzman al-Asghar; in books he is usually just called Ibn Quzman, ignoring the unexplained 'Asghar' ('the Lesser' or 'Junior'). I think of him simply as Muhammad, so clearly does his personality shine through the centuries.

I first met him on opening a loosely bound manuscript, eighty yellowed vellum pages in a coarse binding. The binding, at least, had obviously been around: there is a shopping list on the outside, mostly spices and dried fruits and the obscure 'myrrh of the Patriarchs'. It had travelled a lot further than to the souk, from Safad in Palestine, which the thirteenth-century copyist calls in the colophon *al-mahrusah*, the well-guarded or secure – this was the time of the Crusades, after all – to Leningrad, as it was at the time. A wandering Russian collector of orientalia, a Jewish Baron named Gunzburg, had brought it home from his travels. After the Revolution, it came to rest in the Institute of Soviet Peoples, which now, following yet another upheaval, is known as the Ethnographical Museum in St Petersburg. Were it not for the survival of that small and battered packet, Muhammad's name would be unknown except in a few citations, and we would be deprived of some remarkable poetry.

He was born and raised in Cordoba, at a time when it was possibly the most civilized city on Earth, but already past its prime. His birth came just too late to witness the famous victory of the Muslim army against the Christians at Zallaqa in 1086, being, as he put it, 'in my father's purse' at the time. The battle was won by the Almoravids, fierce tribesmen who would be called 'fundamentalists' today. They had been invited across from Morocco by the poet-king of Seville, whose city-state was threatened by the Christian armies advancing from the North. Predictably, the Almoravids decided to stay and rule Spain after Zallaqa, and their martial presence slowed down the Reconquest by about a century.

Muhammad's was an unquiet time: in the four centuries since the Arab conquest of Iberia, the descendants of the nomadic conquerors from the desert had grown soft, more interested in the refinements of poetry, architectural embellishments and general dissipation than in martial arts; central government had all but collapsed. The Almoravid warriors who filled this vacuum veiled their faces (yes, the men), taking a dim view of wine and fornication, two of Muhammad's favourite pastimes, God forgive him. Fortunately they had no problems with poetry, when they understood it, and indeed Muhammad could just about make a living writing panegyrics to the half-educated rulers and the native Andalusis they appointed to positions like *qadi* (judge).

Muhammad's poems are startling to anyone familiar with the canon of Arabic poetry, on several counts. Form first of all: he chose to write in the spoken Arabic of his day, the first recorded instance of this, other than a few snippets; and in ballad-stanzas, not the long monorhyme odes of Arabic tradition, tantalizingly suggesting that they were meant to be sung to irretrievably lost tunes. Besides the innovation of writing in spoken Arabic, he sprinkled his poems with words, proverbs and whole lines in Spanish, that is, in the spoken Romance vernacular of his Christian neighbours. His poems and a few others of the same time incidentally provide us with some of the earliest recorded examples of colloquial Hispanic dialect. He wrote some perfectly good verses in Classical Arabic; but his heart was in the colloquial ones, where you can sense the buzz and flow of street life in medieval Andalucia.

But the real interest of his work is, unsurprisingly, in its content. His long poems praising the wisdom and power of the Ibn Hamdis family of *qadis* are readable because he makes them lively, spicing them with anecdotes and vignettes which are also unique, but his best passages are in the lyrical love-songs written to real women. He was no fanatic despite living in a time of increasing tension between the faiths; his loves and lusts included a Christian girl he called his little star, *nujaimah*, and a Berber girl seen sitting on a doorstep with a diadem in her hair, along with many others. One of his poems describes a party at his house, where as entertainment (besides food, wine, music and dancing) the guests and invited actors put on a play or skit depicting bedouins coming to adore the baby Jesus in the manger.

Ibn Quzman was not really a bad Muslim, or he did not think he was. But he did love his drink, at least when he was young: taking a leaf from the poems of the great Abbasid poet Abu Nuwas in describing drinking-parties with his friends, but dwelling more on the quality and beauty of the wine than on getting drunk. I think he would have a good laugh if anyone suggested his wine was a spiritual allegory, however. In Classical Arabic poetry, the lover to whom verses are written is often addressed as a male, whatever his or her gender may have been. Muhammad ignores this convention, vividly describing his women and – in a few cases – graphically telling us what he did (or, more often, hoped to do) with them, but also writing a tender love-song about *sabi min as-souq*, a market-boy . . . Nonetheless, his faith was sorely tried by the holy month of Ramadan, and every year he dreaded the new moon that announced it. He mentions in several poems how he anxiously awaited the next moon, herald of the month of Shawwal and the end it brought to fasting. If he did not keep the fast pretty scrupulously, it would not have bothered him so much; but then again, this is poetry, so who knows.

Money was definitely a problem. He calls himself a *wazir* or functionary, but there is no evidence that he ever held any real post or did any significant work other than writing poetry and cadging money from the rich and powerful. He used all the usual tactics of praise, and when those were exhausted, tried pity: it is the *Adha*, the Feast of Sacrifice, and what did *I* have to sacrifice? An onion, a paltry onion, so I cut off its head and dreamt of mutton . . .

He loved his city, making only a few short trips around Andalusia, and – in one late poem – tells us in passing that he had never seen the sea. There had been a decline in civil order in the century before his birth, as the strong and centralized Caliphate gave way to the city-states ruled by 'Party Kings'. They vied with each other to attract the best artists and poets, and paid them handsomely (Muhammad really should have been born a hundred years earlier). By his middle age, Cordoba was showing physical signs of decay:

> Oh Ibn Quzman,
> You weep in vain:
> Stirring through ruins
> Brings only pain.

> Where is Ibn Zaid's Lane, with its bustle?
> Where's the Mosque Quarter, and its beauty?
> Laden it is with more spite than it can bear-

> Come close! You'll see a
> Field to plough and seed;
> The rest infested
> Head-high with weed.

As he grew older he became more religious, though he imagined his friends laughing at him:

> Ibn Quzman has reformed – bravo! (if it lasts);
> His every day was a feast among days,
> All drums and tambourines and dancing sleeves rolled up;

> Now it's to the minaret
> Up and down,

Or genuflecting in his
Priestly gown.

Muhammad's poetry is personal at a pre-Romantic time when most poets were working within a canon of conventional genres, stringing together formulas, occasionally achieving originality but in the nuance rather than the very fabric and meaning of their work. His work is a departure from all of this at once, describing himself even in unflattering terms, pushing the envelope of what was decent or permissible (he makes fun of the Almoravids in two poems), and leaving us with an irreplaceable window on Moorish Spain just before its long and terminal disintegration. His was not a 'voice in the street' as he has been called, but an educated writer's pastiche of life in the streets of Cordoba and a record of some aspects of his own life.

In his last poems, he left us some poignant verses on old age itself:

> When I was young, I walked straight as an *'alif* –
> Now I am bent as a *waw*, as though searching
> For my lost youth in the dust.

The *'alif* is the first letter of the Arabic alphabet, a single vertical stroke; the *waw* comes towards the end: a small loop at the top, then a curve like a large comma or a closing parenthesis.

He died in 554 of the Hijra, 1160 of the Christian calendar, on the last day before the start of Ramadan.

The Last Caliph and his Daughter

PHILIP MANSEL

LONDON IS NOW a Muslim as well as a Christian, Hindu and Jewish city. Sixteen percent of the population is Muslim: the city contains at least two hundred mosques, probably more. It is also a haven for exiles from Muslim countries. Many Iranians, Iraqis and Algerians find our multicultural megalopolis more congenial than the Muslim cities of Tehran, Baghdad or Algiers. One forgotten Muslim diaspora is the Ottomans who, appalled or expelled by Mustafa Kemal's radical secularist regime, moved to London. The most remarkable survivor of this lost world is Durrushehvar, Princess of Berar – the last living link with the Ottoman empire. When I went to see her in 1997 in her first-floor flat in South Kensington, I found a stately woman with the profile of a sultan and the manners of an empress. 'Won't you pour yourself some coffee, Mr Mansel?' she offered, as I perched on her sofa. Unfortunately her memory of the decisive years in Istanbul, between her birth in 1912 and her dynasty's expulsion in March 1924, is sketchy – although she said that Dolmabache Palace was better maintained by the Turkish republic than it had been by the Ottoman dynasty. Possibly, like many other Ottomans, she found it so hard to reconcile her resentment at her family's expulsion and humiliation by Mustafa Kemal, with her veneration for the saviour of modern Turkey, she preferred to forget.

Having lived between Istanbul, Nice, Hyderabad and London, the Princess of Berar shows that Muslim piety can be combined with immersion in English and Indian culture, and a commitment to changing women's lives. The Nizam of Hyderabad, wealthiest and most independent of Indian princes, had long supported the Ottoman dynasty with money as well as admiration. On 12 November 1931 in Nice Princess Durrushehvar was married to the Nizam's son and heir Azam Jah, at the same time as her cousin Nilufer was married to his younger brother Muazzam. The simple ceremony was attended by relations, a few Hyderabad officials and Marmaduke Pickthall, the English Muslim and translator of the Qur'an.

In Hyderabad, far from Nice and Istanbul, she was in a new world. Cecil Beaton admired her looks, her climate of 'restfulness and serenity', her love of philosophy and literature, and her knowledge of languages: she soon learnt Urdu. The great Turkish feminist Halide Edib, once an admirer now an exiled adversary of Mustafa Kemal, admired the Princess's Indian transformation: 'She had ceased to be anything but an Indian princess, so well does she seem to have adapted herself to her environment and taken to heart the duties that go with her position, both as a wife and mother and as a woman of an unusually deep culture ... In spite of her queenly and dignified figure she has a modest and somewhat timid air.' With her large, wide-apart eyes, high Ottoman forehead and prominent Ottoman nose, she reminded Halide Edib of Bellini's famous 1480 portrait of one of the greatest and most cosmopolitan of Sultans, the Conqueror of Constantinople and restorer of the Oecumenical Patriarchate, Mehmed II. She admired the princess's judgement and her belief, revolutionary in its time, that: 'Every woman ought to be in a position to support herself by means of an honourable livelihood should the occasion arise. It is a matter of pride and not humiliation to add to the meagre family income by one's own endeavour'. This modern Muslim from Istanbul helped many Hindu women of Hyderabad escape the prison of *purdah*, and encouraged the construction of hospitals. Some considered her the only man in the Hyderabad family.

Her sons' tutor Philip Mason, the historian of British India, wrote: 'she wore superb saris which suited her most impressive height. No one could ignore her or slight her. She was always essentially and indefinably royal'. Lord Monckton, legal adviser both to Edward VIII and to the Nizam of Hyderabad, described her as 'in many ways the most remarkable person in Hyderabad, a woman tranquil yet resolute whose personality dominated any room she entered . . . I learnt from her what any person must learn who has Muslim friends – how unnecessary it is to talk just for the sake of talking, and that there is no unfriendliness and there would be no awkwardness or embarrassment in silence'.

Her London flat contained dominating portraits of Ottoman sultans: when she stood in front of them, across the centuries the family resemblance was clear. They were painted by her father Abdulmecid Efendi, the last Ottoman Caliph (1922–24). Throughout his life, like his daughter, he showed a confident combination of Islam and modernisation. Members of the late Ottoman elite felt no sense of inferiority. As Ottomans, they spoke to the Russians or British as rulers of one empire to another: the language of communication was French. Born in 1868, a son of Sultan Abdulaziz (1861–76), and first cousin of Sultan Abdulhamid (1876–1909), Abdulmecid had received an education in both traditional Ottoman and modern French cultures at the princes' school in Yildiz Palace. He lived below the isolated wooded hill of Camlica on the Asian side of the Bosphorus, in a kiosk built in Turkish style and decorated with Iznik tiles.

Autocratic and suspicious, during his reign Sultan Abdulhamid forbade his cousin to cross the Bosphorus to Istanbul. In his years of enforced leisure Abdulmecid practised traditional Ottoman calligraphy, read the works of Victor Hugo, wrote poems and cultivated his garden: he boasted that the goldfish in his pools could recognise the sound of his voice when he came to feed them. Finding no contradiction between European culture and Muslim piety, he learnt to speak French and German almost as well as Ottoman and Persian. He also became an accomplished musician, playing the piano, violin and cello, often with his wife, and composing both classical western music and Turkish music. In her introduction to a recent book on the prince, Gunsel Renda writes: 'His music library was of rarely surpassed scope, containing a vast collection of written music and books of both Western and Turkish musical theory and demonstrates the full extent of his musical culture. Regrettably most of his own compositions are now lost.'

Painting was another favourite occupation. He took lessons from the Director of Imperial Museums and Ottoman Orientalist Osman Hamdy

Bey and had a studio in his kiosk. Admiring both the Western paintings and the Ottoman calligraphy panels hanging in Ottoman palaces, he was able to paint in both styles. Surviving works include pictures of Ottoman soldiers in traditional dress; portraits of the sultans Selim I, Murad IV, Selim III, Mahmud II; and of his own father Abdulaziz on a white horse. Abdulmecid was not a professional painter: in some pictures the hands are lumps. Nevertheless he painted with vigour. Moreover, reflecting the educated elite's interest in Turkish and French cultures, the pictures are themselves historical documents.

In politics Abdulmecid sympathised with the 'Young Turk' reformers who were enemies of his cousin Abdulhamid. One of his most famous pictures, in a style like the Paris Symbolists, was called *The Fog*. It was a political picture, an attack on Abdulhamid, inspired by a poem of the same name by Tevfik Fikret comparing Istanbul under Abdulhamid to a senile sorceress, shrouded in a fog of hypocrisy, jealousy, greed and dishonour. No longer the 'queen of the world', it had become the 'whore of the world'. Inscriptions on tiles in the prince's kiosk also have a critical note: 'the leader of the tribe is he who serves the tribe'; 'he who is learned has the highest rank'; and, prophetically, 'the powerful do not know that their palaces are sometimes destined to be a sparrow's nesting place.' Above the gate was written: 'There is no victor but Allah.'

After the overthrow of Abdulhamid by Young Turk revolutionaries in April 1909, Abdulmecid was so overjoyed that he executed a painting of the moment when four deputies of the Ottoman Parliament informed the Sultan in Yildiz palace of his deposition. The four deputies in question (Essad, Karassu, Aram and Arif Hikmet – an Albanian, a Jew, an Armenian and a Laz) were summoned to his kiosk to give the picture authenticity. The only picture of a monarch's deposition painted by a member of his dynasty, *The Dethronement of Sultan Abdulhamid II* shows the truth of the proverb 'revenge is a dish best eaten cold', and the bitterness of the struggles for power within the Ottoman dynasty between traditionalists and modernisers, supporters of absolute or constitutional monarchy.

During the relative freedom following the 'Young Turk' revolution, Abdulmecid frequently crossed the Bosphorus to Istanbul, exhibiting paintings at the *salons* of the Society of Ottoman Painters (founded in 1908, of which he was the energetic Honorary President). He visited mosques, attended concerts, became a patron of Turkish charities, poets and painters. Concerts of Ottoman music and performances of modern Turkish plays, attended by writers and intellectuals from the city, were held in his kiosk. The prince painted portraits of famous writers of the period, Recaizade Mahmud Ekrem (1911), Abdulhak Hamit (1917). His portrait of Selim III instructing Shehzade Mahmud (1912–14) is a tribute to two great reforming sultans of the past. *The History Lesson* of 1912, showing his adored son Omer Faruk and Durrushehvar looking at a map of the provinces lost to Bulgaria, Serbia, Albania and Greece by the Ottoman Empire in the Balkan wars of 1912–13, reflects the patriotic resentment at defeat – and the expulsion of hundreds of thousands of Muslims from the lost provinces – which Abdulmecid shared with other Turks. Far from the Ottoman dynasty being incompatible with modern Turkish nationalism, one of the most prominent Ottoman princes was one of Turkish nationalism's most vigorous patrons.

In October 1914 the Ottoman Empire entered the First World War on the side of Germany and Austria. Abdulmecid was disillusioned with the Young Turk leaders, led by Enver Pasha, who had dragged the country into the war against the wishes of the Sultan, the ministers and the population. However, he was first and foremost a patriot. Pictures by Abdulmecid of Ottoman princes and princesses playing Beethoven in the palace, watched by himself (1915), and of a harem lady reading Goethe (1917), were intended to affirm both the Ottoman Empire's alliance with Germany and Austria and the palace's embrace of western culture: they were shown at an Ottoman exhibition in Vienna in 1918. However in November 1918 the German, Austrian and Ottoman empires were forced to sign armistices with the allies. That month British, French, Italian and Greek forces occupied Istanbul.

The prince was too intelligent not to be appalled by the pro-allied policy of his cousin, the new Sultan Mehmed VI. In June 1919 Abdulmecid Efendi was reported by British and other sources to be 'at the head of the nationalist party'. He feared 'the gravest eventualities' for the imperial house and called the Sultan 'the ruin of the country, the Caliphate and the Sultanate.' He called for immediate elections and the formation of an all-party government including nationalists. Both in 1919 and in 1920 he and his son Omer Faruk were the only princes who considered going to Anatolia to join the Nationalist movement of Mustafa Kemal, whose forces, in the summer of 1920, approached the Asian shore of the Bosphorus. Again showing the close link between the Ottoman dynasty and Turkish nationalism, Mustafa Kemal frequently corresponded with Abdulmecid and in the summer of 1920 expressed a desire for Omer Faruk to join nationalist forces.

When the Nationalist general Refet re-entered Istanbul in triumph, on 19 October 1922, Abdulmecid sent an ADC to welcome him. After the Turkish reoccupation of Istanbul, Mehmed VI left Istanbul on a British battleship. But even after Mehmed VI's catastrophic reign, Turkish nationalists were not yet willing, or able, to break with the Ottoman dynasty. On 19 November, as 'the most moral, learned and pious of this dynasty', Abdulmecid was chosen by the Turkish Grand National Assembly in Ankara to be Caliph of the Muslims.

At first, Abdulmecid was reluctant to accept the title of Caliph, correctly stating that it was reserved for 'the most powerful monarch in Islam'; he did not want to be 'a mere phantom'. He yielded when the Nationalist general Refet promised that the sultanate would eventually be restored, and hinted at 'consequences of a regrettable nature' if he refused. In effect he was blackmailed into the position, because Mustafa Kemal could not dispose of the Ottoman dynasty at once. Believing in parliamentary government, Abdulmecid was in some ways more modern, certainly more familiar with European culture, than Mustafa Kemal. Both favoured modernisation. The difference was that he was a pious Muslim who went to mosque every Friday and Kemal was not.

On 29 November 1922 the new Caliph received the homage of *ulama*, deputies and senior officials, in Topkapi Palace. Any ceremony which implied political sovereignty or military authority was dropped from his inauguration. Thus he wore white tie and tails rather than military uniform, and received homage standing in front of, rather than sitting on, the golden throne of the Ottomans. He did not receive the traditional Ottoman inauguration rite of being 'girded with the sword of Osman' at Eyup. However, as His Imperial Majesty the Caliph Abdulmecid II he drove from Topkapi to the mosque of Fatih in a state carriage, with Refet beside him. They were escorted by horse guards and followed by a procession of cars and carriages. As a film of the event shows, there was steady hand-clapping from crowds lining the route, many of whom climbed trees and onto roofs in order to obtain a better view. The city seemed to have turned scarlet with Turkish flags. In the mosque, thanks were offered for the preservation of the Turkish people from extinction; for the first time prayers were in Turkish, not Arabic. After victory in one holy war, there was a call for another holy war, against ignorance and in favour of commerce and agriculture. On the return journey, in accordance with tradition, the new Caliph offered prayers at the mausoleums of Mehmed II, Selim I and Mahmud II.

Although it added to the surface glitter of the city, and gave an Islamic cover to the government's modernisation programme, the Caliphate was doomed. Mustafa Kemal wanted no rival as a Turkish father figure, and was determined to de-islamicise the state. As early as January 1923 he told a group of journalists that he planned to abolish the caliphate – once they had, on his instructions, 'prepared' opinion. On 2 October 1923 the last of the allied occupying forces left Istanbul – from outside Dolmabache Palace. On 13 October Ankara was proclaimed capital of the Turkish state; On 23 October Refet, the only nationalist who had paid court to the Caliph, was deprived of the military command of Istanbul. On 29 October Turkey became a republic, with Kemal as President. Abdulmecid sent Kemal his congratulations. Nevertheless his dynasty was doomed.

In the winter of 1923–4 the Caliph's budget was cut and he was deprived of his state *kayik* and guard. The last Ottoman *selamlik* took place on 29 February 1924 at the mosque outside Dolmabache Palace. On 3 March the Grand National Assembly in Ankara abolished the caliphate. Dolmabache Palace was surrounded by troops. Abdulmecid was reading the Qur'an (by some accounts the essays of Montaigne) late at night when Adnan Adivar, husband of the great Turkish writer Halide Edib and Ankara's chief representative in the capital, and the Prefect of Police came to tell him that he had to leave at dawn.

The abolition of the caliphate was far from popular. Ismet Inonu wrote in his memoirs, 'we encountered the greatest resistance when we abolished the Caliphate.' The Caliph took his son Omer Faruk and daughter-in-law Sabiha, their daughter Nezlishah, his daughter Durru-shehvar, two servants, two wives, three officials and seventeen suitcases. At five thirty in the morning, having bidden farewell to a small crowd at the palace gate, they were taken in three cars, followed by a lorry-load of luggage, along the Bosphorus, over Galata bridge, past the Bayezit mosque, out through the Edirne gate, and then on to Catalca. At eleven o'clock, sad, tired, and hungry, the party arrived at Catalca railway station. The Caliph tried to smile when the police and gendarmerie gave him his last salute. The Orient Express arrived at midnight. As the party began to board, watched by the other passengers, the governor of Istanbul gave the Caliph an envelope containing passports valid for leaving Turkey, visas for Switzerland, and £2000 sterling.

The last Ottoman Caliph never saw his country again. As a prince he had called France his 'second fatherland'; it now became so in reality. He lived in a villa in Nice, continuing, as he always had, to read, to paint, to play the piano, and attend concerts. He generally wore a fez (supplied by an Armenian tailor in Paris). His verdict on Kemal's reforms was: 'It is not constitutions which shape souls but souls which shape constitutions. Suddenly to make a clean sweep is blindness.' The month that the caliphate was abolished, all Muslim religious courts and schools in Turkey were closed down. To this day Turkey remains a secular state. Every aspect of Islam is, in theory, controlled by the government.

Like many Muslims, both in India and the Middle East, Abdulmecid never accepted the abolition of the caliphate. He died at the age of seventy-six on 23 August 1944 in Paris, as German soldiers were leaving the city. The battle for the soul of Turkey between secularists and Islamists, which the caliphate might have defused, continues.

Ziryab on My Mind

PHILIPPA SCOTT

LOOKING BACK, it seems inevitable, *kismet*, that Ziryab, father of *cante jondo* and the Andalusian guitar, should enter my life.

Unconsummated romance is best if the longed-for person is completely and utterly physically unavailable, for then frustration is sublimated to something more exquisite, and bliss attained in a mental, emotional and spiritual state of heightened ecstatic yearning. There is no need for the focus of one's fascination to be in the here or now, they may be long dead, or not even human, existing only through the powers of belief or imagination. Both these are strong enough to enthrall and sway the heart. Long distance or otherwise difficult love affairs are the next best thing, and music has the power to recreate and make us relive every cherished or imagined experience anew. Since our paths crossed, Ziryab has been my heart's companion on such journeys.

Passion led me from wistful ballads to anguished opera, then to the poetry and songs of medieval troubadours, those somewhat sufi Christians whose ethos of romantic longing for a distant beloved were expressed in the strange irresistible twangs of 'langue d'Oc'. The more I listened to troubadour music with its ethos of amorous longing, the more of those eastern resonances I hungered for. I followed the trail south from Cathar country across the Pyrenees towards the urgent sorrows and heartache of guttural flamenco, sobbing to Arabic and Kathak rhythms. For weeks I played nothing except Harmonia Mundi's 'Musique Arabo-Andalouse', familiarity increasing pleasure.

The alchemical mix of my own nature and a certain doomed, long-distance, overflowing with yearning, but very definitely consummated love affair added potency to poets' words, and in the 1980s desire called me frequently to France. Nineteen eighty five saw me living in Paris, where a small music shop in the midst of St Germain's wine and caffeine-fuelled heart proved a source for many wonderful recordings of early music and vintage flamenco. Not today's popular 'flamenco lite', but the *cante jondo* of such singers as the great Nino de Almaden, Juan de Varena, Antonio Chacon, Pepe de la Matrona, Pepe Marchena. These tapes were discreetly packaged in black with white writing, free from distracting images – no pomaded black hair or taut poses flaunting bright carnation frills – this was Amencopura, the essence of soul music. I coursed along motorways to assignations and stolen (though of this I was still happily unaware) pleasures, music from Provencal Courts of Love accompanying me on the outward-bound journey, and returned car vibrating with the crisp staccato of hand claps, the irresistible per-suasion of plucked strings, and voices whose tingling physicality felt like a cat's tongue rasping my skin. Ah, love, sweet love ! There's no high, no adrenalin rush quite like it, is there? Fate cast me as a long-distance traveller on love's journey; I will, I must, stay the course, despite, some-times, stubborn and wayward as I am, even *because* of obstacles, and when the beloved companion chooses another path and our ways part, despite pain and fury, love still lingers in the ashes of each burning affair. The heart's ways by-pass logic, and love is wilful.

And so there came a day when to feel the music, to drown in the emotions it expressed and echoed, was no longer enough. Once dis-appointment and the rawness of betrayal begin to lose their first sharp pain and feelings settle, the mind sees and seizes its chance. From healing empathy, music now offered a pathway out of my morass of suffering. Now ignorance became my burden. I needed to understand the music's own journey, where it came from, how it came about, the overlaps and interweavings of its evolution, its story. I escaped into another colour, a different mood, a new level of the music I had so far been listening to from a purely emotional and instinctive state. Every love affair leaves its mark and its gift.

Oh, he's is not mine alone, I accept that. Ziryab has always been famous. Today the Kurds broadcast their claims on the internet, I can listen to my CD of Paco de Lucia's guitar homage *Ziryab*, and after a visit to the Institut du Monde Arabe in Paris, pause for coffee in its Café Ziryab. No matter. This is merely the nature of fame; my personal relationship with him, as indeed with every relationship of fascination, is just that: *personal* and *mine*. My Ziryab is a romantic figure of my own conjuring, gleanings from dry history moistened and coloured with imagination, and spiced with fantasy's zest. Each relationship is unique to those involved in its experience, and for me Ziryab has been an invisible but sometimes almost palpable presence, a wise companion and guide, a happy haunting.

Abu al-Hasan Ali ibn Nafi, was born sometime around 789, probably in Baghdad, where his father had been a musician at the court of al-Mansur. He was nicknamed Ziryab, 'black songbird', for the sweetness and clarity of his voice. Historians differ as to whether he was Syrian, Persian, Kurd, or whether the blackbird's colouring owed something to African ancestry. All agree he was a musical genius.

I see him cross-legged, thoughtful, intense, a slender youth in the court of Haroun al-Rashid, where he is a student of the great Isaak al-Mawsli. Hand raised above the pieces, he considers his next move in a game of chess. The game is set out on a silk cloth, a collage of carefully stitched squares, emerald green and ruby red. The pieces, carved in India, are representational, unlike the abstract shapes preferred in the Abbasid court. Ziryab touches an ivory elephant, *fil*, stained red with Indian *lac*. He tries to concentrate on the game, but other thoughts intrude and he remembers his teacher's face, dark with fury, when he performed for the Caliph. Ziryab was right to be concerned, his action had set in motion a train of events which would result in exile from his homeland, and take him to the farthest reaches of the Muslim world. In his wildest imaginings he could not have foreseen what lay ahead. Yet if he had not risked everything in Baghdad, in what seemed to the entire court an act of arrogant madness, the life that lay ahead, of power, far-reaching influence and immense riches, would never have been his. Ziryab followed his pounding heart, and accepted Fate's challenge.

Haroun al-Rashid's was a court of luxury and learning, of immense refinement and sophistication, where Arab and other scholars adopted the ideas of Pythagoras and Aristotle, whose writings taught that music was an echo of the cosmos' music, produced by the movement of celestial bodies, and reflected the harmony of the universe. The melodic archetypes of oriental music known as *makams* correspond to the modes of ancient Greece, and it was believed that music could produce a perfect emotion which would exalt the soul and repel ugliness; it was an echo of the divine. There is more than one way of attaining the state of bliss, and music is a guide that speaks the language of the human soul.

The seventeenth-century Arab historian al-Maqqari says in his *Nafh al-Tib (Fragrant Breeze)*: 'There never was, either before or after him, a man of his profession who was more generally beloved and admired.' But extraordinary talent and unusual gifts bring their own challenges and Ziryab believed his own compositions were divinely inspired, for they came to him in the moments between waking and sleeping.

One day the Caliph asked to hear the student play. Ziryab sang for the Caliph, and then asked permission to perform some of his own compositions, which no ear had ever heard before. Curious, the Caliph assented. Ziryab then declined to use his master's proferred 'ud, saying he had brought his own because his compositions had been created specifically for this instrument. It was, he explained, lighter in weight, two strings were of lion gut, the others silk which had been reeled but not soaked in hot water, and he had added a fifth string. Some of Ziryab's compositions were based on the observations of the astronomer, Ptolemy, which he had set to music. The traditional Arab lute had four strings, representing the humours of the human body, and coloured accordingly. Ziryab's fifth string was coloured red, representing breath, or soul, and his pick was a sharpened eagle's claw.

Ziryab must have known that exposing his secret studies, openly competing with his master for the Caliph's attention would cause a stir and that there would be wider repercussions. He gambled, but instead of arousing his teacher's admiration, he provoked fury and fear. Whispers circulated. It was said that Ziryab was mad, possessed by spirits, a conjuror of demons, and Ziryab realized that if he wanted to live and prosper, it could not be at Haroun al-Rashid's glittering court. He went

first to the furthest reaches of the Abbasid territories, the court of
Ziyadat Allah I at Kairouan.

Court scandal travels fast and wide. One of Cordoba's most distinguished musicians, a Jew named Abdul-Nasr Mansur, heard, via the
extensive Jewish trading grapevine, about the drama at Baghdad. Al-
Hakim I, Emir of Cordoba, considered himself a poet and patron of the
arts, no less than the Caliph of Baghdad. Mansur easily persuaded him
that here was an opportunity to bring one of the brightest stars of
Baghdad court culture to al-Andalus. Ziryab was sent for, and the
musician duly sailed to Spain with his wives and four young sons.
Disembarking at Algeciras he learned that although the Emir had
meanwhile died, Mansur had persuaded the new ruler, Abd al-Rahman
II, that this was a unique opportunity to steal a gem from the crown of
Haroun al-Rashid, and should not be allowed to slip away. A messenger
arrived, announcing the imminent arrival of a deputation from the new
Emir, and shortly afterwards a portly and elegantly dressed eunuch, all
praise and promises, arrived with a convoy of mules and attendants
bearing gifts to welcome Ziryab and his family, and to convey the party
to court. And so it was that Ziryab arrived, eventually, after many a stop
and adventure, at the Cordoban court in 822. He arrived, it is said 'with
one thousand – no, two – no, ten thousand stories and songs . . . '
Determined to keep Ziryab, and keenly aware that the musician would
constantly compare everything in Cordoba to the glittering court he
had left behind, the new Emir denied his new court musician nothing.

Ziryab's repertoire consisted of his own compositions as well as
those of his teacher al-Mawsili, Arabic poems, and the music of the
Abbasid court whose melodies and rhythms were largely influenced by
Persia and India. Like classical Indian *rhags*, which correspond to the
hours of the day, Arabic-Andalusian music evolved a series or suite of
songs grouped together in different movements, played in a pre-
established order. There were twenty-four of these *noubas*, also
corresponding to the hours of the day, and Ziryab set down written
rules for their interpretation. He established a music conservatory at
Cordoba, open to anyone of talent, girls as well as boys.

I imagine him in his later years of maturity, his figure still trim, his bearing straight. He has spent his life studying breathing and vocal exercises, diet and healthy living, in order to constantly improve his singing and to teach it his pupils. Ziryab was always the epitome of elegance, and his words were honey to the Cordoban court. 'In Baghdad we do . . . thus,' he would say, and the entire Cordoban court would rush to cut their hair, dress in certain colours at certain seasons.

Ziryab's role in my life extends beyond music, for when I followed his story, it clarified a medieval puzzle woven in silk. I was writing about this most magical of fibres, and was puzzled by an apparent fashion for elephant-patterned silks in Moorish Spain. The generally accepted explanations for this fashion – coins of Hannibal found in Spain, or Persian influence on silk-weaving – worried me. For a particular fashion, surely there had to have been a more specific inspiration, perhaps even a real elephant, and a story. In time I found the elephant. Why should his story intrigue the Arabs of Spain? For that a skilled storyteller is needed. There was no more skilled teller of stories than Ziryab, and Ziryab knew the elephant and his romance.

His influence pervades even the meals we eat today, in the order of separate courses which he introduced to Spain, a custom which rapidly spread from court to court, and courtier to courtier. Asparagus was introduced to Andalusia by Ziryab. I like to imagine this was as much to assuage occasional pangs of homesickness as for the culinary education of the Cordoban court. Each spring when thin, spindly young asparagus appears on the stalls of Portobello Market I buy quantities to cook and puree for an utterly delicious lamb fricassee. This is my Ziryab feast, and I pig out. Bliss, sheer selfish bliss. Occasionally I invite friends to share my asparagus lamb, and serve it with celeriac mash, a happy pairing of tastes 'Oh this? Just something seasonal, based on an old Baghdad recipe,' I say.

Nobody ever refuses a second helping.

Nor was this the last of our lingering encounters. I wanted to replace some of my old cassettes with CD's, and went on to a flamenco website. An old LP cover featured a lurid technicolour photograph of Marchenita, who used to play with Pepe Marchena. Marchenita wore a Nehru-type hat. Curiousity piqued, I investigated further. Marchenita's original name was Aziz Balouch, he was a sufi from what is now Pakistan, who arrived in Spain in the 1930s. This famous exponent of *cante jondo* believed himself to be the twentieth-century reincarnation of Ziryab.

But that's another story.

About the Contributors

After travelling and working in other people's bookshops, **Sarah Anderson** founded her own shop in 1979. She stayed with the Travel Bookshop in Notting Hill for twenty-five years before leaving and now travels, writes and teaches. She is the author of *Anderson's Travel Companion*, *The Virago Book of Spirituality* and *Inside Notting Hill*.

Glencairn Balfour Paul was born in 1917 in Dumfriesshire. He served throughout WW2 as an infantry officer, then as an administrator (and archaeologist) in Sudan until its Independence in 1955. Thereafter he was in the diplomatic service, serving as Ambassador in Iraq, Jordan and Tunisia. He directed the Middle East Association in London for two years, resigning to take up a Research Fellowship at Exeter University in 1979. He has published widely on Arab affairs and a poetry collection, *A Kind of Kindness*, came out in 2000. *Bagpipes in Babylon* is his forthcoming memoir.

Alberto Cairo has a degree in law and would have practiced as a lawyer but has instead worked for the Red Cross in Kabul for the last fifteen years making prosthetic arms and legs and teaching disabled Afghans to walk. In 1996 the front page of the *International Herald Tribune* described him as 'the most beloved foreigner in Afghanistan'. He returns to Italy to lecture and has written about Afghanistan and its needs, achieving spectacular success in 2003 when his book *Storie da Kabul* was published in Turin and immediately entered the bestseller lists.

John Carswell is an artist, writer and art historian, who started off life as an archaeological draftsman in Jericho. He taught at the American University of Beirut 1956–76, was Visting Professor at SOAS and then Curator of the Oriental Institute and Director of the University of

Chicago's Museum. He subsequently became Director of the Islamic Department at Sotheby's and now lives in Andalucia.

Horatio Clare was born in London in 1973 and raised on a sheep farm in South Wales. He was a trained lifeboatman, barman and journalist when he joined BBC radio in 1998. There he researched and produced many programmes, including *Front Row, Night Waves* and *The Verb*. His writing has appeared in the *Guardian, Spectator, New Statesman* and in the collection *Marrakech: The Red City* (Sickle Moon 2003). His first book, *Running for the Hills* (the story of an upbringing on a Welsh mountain, and a biography of his parents' relationship), is published by John Murray in 2006.

Peter Clark worked for the British Council for over thirty years, mostly in the Arab world. He is the author of *Marmaduke Pickthall: British Muslim* and *Thesiger's Return* and a contributing editor of *Banipal*. He has translated eight books from Arabic.

Mary Clow has worked on feature films in Turkey, Egypt, Italy, France, Greece and Liverpool. She has travelled in Bangladesh, Pakistan, Burma, India, Bolivia and Bali. She lives between Lindos, London and Manhattan.

Angela Culme-Seymour was a celebrated beauty, much pursued and loved. Amongst her husbands were the painter Johnny Churchill and the writer Patrick Balfour (later Kinross), although she would only find contentment as the partner of Ali Bulent. Together they set up schools for the study of Ibn al-'Arabi and other mystics.

William Dalrymple is a writer, broadcaster and historian. He was born in Scotland. He researched his bestselling first book, *In Xanadu*, by travelling during the Cambridge summer holidays. It was published when he was just twenty-two. In 1989 he moved to Delhi to work as a journalist for six years, producing *City of Djinns*, followed three years later by *From the Holy Mountain: a Journey in the Shadow of Byzantium*. His collected Indian travel essays, *Age of Kali*, appeared in 1998 and *White Mughals* in 2002.

Laurence Deonna is a reporter, author and photographer. Her major 'beat' is the Middle East, from Yemen to Iran, and the Islamic Republics of Central Asia (ex-USSR). Her books have been translated from French into English, German, Spanish, Italian, Arabic and Hebrew. One-woman photo exhibitions have been held in Europe, New York and Canada. In 1987, she was awarded the UNESCO Peace Education Prize.

Jason Elliot studied Persian and Arabic at SOAS. His first journey in the Islamic world, at the age of nineteen, was as a clandestine guest of the Afghan *mujahadin* during the Soviet occupation of Afghanistan. His first travel book, *An Unexpected Light*, was published in 2000 to broad critical acclaim in the UK and became a *New York Times* bestseller in the USA. His forthcoming book, *Sons of Adam*, is the result of several years' travel and investigation into the arts and culture of Iran, and will be published by Picador in 2006.

In 1997 **James Fergusson**, a freelance British journalist with nine years of foreign reporting behind him, met Mir, an interpreter in rebel-controlled Afghanistan. They became friends as well as colleagues. When Mir was forced to flee his homeland, James was able to guide him through the complexities of London life. His account of this tale of two worlds is the critically acclaimed *Kandahar Cockney*, published in 2004.

Sylvie Franquet was born in Belgium and studied Arabic at the University of Ghent before moving to Cairo, where she lived for many years. She has spent much of the past decade travelling through and writing about the Middle East and North Africa, where she has worked as a model, guide, television producer and teacher.

Eamonn Gearon is a writer, freelance journalist, photographer and film-maker. He has lived in the Middle East for most of the past decade as well as in Burundi, the Democratic Republic of Congo and Rwanda. Under the tutelage of bedu in Egypt's Western Desert, he learnt the traditional skills needed to live and travel in the desert. He later moved to the oasis of Siwa, where he lived for eighteen months. Siwa and his desert treks form the basis of *Footnote*, the manuscript of which (*Insha'allah*) is near to completion.

Ted Gorton was born in Texas in 1947, educated in Argentina, Lebanon, France, America and finally Oxford. He left his first job as a lecturer in Arabic Studies at St Andrews for a short assignment with Shell in Oman, which turned into a long career working for oil companies in the Middle East, London, and more recently Russia. He has published extensively on Hispano-Arabic poetry in scholarly journals, and is currently translating the poems of Ibn Quzman and other Moorish poets.

Kevin Gould has been a chef, DJ, jazz singer, carpenter, grocer, caterer and restauranteur, and is a writer, trend predictor and photographer. Like his mum he is interested to find out what he'll do when he grows up.

Shusha Guppy was born and grew up in Tehran. After school, she went to Paris to study at the Sorbonne. In the '60s she met and married English writer and explorer Nicholas Guppy and settled in London. She is the author of *The Blindfold Horse: Memoirs of a Persian Childhood*, which has won several literary prizes in Britain and France, and of *A Girl in Paris, Looking Back* and *Three Journeys in the Levant*. She is also a well-known singer and songwriter and has made numerous records of her own and other contemporary singer/songwriters' works.

Robin Hanbury-Tenison is an explorer, conservationist, broadcaster, filmmaker, author, lecturer, campaigner and farmer. Named by *The Sunday Times* in 1982 as 'the greatest explorer of the past twenty years', he has been on over thirty expeditions. A Gold Medallist of the RGS, he was one of the founders of Survival International and is now its President. Author of some twenty books, twelve of which are currently in print, he campaigns actively for the protection of the world's rainforests and its indigenous peoples.

Fraser Harrison was born in 1944. He worked in publishing before becoming a freelance writer in 1974 and has published eight books, among them *The Dark Angel* (1977, a study of Victorian sexuality), *A Father's Diary* (1985), *The Living Landscape* (1986, a collection of essays about conservation and the countryside) and *High on the Hog* (1991, his first novel). In 2001 he completed an MA degree in Human Rights at Essex University. He currently works as a legal representative giving advice to detained asylum seekers.

Mark Hudson is the author of *Our Grandmothers' Drums, Coming Back Brockens* and *The Music in My Head*. He is a regular contributor to the *Daily Telegraph* and the *Observer*.

Michael Jacobs is an art historian, travel writer and hispanist. His numerous books include *Between Hopes and Memories: A Spanish Journey; In the Glow of the Phantom Palace: Travels from Granada to Timbuktu; Alhambra;* and *The Factory of Light: Tales from my Andalucian Village*. His latest travel book, set in Chile and Bolivia, will be published by John Murray in May 2006. He is a Senior Honorary Research Fellow in the Hispanics Department at Glasgow University.

Ghada Karmi is a writer and academic. She is the author of a highly acclaimed memoir, *In Search of Fatima*, and is completing a book on the Arab-Israeli conflict. She is Research Fellow at the Institute of Arab and Islamic Studies, University of Exeter, and is currently on assignment to the Palestinian Authority's Information Ministry in Ramallah.

Born in India and schooled at convents in the UK, **Brigid Keenan** started journalism on the *Daily Express* and went on to be Fashion Editor of *The Sunday Times*, Assistant Editor of *Nova* and Woman's Editor of the *Observer*. She married a diplomat and has spent the last thirty years as a 'trailing spouse', following her husband to postings in India, the Caribbean, Africa, Syria and Kazakhstan, where she wrote her most recent and highly entertaining book, *Diplomatic Baggage*.

Sabiha al Khemir was born in Tunisia. Her fiction includes *Waiting in the Future for the Past to Come* (Quartet) and *The Blue Manuscript* (forthcoming). She has illustrated *The Island of Animals* (Quartet) and *Le nuage amoureux*, (Maspero, Paris). Her work in Islamic art includes consultancy for the Metropolitan Museum of Art, New York, and two television documentaries which she wrote and presented for Channel 4, London. She is currently chief curator of the Islamic Art Museum Project in Doha, Qatar. She has finally accepted that she is a nomad who hopes to be free of place!

About the Contributors

Marius Kociejowski, poet, essayist and travel writer, lives in London. He has published three collections of poetry, *Coast* (Greville Press), *Doctor Honoris Causa*, and *Music's Bride* (both Anvil Press). Most recently, he published *The Street Philosopher and the Holy Fool: A Syrian Journey* (Sutton Publishing) and is currently working on a second book, *The Pigeon Wars of Damascus*. He is also editing a collection of travel writings on Syria.

For the past twenty years **Tim Mackintosh-Smith** has lived in the Yemeni capital, Sana'a, a place he describes as 'the nearest thing I've got to a muse'. His most recent book, *The Hall of a Thousand Columns*, is set in India and is one of a series retracing the travels of the great Moroccan wanderer Ibn Battutah.

Gerald MacLean is Professor of English at Wayne State University in Detroit and Visiting Professor at the Institute for Arab and Islamic Studies, University of Exeter. His recent publications include *The Rise of Oriental Travel: English Visitors to the Ottoman Empire, 1580–1720* (2004) and the collection *Re-Orienting the Renaissance: Cultural Exchanges with the East* (2005). He has travelled and lectured extensively in North Africa and the Middle East.

Philip Mansel is a historian of France and the Middle East. He has written lives of *Louis XVIII* (1981) and the *Prince de Ligne* (2003), and histories of *Constantinople: City of the World's Desire 1453–1924* (1995) and *Paris between Empires 1814–1852* (2001). His latest book, *Dressed to Rule* (2005), is a study of royal and court dress from Louis XIV to Elizabeth II. He has written for the *Financial Times*, *International Herald Tribune*, *Spectator*, and *Apollo*. He is a Fellow of the Royal Historical Society and the Institute of Historical Research and editor of *The Court Historian*.

Justin Marozzi is a writer and journalist who has been travelling regularly to the Middle East for the past eighteen years. His first book – *South from Barbary* (2001) – was the story of a 1,200-mile crossing of the Libyan Sahara by camel. His second book *Tamerlane: Sword of Islam, Conqueror of the World* (2004), was a biography of the fourteenth-century Tatar warlord. He is currently researching a travel history of Herodotus for John Murray.

Henrietta Miers read classics at Oxford and then took an MA in Development Studies at SOAS. Since then she has worked as a consultant all over the developing world. This includes living in Pakistan for five years, travelling into Taliban Afghanistan, working with Rwandan refugees just after the genocide, interviewing nomads in the Mauritanian desert, conducting research in a former nuclear test site in Kazakhstan and getting caught up in the Kyrgyz revolution. She is now living in London and working on her first book about these adventures.

Formerly a member of the BBC Music Division, the writer and record producer **Ateş Orga** was for many years Lecturer in Music and Concert Director at the University of Surrey before being invited in 2000 to initiate and direct the Music Administration programme at Istanbul Technical University (MIAM). His books include biographies of Beethoven and Chopin, and he contributes regularly to *Cornucopia*, *Andante* and *International Piano*. Home is a forgotten forested hamlet up in the Rhône Alps.

Following a career in languages (and widowed in her early forties with four children), **Sheila Paine** has spent the last twenty-five years travelling, alone and often to remote and dangerous places, to record embroidery traditions before they disappear. She has written three books on embroidery, one on amulets and three travel narratives: *The Afghan Amulet*, *The Golden Horde* and *The Linen Goddess*.

Following a parsimonious History of Art degree at the University of Edinburgh, Juliet Crawley followed her true interest and in 1985 left a London office and travelled east to Peshawar to work on emergency support for Afghanistan. In 1991 she moved to Moscow with her husband, war cameraman Rory Peck, and together they covered the break up of the Soviet Union. 2005 finds **Juliet Peck** weary of life but back at University, in York, where she is studying for a PhD in Post-Conflict Reconstruction when not hunting to hounds.

Born in India, **Philippa Scott** grew up in Scotland before turning twenty-one in Istanbul. A one-time dealer in carpets, textiles and Islamic art, she is now a freelance writer based in Notting Hill. Her books include *The Book of Silk*, *Turkish Delights* and *Gourmet Game*. Her writing has also appeared in *India of the Rajahs*, *The Englishwoman's Kitchen* and *Reflections of Paradise* and she is a Contributing Editor to *Hali* magazine. She is always pursuing mermaids and red herrings, and always ready to drink champagne and listen to opera.

Tahir Shah is the author of ten books, chronicling a wide range of unusual and outlandish journeys. Nothing is so important to him as deciphering the hidden underbelly of the lands through which he travels. Shah's books, which have appeared in many languages, are regarded as extremely original and peculiarly observant, combining hardship and humour. Tahir Shah lives in a sprawling mansion in the middle of a Casablanca shantytown, with his small son, daughter and his Indian-born wife.

Bruce Wannell is a researcher, translator, lecturer and linguist with a long and detailed experience of the Muslim world. He is currently immersed in an annotated translation of the Persian courtier-historian Shushtari (with William Dalrymple), an account of his youthful travels through the Islamic world (for Constable-Robinson) and a series of lectures on sufism at the invitation of the Ismaili Institute.

Jasper Winn is a writer, photographer, broadcaster and filmmaker with an interest in pastoralist cultures and traditional horsemanship. A Winston Churchill Travelling Fellowship paid for a neurotic mule, ('Mrs Bottom') which carried him for 1,500 kilometres across Morocco to study the seasonal movements of Berber tribes. He lived and worked with one Ait Atta family through a year's travel as they walked their sheep, goats and camels between their winter caves in the pre-Sahara, and the summer tents in the Central High Atlas Mountains. He is currently researching a book on horse-based cultures of the world.

Emily Young was born in London and was raised there and in Italy and Wiltshire. As a young woman she travelled the world. She is one of Britain's most successful stone sculptors, and lives and works in London and Italy. She has one son.